Data in Decline

Why Polling and Social Research Miss the Mark

Steve A Wood

Data in Decline: Why Polling and Social Research Miss the Mark

ISBN-10: 1-7328897-0-8
ISBN-13: 978-1-7328897-0-5

Figure 9.2 images reproduced with permission from Royce Bair.

Table of Contents

Acknowledgements

I would like to thank my editor, David Ferris, for his prompt feedback and concise edits; my co-founder Doug Williams for his organizational insights; my colleagues Jessica Tercha and Alyssa Darmanin for our work together and their insights which informed several portions of this book regarding how high quality data must be collected; my professors at the University of Cincinnati, whose teachings greatly influenced the details of this book; Dr. Walter Barbe for his insights on publishing; Dr. Phillip Magness for his feedback and content suggestions; all my published sources for the thorough nature of their research; and of course my loving wife Ammy, who managed to keep our son entertained enough that I could turn this collection of thoughts into a completed book.

Acknowledgments

[illegible]

Introduction

Once upon a time, the social sciences produced objective insights into our world. Research findings helped individuals and organizations optimize outcomes by aligning their activities with what studies indicated that society preferred. The citizens of Western nations were connected through networks that spanned entire continents and had nearly universal buy-in. With a few exceptions, those societies were sufficiently homogenous, so a relatively small sample could give an accurate representation of the entire population.

That is no longer the case.

The foundations of social science research were largely predicated on these ubiquitous networks and assumptions of relative homogeneity, but the reality that underpinned these assumptions has broken down. However, social science research and its practitioners have yet to adapt to the new reality.

The high cost of thoroughness when using traditional methodologies leads to less reliable research, as does a lack of reproducibility or adequate incentives for accuracy. The politicization of social science research additionally contributes to a climate in which findings often reinforce a predetermined narrative. Research in the social sciences already suffers from poor social perception compared to the robustness of physical science research, and it is further degraded by these methodological problems.

The social sciences can learn a lot from the approaches used by the natural sciences, and fields such as medicine or nutrition already contain substantial overlap between those two realms. Their approaches represent a step in the right direction but are insufficient, as they often suffer from the same reproducibility concerns that plague fields like psychology. By adopting much higher data quality standards and collection methods, however, the vast majority of these issues can be overcome.

All data in a given dataset must have several characteristics in order to be effectively used in research. Objective measurability, internal comparability, pertinence to the subject matter, and static meaning are all crucial attributes. Current social science methods produce data that is consistently lacking in these metrics. The results speak for themselves—with each passing year, research findings paint a picture that is further and further removed from the real world.

Though researchers are attempting to respond to these developments by changing up their methodologies and invoking new data sources, they fail to understand how deep the changes run. Too often, they believe that merely applying a 21st century overlay to 20th century techniques can correct the issues when in fact a novel approach is required.

As Einstein once said, no problem can be solved with the level of thinking which created it. The problems facing the social sciences cannot be addressed through modifying traditional methods any more than alterations to Newton's equations could accurately predict the orbit of Mercury. They may get "close enough" for a casual observer, but political campaigns, product marketers, and anyone whose livelihood depends on knowing what people genuinely want will face disaster when acting on flawed findings.

This is not to say that existing approaches have zero value; they will likely continue to provide valuable insights, reveal areas where further inquiry is merited, and provide supplemental information that newer approaches are not as suited to collect. However, that sort of data does not meet current standards of scientific rigor and cannot be used to draw accurate conclusions about the world.

This book focuses on how the issues surrounding traditional modes of inquiry are applied to political research and public opinion polling. There are several reasons for this focus, including but not limited to the pervasiveness of this type of research, the accessibility of historically comparable data, and the fact that election polls are one of the few sectors of social science research with an objective measurement against which the accuracy of the research can be judged. The problems in research methodology are far more pervasive, but focusing on how they affect political research shows the extent of the underlying problem.

The first five chapters consists of a discussion of the fundamental shifts in how people have engaged with each other and with the world. This takes the form of a demonstration that these changes have an ongoing deleterious effect on the efforts of researchers in a wide array of fields, such that in many instances a coin flip would be just as likely to be accurate.

The last five chapters are dedicated to discussing what format social science alternatives to action-reaction/ask-answer approaches take. Since circumstances have changed, there is a need for new methods that do not require active and conscious participation. The second half of this book investigates how new data collection methods can overcome the problems faced by traditional approaches.

Such solutions must be built from the ground up. No existing data sources fit the needs of the social sciences, regardless of whatever other value they may offer. The requisite data cannot be repurposed from social media giants, search and browser histories, consumer financial data, or any public records. It must be pure, clean data gathered in a manner which limits the many biases that present themselves in the troves of collected information.

It can be difficult, if not impossible, to implement standards and collection methods which adequately and consistently reflect the realities of human behavior when approaching the problem from a traditional perspective. The shift towards a digital society has profound ramifications on the social sciences, and it presents the opportunity to elevate such fields to a more robust science. Doing so correctly is of the utmost importance if we are to properly understand ourselves and build a society we want to inhabit.

Chapter 1 - Traditional Social Research Is Increasingly Ineffective

Something is rotten with the state of opinion research and polling.[1] For almost a century, nearly every respected researcher in the field has taken a similar approach to producing the data and reports that keep them in business. The methodologies employed have been incrementally adapted to evolving societal conditions, but by and large the core concepts remain strikingly similar to those used in 1936, when the first historically accurate presidential election poll to use simple random sampling was conducted.

The straw polls used at the time were conducted by researchers who generated mailing lists of millions of potential respondents from assorted contact lists. They would then send a mock ballot to these individuals, asking them to fill out and return the ballot. This method created a *sampling bias* because the sample group represented by these contact lists excluded large swaths of the population, particularly those with lower incomes.

Civic, service, and social groups are primarily comprised of individuals from upper income brackets. Even though the method generated a large sample size, sample representativeness is more important than sample size. A large sample that is not randomly generated from the entire population of interest is substantially worse than a smaller, more representative one.

Except in instances such as the U.S. Census Bureau's American Community Survey, to which a response is currently required by law, the data collected from these types of polls is also subject to *self-selection bias*, as those who responded selected themselves into the group by choosing to send back the sample ballot. This creates inherent bias, as those with less interest in participation are excluded.

Literary Digest's[2] 1936 presidential election straw poll, the last of its type conducted and taken seriously, was predisposed to both[3] *sampling bias* and *self-selection bias*. The use of a 10 million person mass mailing to which only 2.4 million responded resulted in wildly inaccurate predictions. The poll predicted that Alfred Landon,[4] the Republican candidate running against incumbent

Franklin Delano Roosevelt, would be overwhelmingly victorious with 370 electoral votes and 57% of the popular vote.

By contrast, George Gallup used a 50,000-person random sample as an effective method for eliminating—or at least significantly reducing—the extent to which these aforementioned biases affected his own results. He correctly called the election for FDR, who won with nearly 61% of the popular vote and 523 electoral votes. This launched a new era of public opinion research, although Gallup's prediction[5] understated Roosevelt's margin of victory by nearly 13 percentage points.

While this paradigm has been a somewhat effective approach for over half a century, recent events have shown that history is beginning to repeat itself. Some of the major problems that first created the structural issues of the past are beginning to resurface. High-impact election outcomes have diverged from what the polls predict, and the trend is only accelerating. Significant changes are necessary for almost the same reasons as in the 1930s, with some 21st century twists.

There is a good reason why the established approaches to public opinion and market research are the way they are: they have worked well enough for a long time. It wasn't until the mid-2000s that societal and technological trends moved sufficiently in a direction that existing methods were ill-equipped to handle to have a significant effect on results. Since it can be difficult to detect how closely research results align with reality, the problems caused by such gradual shifts are not always readily apparent.

The only true checks on public opinion polling accuracy are election results. For the United States and several other nations, this means that presidential elections are the primary indicator. Nearly every polling organization examines every presidential election cycle at some point in some form.

However, since these elections only occur every four years and provide a single real-world data point per cycle, it can take some time to discover trends in polling accuracy. Some other elections, such as those which are regularly contested or those on specific hot-button issues, can provide additional checks, although the datasets in such instances are rarely as robust. They frequently have smaller sample sizes and are conducted by fewer organizations conducting polls which collect data less often. It is uncommon for most of these less-significant political races to receive the level of attention necessary for pollsters to properly check how well the predictions align with real-world outcomes.

Validating market research faces even greater hurtles. While market activity can somewhat confirm or deny the validity of market research, there are often too many variables at play to isolate whether bad research data or poor execution of market strategy was to blame for negative outcomes. Since there is no specific event for which market research results are attempting to accurately determine the outcome, the findings are not falsifiable and thus unscientific at their core. Definitive accuracy checks can rarely, if ever, be conducted under these circumstances.

If the U.S. presidential election is the best case study for the accuracy of the opinion research industry, then it is safe to say that since the start of the 21st century, the practice has seen an increasing decline in reliability. Many of the tactics used to collect information are based on concepts that have been demonstrated to be outdated in other sectors of the economy. Much of the polling industry has yet to fully adapt to the newer ways in which information is both conveyed and collected.

Elections as Research Accuracy Barometers

The Gallup polls illustrate the degrading accuracy of election projections. Because they have used fairly consistent methodological approaches for the better part of a century, Gallup's data provides the best data set for historical accuracy comparisons. In recent years, many more research organizations have started to make their more recent data publicly available, but the Gallup's record is by far the most historically comprehensive.

Prior to 2000, the Gallup Organization[6] incorrectly predicted the outcomes of only two presidential elections since 1936: the infamous "Dewey defeats Truman" findings of 1948 and Jimmy Carter's first race in 1976, against unelected incumbent Gerald Ford. This gives Gallup an 87.5% accuracy rate over 16 election cycles, a respectable rate by any standard.

From 2000 onward, issues begin to arise. Looking more closely at the polls conducted from 2000 to 2016 provides a better glimpse into the problem. Gallup has a 40% prediction success rate over the 21st century's first five presidential elections, evidencing a significant decline in accuracy over time. This trend shows no sign of slowing down. The only presidential elections that

Gallup called accurately after the turn of the millennium were those in which Barack Obama was a candidate, though Gallup was still incorrect about a key factor in the second of those races: turnout.

Both of Obama's elections were decisive enough that the growing problems in the opinion research industry went largely unnoticed during the eight years he served. During that period, the quality of data collection declined as a result of societal and technological changes. The shift in prediction accuracy lowered Gallup's overall accuracy rate to a little over 76%. This relatively high overall accuracy metric, along with the accuracy of its predictions in 2008 and 2012, somewhat cover up the problem with Gallup's predictions as well as those of the industry as a whole. This is one reason the problem has grown, and now many polls no longer predict results within their stated margins of error.

Gallup hardly faces this issue alone.[7] The problem of declining reliability is not confined to specific data collection organizations and does not appear to be the result of the unique internal bias inherent to each firm. Of the 21 national presidential election polls conducted the day before the November 8th, 2016 vote, only two correctly projected Donald Trump as the winner. Only one of these predictions, from Rasmussen Reports,[8] correctly predicted the popular vote outcome.

The situation at the state level was little better that cycle. The majority of the polls in Florida,[9] Pennsylvania,[10] and Michigan[11] projected wins in those states for Hillary Clinton. All of these states went to Trump, but they would have swung the election had at least two of those predictions been correct. None of the polls in Michigan or Wisconsin, which also went for Trump, were accurate to within the stated margin of error, a problem also true of several national polls.[12][13][14]

Wisconsin[15] was considered so likely to vote for Hillary that no polls were conducted there in the final days before the election. This was one of the major mistakes made in the blown 1948 call, a lesson which has apparently been forgotten. When speaking about the poll later that year, George Gallup Jr. said, "We stopped polling a few weeks too soon...We had been lulled into thinking that nothing much changes in the last few weeks of the campaign."[16]

Little improved in the months that followed these inaccurate polls. The Georgia 6th Congressional District's 2017 special election, which took place on June 20th, was projected to go to Democrat Jon Ossoff by wide margins for almost the entirety of the race.[17] This was the most expensive Congressional race in history and occurred outside of the normal election cycle.

Opinion researchers paid the election a great deal of attention, but at no point during the race did any poll come close to correctly predicting the final outcome.[18] Only three of 15 polls correctly named Republican Karen Handel the winner, and those all underestimated her margin of victory by nearly 50%. Of the 10 polls which called the election for Ossoff, only one was within its relatively large 4.2% margin of error.[19]

There were 15 polls conducted for this race, the first of which was taken three months prior to the vote, but only four of which were accurate to within the given margin of error. Of the five polls that were conducted through the week prior to the election, only three accurately called the race within the provided margins of error, and only one accurately projected the winner.[20]

Montana and Kansas also held special elections to fill vacancies created after Trump appointed the Republican congressmen who held those seats to his administration. As was the case in Georgia, these races were given more attention than they traditionally would have merited because early polling suggested possible upsets, amplifying the perception that these races were early referendums on the new president. Polls did correctly predict the winner in these cases, although many of them substantially overestimated the margin of victory.[21]

In the related 2017 Virginia gubernatorial election, most polls predicted the correct winner but greatly understated the margin of victory. Of all 13 polls conducted in the week before the November 7th election, only two accurately projected the outcome to within the stated margin of error.[22] A number of those polls missed the mark by more than double that margin.[23][24][25][26]

The 2016 general election, the 2017 Georgia special election, and to a lesser extent the 2017 gubernatorial elections were very high-stakes events and were examined by scores of researchers. In the end, that didn't matter. Although researchers in 2017 had several months to examine errors in their methodologies after the 2016 presidential election, they failed to adapt.

This is surely not for lack of trying—the ongoing inaccuracies have publicly called their competence into question and now pose a threat to their livelihoods. Dr. Alfred Tuchfarber, *Professor Emeritus* of Political Science at

University of Cincinnati, indicated as much when he noted that "recent mistakes call for more soul-searching than the discipline has been willing to make."[27] Unfortunately for individual researchers, organizations with a lot of momentum that have historically produced returns are generally the most difficult to change.

Dying Methodologies

Both moving objects and organizations have inertia, and just as it requires a lot of energy to change the direction a large moving object, bigger organizations are naturally resistant to change. Unfortunately, this means that when they are heading towards or are already in treacherous waters, it may not be possible to avoid running into icebergs.

Adapting new and often disruptive technologies to firmly-entrenched business practices is difficult, and few companies successfully do so without acquiring smaller competitors who have already successfully deployed their own solutions. Even when they do, organizational inertia can make integrating new methods difficult, leading to collisions with unexpected icebergs that can seriously damage the biggest of ships.

Organizational inertia is evident in the polling industry. The fact that traditional methods have historically been successful in producing acceptably accurate predictions has generated little incentive to re-examine how things are done. The standard script for polling makes many assumptions which are poorly tested. The largest and most basic of these assumptions is that the pollsters effectively know everything they need to know about the needs of the client, the population to be examined, and how respondents will behave in advance.

There is also a general presumption that when polling takes place, a meeting of the minds occurs wherein the respondent fully and properly understands what is being requested by any given question. While there are points in the process where it is understood that this is not the case, large organizations that have been polling for decades often fail to consider that they might not have all the information they need to properly conduct a study before the project is underway.

When a polling or research organization is asked to collect data, there are several steps in between making an agreement with the client and delivering the final product. The process is very similar to the waterfall methodology in software development, a process in which all the anticipated components of the final product are gathered in advance and analyzed to determine the best approach, which is then designed, built, and tested before it is released.

This logically-ordered approach, depicted in Figure 1.1, became quite popular after it was officially documented and released in a 1970 report titled "Managing the Development of Large Software Systems." However, the model was never intended to work as simply as depicted which Winston W. Royce, Ph.D., indicated when stating that the concept as he outlined it was "risky and invites failure."[28]

Figure 1.1 – Software Development Waterfall Methodology

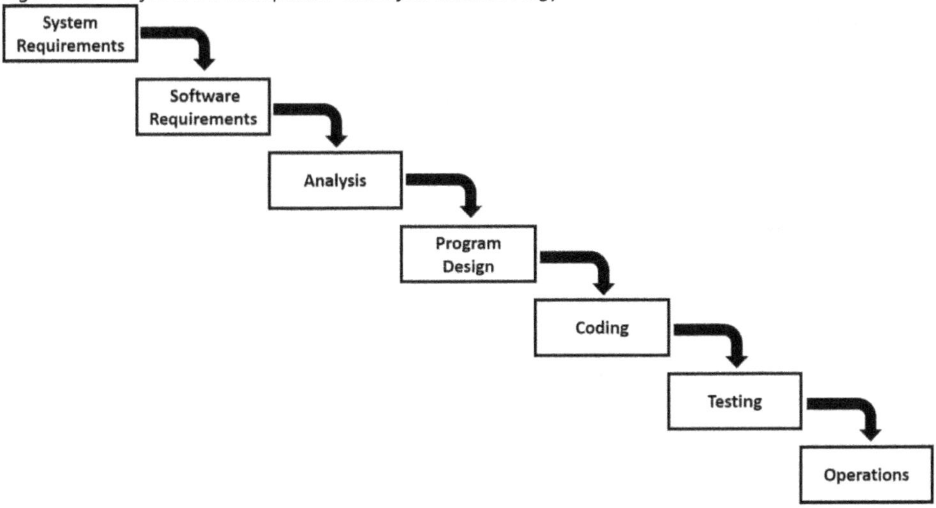

On its surface the concept is sound, but when put into practice, problems surface regardless of the industry in which this approach in implemented. Computers and processing time used to be much more expensive than employee time and labor. The waterfall approach was built around this constraint in order to minimize costs. However, this meant that errors made in stages 1 through 5 were unknown until stage 6. Since testing didn't occur until the very end of the process, locating the source of problems entailed repeating the entire process from at least the second step.

This approach to problem solving and project management has been applied to many industries due to its straightforward nature and superficial appeal. However, after witnessing the many problems posed by using the waterfall methodology, many cutting-edge organizations such as software development firms are moving away from this model.

It is easier for younger companies in newer industries to make such shifts; they lack much of the inertia that causes resistance to change, but established public polling and market research organizations have followed such a template for much longer than most software companies have existed. As such, pushing a firm to abandon something that has served it well for longer than many of its employees have been alive is a long, uphill battle.

Most public opinion researchers implement this waterfall approach by discussing all details of a research effort with their clients up front. By the end of this stage, the research company believes it has a comprehensive understanding of the client's needs. A questionnaire is then constructed based on the researcher's understanding of the client's needs and drawn from past experiences with collecting similar information. The questionnaire is then given to staff, who deploy it. The resulting data is synthesized into a report which is then released to the client, to the public, or both.

Figure 1.2 – Opinion Research Waterfall Methodology

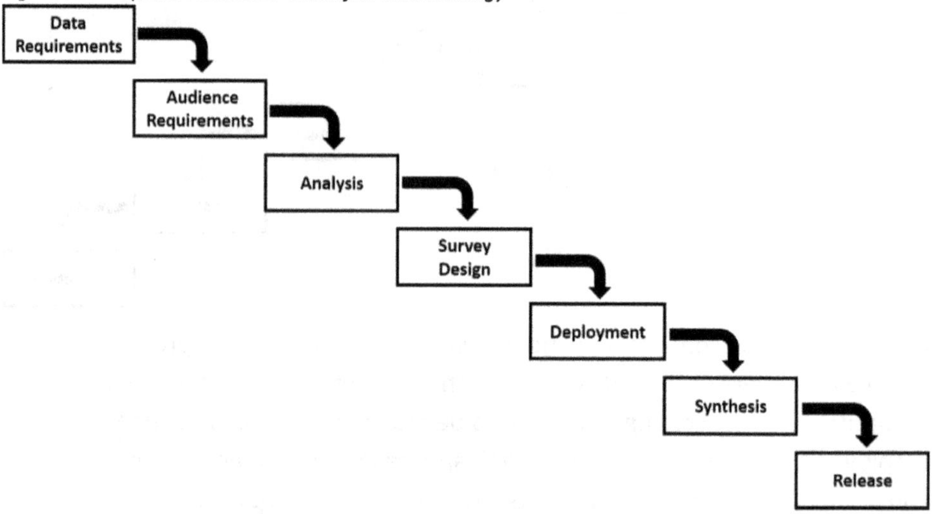

As in software development, issues with survey data collection don't present themselves until the gathered information is synthesized into final reports. This issue is somewhat understood by researchers, who end up taking the results of the initial research and using them to revise the questionnaires, then repeating the data collection process. In some cases, the researchers may even have to go back to the client to verify or revise the data and audience requirements.

Identifying and soliciting response data is the costliest and most time-consuming part of conducting a research survey; ensuring that survey research is viable for more than the most well-funded and patient clients means this step cannot be repeated. It is delayed until researchers believe everything else to be in place. Thus, whereas the cost and difficulty involved in securing computer time to run tests was a primary driver behind the waterfall approach when used in software development, the difficulty and expense involved in reaching individuals for a survey is a key reason why this methodology is still used by researchers today.

There isn't much overlap between the group of people who researchers need to respond to a given survey and the group of people who will do so willingly. Offering incentives for responses increases the overlap between these two groups, but it also increases cost and thus runs counter to the cost-cutting mindset behind taking this approach. A rewards-based system also requires that the incentive be sufficient enough to compel a response. An offer of $5 to take a 10 minute survey will not help much to reach iPhone users, whose annual income averages $85,000 per year.[29]One way in which the industry adapts to this issue is by using focus groups, small panels of well-compensated individuals with a vested interest in the issue being examined, to help shape broader research efforts. These groups average 4-6 people and participating individuals are typically paid in the neighborhood of $100 for more of their time than would be required to complete a survey.[30]

Table 1.1 – Focus Group Compensation

Group	Hours	Compensation	Hourly Rate
Business and Politics[31]	2.00	$150	$75
Richmond, VA Residents[32]	1.00	$150	$150
Truckers & Logistics Pros[33]	2.00	$250	$125
Money Transfer Services[34]	2.00	$150	$75
Phone Interviews[35]	0.50	$100	$200
App Testers[36]	0.25	$50	$200
Russian & Mandarin Speakers[37]	0.50	$50	$100
San Francisco Residents[38]	0.33	$50	$150
Women's Fitness[39]	5.00	$500	$100
Child Care Workers[40]	0.50	$50	$100

Such high hourly rates are effective and leave participants feeling very highly valued, which when combined with how individuals in focus groups are generally "genuinely interested in expressing their opinion"[41] and "like to hear about new ideas coming down the pipe,"[42] according to Diane Hagglund of Dimensional Research, provide massive incentives for thorough participation by imparting substantial value to participants on multiple levels.

A focus group is an excellent way to gather a lot of information about what a small, select group thinks. Since the participants are motivated by substantial compensation and a pre-existing interest in the subject matter, they tend to provide a lot of detail and insights. The open format of these groups can reveal not just what or how people think or feel about something, but also *why* they think or feel that way.

Focus groups are time-consuming. However, for clients with a lot of time and not a lot of money, they can be effective in lowering the capital outlays required to gather data. They reduce the likelihood that a full survey will require multiple iterations, a process which can cost anywhere from $15,000 to over $100,000.[43] In contrast, it likely costs about $6,000 to study a focus group.[44]

The success of this tactic, however, is a mixed bag. Focus groups can certainly be a more cost-effective way to look at what particular groups think about a certain subject, but they come with other methodological costs that, while less obvious in the short-term, could cause significant problems down the line.

While not as rigid, focus groups are still a waterfall-oriented approach. A lot of back and forth occurs during the actual meeting of the focus group, but the requirements and design are planned entirely in advance. The end results are still synthesized into a report for the client, but the reports delivered typically focus on addressing the client's original requirements. In contrast, they downplay spontaneously-volunteered perspectives which may not be entirely related to the questions asked which could yield avenues for additional investigation not previously considered. Unless the client is present to monitor the focus group or reviews the collected data in its entirety, a lot of the value ends up lost.

Additionally, the information that is collected and reported back to the client is highly subject to bias. Participants are often selected based on known prior engagement with the subject matter, meaning they have openly expressed that they are partial in some way. Because focus groups are small, the breadth of opinions they offer is also limited. Even a very large, 10 person randomly sampled focus group would produce results with margins of error in excess of greater than 31%,[45] which renders unlikely the assumption that the focus group is representative of the population in question.

Having multiple focus groups doesn't solve this problem, as there is still a significant margin of error when attempting to generalize from these findings. If one 10-person randomly sampled focus group says half of the population will like a proposed idea, rest assured that between 19% and 81% of the general population will.

Since focus groups are ineffective at determining what broader populations think, they are primarily used in advance of a full survey to refine and narrow its scope. The problem here is that even though focus group data cannot be generalized, researchers still assume that broader populations will think and respond to questions similarly. Therefore, focus groups can actually end up skewing the results of broader data collection, and the real cost of this method comes from the introduction of a small group's biases into a broader survey.

Some unscrupulous organizations may even take advantage of this effect, using focus groups to deliberately develop surveys that will yield results supporting a predetermined conclusion. While still a concern, this is a distinct problem from the one posed by outdated research methodologies.

Even running multiple focus groups cannot entirely erase this problem, and if the objective in using them is cost reduction holding many focus groups in advance of the full survey runs counter to that goal.

This isn't to say that focus groups serve no good purpose or that they are solely damaging. On the contrary, they can be quite effective at uncovering some of the thought processes that go in to reaching a conclusion. They're also a helpful method for finding new ways to reach a very specific audience that thinks very similarly to those who participated. The problems arise when using the collected data to generalize how broader populations think or behave in response to certain stimuli. Focus groups are effectively a waterfall within a waterfall employed with the intent of reducing the risks posed by using the waterfall approach. If this seems counterproductive, that's because it is. In attempting to reduce the probability of errors in the survey design phase, this tactic can actually increase the number of issues while embedding these errors more deeply into the questionnaire so that they are later overlooked as potentially misleading information. The solution to the problems posed by a waterfall approach is not to increase the number of waterfalls.

Data Integrity Issues

Research by Mary and Tom Poppendieck, published in 2006, has shown that when a project is handed off from one person or group to another, substantial information loss occurs.[46] The loss rate is around 25% on average, but Poppendieck's estimates show that "each handoff leaves behind approximately 50% of the knowledge we intend to transfer."[47]

The impact is not uniform across an organization's operations either.[48] Many organizations recognize the ramifications of handoffs and work to minimize it by reducing employee turnover, but information loss regularly occurs over the course of a single project whenever it is passed from one group to another as part of the organization's workflow. Waterfall approaches generally involve a lot of handoffs, causing information loss to accumulate over the course of the project. In the opinion research field, the team that works with a client to create a questionnaire is rarely the same team that fields that survey.

In order to fully appreciate this problem and how severely it can distort data collection, we should examine a case with quantifiable effects. By looking at instances where survey respondents are organizations that follow a membership structure in which each member contributes a portion of the final response, we can see how a mere two degrees of separation from the stakeholder affects the response.

For this example we will examine a case from a national non-profit association which has conducted annual surveys of its membership since 2006 to collect basic statistics about the state of the industry which it represents. The findings from these surveys are published in various documents and are considered the gold standard for data on this subject. They are used by other public education and advocacy organizations as well as policymakers at the state and federal levels to help determine funding and legislative priorities. This association's membership is mostly comprised of other organizations and agencies, which themselves often represent multiple other companies or groups.

In one annual survey, which was conducted for the 11th time in 2017, an issue with one set of responses highlighted how handoffs can result in significantly skewed results. This particular survey is sent to a single point of contact in every U.S. state. The recipient is usually someone within the state government office that licenses certain educational programs or someone who works for the association's largest member organization within that state.

Respondents are asked to gather a broad range of aggregate statewide figures. Some can do so very quickly by using statewide systems that track and compile the information requested by the survey. In such cases, there is only one handoff. Due to the relatively small number of respondents, the research team is able to work very closely with them to resolve any issues and vet responses for potential errors.

In some other states such systems do not exist or are inaccessible for the purposes of this survey, so the data must be aggregated from multiple systems that are run by separate groups. In these cases, the single respondent works with their counterparts at smaller regional organizations within the state to put together an aggregate statewide response. This means there are at least two handoffs between the original stakeholder, the national association's policy and research department that designed the survey, and the individuals from whom the requested data would actually be sourced.

Sometimes the regional team staff members cannot process the data requests from the state respondent. When this happens, the regional staff member must pass the request along to yet another individual to retrieve the numbers, adding another handoff to the process. By this point, the original request is so far removed from the respondent that the cumulative misinterpretations and omissions mean we can expect over 50% information loss.

In 2017, one respondent from a state without access to a statewide system responded unusually late. The research team's attempts to follow up individual were unsuccessful. Eventually, when they managed to connect to a regional organization representative, the team discovered that the state point of contact had moved on after distributing the request to the regional groups.

After working closely with members from each of that state's regional groups, the research team was able to compile that state's aggregate response. The direct collaboration between all regional organizations revealed that each regional point of contact had interpreted the specifics of the requests somewhat differently. Some contacts felt the criteria to be broader or narrower than others, meaning that each had compiled their portion of the aggregated data using different filters, and they had each excluded different data types from their totals.

When this aggregate was analyzed and compared to one that had been generated previously, it was quickly discovered that the 2017 aggregated figures, which were generated after two handoffs, were only 55%-75% accurate. The nature of these disparities varied significantly from region to region; some had managed to correctly deduce the actual criteria for most data points while others missed the mark on every measure. Many were correct on some metrics and wrong on others, with little consistency from region to region. The only responses that could effectively be analyzed for comparative accuracy were for questions with purely quantitative answers.

The specific circumstances allowed the research team to do it right—the stakeholders and the team that crafted the research questionnaire were the same party. Thus, when the research team worked directly with the regional respondents to re-generate the state's aggregate response, the respondents and client were working together with only one degree of separation.

Very rarely is this the case. In most instances, the client seeking data is not the same group that executes the research. This work is usually outsourced to a third-party professional research organization, as this national association had done intermittently in the past before bringing the process back in-house.

Additionally, the fact that the general respondent pool was limited to one respondent per state and that conducting this survey was a top priority for the research team made it possible for the team to work directly with respondents. This is another rarity, as most research teams have multiple clients competing for their attention and hundreds or thousands of respondents to manage for each of them.

Because polling organizations cannot often afford to invest heavily in ensuring high-quality data, they tend to rely on automated processes to fill the gaps. The advent of artificial intelligence may end up making efforts to follow-up with individual respondents much more cost effective, but as of this writing, the automations employed by the industry are not nearly so advanced; generally, they are limited to email reminders. Even in the best case scenario, the use of AI still amounts to hounding respondents with messages that may annoy them, get caught in spam filters, go unnoticed, or otherwise fail to result in a completed response set.

Digital questionnaires are one way in which polling and research organizations have attempted to adapt to our hyper-connected world. They need not involve a handoff to additional personnel, assuming a member of the team that created the survey is able to process it into a format for distribution. Still, digital questionnaires create a layer of separation between the team that built the survey and the person responding to it.

Individual respondents may have significantly different understandings of what is meant by a given word or phrasing in a survey. Even when a client and the researchers are in perfect sync, there is significant information loss as soon as the research team distributes the questionnaire to respondents with whom they have no other direct contact.

These handoffs and their respective information loss are symptoms of the industry's waterfall-style approach. The inability of hundreds or thousands of respondents to communicate how they interpret what they see reduces data integrity, and it threatens the validity of any findings derived from the research project.

The only way to guarantee comprehensive data from an online questionnaire is by building personal relationships between the researchers and respondents, yet this is a very time-consuming process. It's rare that any organization can afford the luxury of working closely with respondents, a process which sometimes takes weeks or months, to guarantee that high-quality data will be retrieved. The aforementioned national association, recognizing the need for data of the utmost quality, invests heavily in getting it right. It's necessary that they do so in order to raise the bar for their industry, ensure the safety of those enrolled in the programs they represent, and secure affordable access to all that require such services. Unfortunately, not everyone employs such a careful approach.

Behavioral Problems

One way researchers and the organizations that employ them increase response rates and data quality is by using skip logic. Skip logic involves asking different sets of questions depending on responses to earlier ones. This tactic helps researchers collect more in-depth data on the topics that are more applicable to an individual respondent while speeding other respondents past sections that may not apply to them.

While using skip logic can help ensure that respondents only see appropriate questions and disqualify individuals who don't fit the sample population, it has some drawbacks. This method makes it more difficult to estimate the completion time for any one person. A questionnaire that takes substantially longer than a respondent expects can be annoying to participants. This method also limits how much can be addressed in any survey without creating a *self-selection bias,* especially when using online digital surveys. Since it's much easier to click away from an annoyingly long online form than to hang up or walk away from a human interviewer, these data collection efforts often only hold the attentions of dedicated survey takers or people with a strong emotional investment in the subject matter. This is a manifestation of the root problems behind the waterfall approach, specifically the implicit assumption that researchers know everything they need to know about each respondent's worldview and that questions will be interpreted in the same manner by each person. The resulting information losses come in the form of collecting less data than might be needed to build a robust sample or by *self-selection bias,* which renders the data incongruent with reality. In cases where both of these factors are present, the research results are highly suspect.

Worse, since in many cases this loss is difficult to quantify or identify at all, it often goes completely unnoticed. When discrepancies are observed between the research results and real-world outcomes, rarely is it attributed to flawed research practices. The number of variables at play means the integrity of the research results can often go unexamined when in fact they may be flawed to the core.

When telephone interviews and canvassing are used for data collection, an entirely new team generally takes over from the survey designers to solicit responses. These people only know what they see on the script in front of them and are unable to provide much in the way of guidance on questions beyond their own interpretations, which may not be any more accurate than the respondent's own understanding. This type of handoff can be even more damaging than those created by a digital questionnaire approach because the respondent is likely to believe the interviewer to be much closer to the material than they actually are.

In cases where a respondent believes the interviewer's understanding of the questions to be better than it is, "clarifications" provided by those interviewers can create additional layers of unrecognized confusion and further affect the respondent's understanding of the question. This means in most cases the respondent's answer accuracy is likely to only be about 50% of what the researchers intended to learn due to the compounded information loss associated with the number of handoffs involved in these approaches to data collection.

Some polling groups may deliberately exploit this effect. A street canvasser working to gauge support for a certain campaign may have no knowledge of what the terms they are using actually mean and could unknowingly convey false information to respondents.

For example, an advocacy group seeking to stop a commercial development which would pave over a small creek may attempt to have it designated by the U.S. Environmental Protection Agency as a "navigable waterway" or a "protected wetland" because it had qualified in the past,[49] though is now too small or shallow. Such a group could hire street canvassers to generate support for the push, knowing they are unlikely to understand that the creek no longer qualifies for protection and thus are more likely to pass along suspect information. This would likely result in overstated support for the measure. Since such polling issues are rarely examined in detail, the level of support would likely be taken at face value.

Another problem that arises is the fact that person-to-person data collection is often much more qualitative than quantitative. Respondents may give more open-ended responses which do not fit into the options presented. For instance, a phone interviewer who asks about which political philosophy respondents most associate with may get a response that doesn't fit clearly with the answer choices.

In a poll on voting preferences, an individual may report that they are liberal on some issues and conservative on others. In these cases, the interviewer may try to get a more specific response but eventually mark the respondent as "moderate" when in fact that respondent places far more weight on the issues where they consider themselves liberal and thus always votes for liberal candidates, or vice versa. If skip logic is used, this classification may change the next set of questions, resulting in erroneous data while ignoring the questions that would have provided more insight.

Canvassing also creates both a *self-selection bias* for the simple fact that people don't often like stopping to talk to people on the street. A canvasser's cause is generally readily apparently, so individuals with a particular interest in a given subject are thus far more likely to stop and talk to the canvasser. In contrast, others may project their negative biases onto the canvasser and deliberately ignore them as a result. While this can help researchers reach certain quotas, it skews the perceived level of support because little information is gathered from those with less substantial interest in the subject matter.

Additionally, evolving societal and technological trends are also contributing to *sampling bias* issues. The federal Do Not Call Registry has affect research institutions by limiting who researchers can call. Laws which vary from state to state sometimes explicitly ban the use of automated dialing systems, robocalls, or unsolicited text messages for the purposes of requesting survey information.[50] Some research organizations can obtain exemptions from these restrictions, but most individuals are unaware of this and may respond with hostility or deliberately provide misinformation to an exempt organization. The trend away from landlines has also hampered efforts to conduct surveys by telephone. Developments such as caller ID and the shift towards social media and mobile apps for communication have led some organizations such as Pew Research Center to move towards mixed-mode surveys for contacting and interviewing respondents.[51]

This opens up an entirely new set of potential problems. The use of multiple data sets creates issues when a respondent completes one part of the survey process using one collection vehicle but fails to respond to the other supplementary modes employed. Additionally, since a mixed-mode model uses qualitative and quantitative methods, the issues previously discussed can be found in the final data set, which compounds the severity of the data integrity problem.

For example, climatologists used ice core samples to estimate the atmospheric conditions that existed before more precise measurement tools such as satellite data were available. They then switched to the far more precise satellite data. However, without a significant overlap between the two sources, this effectively compares apples to oranges.

This issue applies to public opinion research as well. When social scientists attempt to blend two different data sources together, some of which collect more qualitative data while others focus on quantifiable measurements, a substantial body of data must measure responses to the same question from each of the sources. This is necessary to properly create a cross-walk between the two data sources.

Getting respondents who have already answered an array of questions from a live interviewer to respond to those same questions again through other means—often digital and thus impersonal ones at that—can lead to feelings of frustration. The respondent is likely to feel that the researchers should already have this data and be less inclined to provide it again.

This makes it difficult to build comparative datasets. Mixed-mode models that attempt to reduce biases are thus hamstrung by introducing even more *self-selection bias*. Additional *sampling bias* can also be introduced in such instances because it requires that researchers identify populations reachable via multiple formats, which are unlikely to be representative of the general population. Attempts to compensate for biases in data thus have the ironic and unintended effect of making the problem worse.

Chapter 2 - The Rules and Standards are Changing

History tends to repeat itself, and the public opinion research industry is no exception. Revolutionary changes in the way people interact in the 21st century have led to the resurgence of *self-selection bias* and *sampling bias* in research efforts. This problem is the primary driver behind the polling industry's rising inaccuracy.

The industry has made some modifications in order to adapt to changing times, but these efforts have not been enough. Poll quality has declined over time, even though some predictions have still been accurate. High-profile misses are at record highs because an entrenched industry has failed to identify both the root changes and how significant the necessary methodological revisions are.

A casual observer may attribute some responsibility for the decline to events such as substantial changes in laws, though in reality the underlying causes aren't so obvious. Market researchers have managed to secure some exceptions to government regulations[1] such as the Do Not Call Registry and the Telemarketing Sales Rule that enabled its creation. While these exceptions have slowed the decline, the primary barriers to quality opinion research are not grounded in law.

Though legal pitfalls do exist, investing in legislative protections has a high rate of diminishing returns. Short of creating a legal obligation to respond to polling outreach by pollsters, which would likely pose a number of constitutional and ethical issues, legislative approaches are unlikely to resolve the issues as they are primarily sociological and technological in nature.

Best practices in the industry were built on assumptions that revolved around 20th century lifestyle habits, only some of which have been reexamined. The way people now respond to attempts by unknown parties to initiate communication creates an obstacle for pollsters, one which traditional approaches to survey research are ill-equipped to address. One noteworthy technological shift has been the swift rise of mobile communication technologies, particularly the widespread adoption of cellular network operated devices in first-world nations. As recently as 2003, nearly 95% of U.S. households[2] had landlines. When nearly everyone had a landline telephone and regularly answered calls, landlines were a generally reliable way to sample every desired population. This is no longer the case; as of the end of 2016, fewer than half of Americans had landlines.

The rise of wireless-only households means that calling landlines creates a *sampling bias*. According to the Centers for Disease Control and Prevention, at the start of 2018, 72% of renters lived in wireless-only households while only 44.6% of homeowners fall into this category.[3] This uneven distribution of homes that still have landlines means homeowners are around twice as likely to be represented in polls conducted through landline calls. Yet, while we now live in an era when over 90% of Americans had a cell phone,[4] 25% of calls made by researchers at Pew are still to landline telephones in 2018[5], as they did in 2016 when wireless adoption rates were similar.[6] It would still be difficult to reach a representative ratio of homeowners and renters by only calling cellular devices, as 82.9% of renters have wireless devices compared with 63.8% of homeowners, but the sample would be less unbalanced along this axis.

If pollsters call wireless phones, their survey will sample three homeowners for every four renters, while a landline survey will sample eight homeowners for every four renters. Theoretically, the 25:75 landline-to-wireless sampling ratio has the effect of balancing out the *sampling bias* in each medium, but aggregating together two separate samples collected from two different populations is a scientifically questionable approach. Given that there are now multiple types of voice calling including IP phones and services such as Skype or Google Voice, the continued reliance on telephone surveys necessitates dubious practices to achieve samples with are mathematically in line with what other research indicates they should be.

Even though some researchers have acknowledged the need to reach respondents digitally, doing so has posed problems which have confounded them. The disproportionate distribution of respondents leads to weighting—giving higher value to some responses over others—in an attempt to correct for any bias that might be created by this sampling error.

The fact that these samples are not always drawn from a pool representative of the broader population raises additional questions about their broader applicability. Pollsters have tried to address this by using tools like SurveyMonkey to conduct non-probability samples, where presumption of an equal likelihood that any member of the population being studied will be included in the sample is discarded. Scott Clement of The Washington Post describes their process for executing this sort of polling research leading up to the 2016 general election in his article *How The Washington Post-SurveyMonkey 50-state poll was conducted* published September 6th of that year.

> The Post-SurveyMonkey poll employed a "non-probability" sample of respondents. While standard Washington Post surveys draw random samples of cellular and landline users to ensure every voter has a chance of being selected, the probability of any given voter being invited to a SurveyMonkey is unknown, and those who do not use the platform do not have a chance of being selected. A margin of sampling error is not calculated for SurveyMonkey results, since this is a statistical property only applicable to randomly sampled surveys.[7]

The trend away from traditional modes of communication is accelerating over time, indicating that a wholesale paradigm shift is underway. Technological shifts are slowly changing the way people interact with one another. The rise of new media and selectively-curated narrowcast news feeds is making people more likely to only accept inputs which we have previously approved. In turn, we tend to reject that which comes to us from anywhere outside our predefined social circles.

Lower Trust Breeds Lower Quality

While current polls have substantial issues that make them less reliable, some have still been able to call attention to the fact that on average, Americans place almost identical levels of trust in public opinion polls as they do in news and media groups.[8] Their support for all of these sources is currently at an all-time low,[9] and this is not something that a change in methodologies can easily address.

The fact that trust in public opinion polls closely reflects trust in media organizations has several implications. Most public opinion poll data is published by news organizations. When major information outlets are no longer seen as legitimate by substantial portions of the population, the research findings they publish are seen as tainted by association. The irony that polls—

which are currently the only real way to measure where the public stands on such matters—are themselves no longer considered reliable has not been lost.[10]

In the Huffington Post, Natalie Jackson and Grace Sparks address this issue in a 2017 article:

> It's understandable that many people wouldn't trust public opinion polls after the run of election polling errors—or perceived errors—in recent years.
>
> Critics point to Brexit polls, which mostly indicated that staying in the European Union would eke out a narrow victory in the U.K. referendum last year, and to the U.S. state-level polls that failed to indicate President Donald Trump would win in enough key states to take the Electoral College majority and win the presidency.
>
> In light of these recent issues and known difficulties in identifying who will turn out to vote — a key source of uncertainty in the election polling enterprise — more skepticism by the public and the media regarding election polls is probably warranted.
>
> **But even with extra skepticism about election polls, there's no other measure that can give us a broad view of what the public thinks.**[11] [emphasis added]

According to polls conducted in the first few months of 2017, only about a third of Americans trust the media,[12] which declined further in the year afterwards according to a report by the American Press Institute in June 2018, [13] with substantial variation by political party identification. A March 2017 McClatchy Marist poll indicated that of all political identifications, only "strong Democrats" placed at least "a good amount" of trust in polls. This finding is particularly interesting given that most polls in 2016 incorrectly projected the Democratic presidential candidate as the winner.

Due to the issues affecting poll reliability, of course, we cannot be certain how accurate these numbers are. When segments of the population lose trust in polling, this can lead to a substantial bias in favor of those who continue to respond, which partially explains the decline in poll quality.

If strongly partisan Democrats are far more likely to respond to an opinion poll than strongly partisan Republicans—which is arguably the case since these same polls indicate 52% of strong Democrats trust polls compared to 27% of strong Republicans[14]—the results of those polls are likely to contain bias. The effect is comparable to *Literary Digest*'s oversampling of Republicans in 1936 by drawing respondents from populations made up of voters who tended to be more Republican than the overall electorate.

That this disparate impact comes at the same time as the rise in narrowcast media, which allows individuals to curate and filter which information makes its way into their consciousness, makes obtaining participatory buy-in from study population members much more difficult than it has been in the past. People are becoming far more accustomed to actively filtering what information they take in. Everything from ad blockers to phone call filters have allowed *confirmation bias*, "the seeking or interpreting of evidence in ways that are partial to existing beliefs,"[15] to flourish in our daily lives.

According to polls conducted in September 2018, a 68% majority of Americans get their news from social media,[16] and 43% specifically did so from Facebook. These polls also report that for those Americans who get their news from Facebook, over 60% of them indicate the fact that news was shared from within their network is a major factor in how trustworthy they consider the information to be. [17]

These findings are supported by research from the American Press Institute indicates that people believe that their personal sources of information are fairer and more accurate than other information sources.[18] If a majority of Americans favor information from within their network, this poses problems for researchers and pollsters, who are unlikely to be "in-network" for the entire populations they need to study.

A substantial level of individual *confirmation bias* necessarily increases the magnitude of *self-selection bias* present in research findings. Potential respondents who believe their responses will be misinterpreted, or that they will not be adequately represented, or that the results of the research will be used to further a partisan agenda to which they are opposed will be far less predisposed to participate even when they are appropriately included in the sample.

The momentum within the polling industry makes it difficult for any organization to execute the pivots necessary to adapt to the shifts which have led to the bias resurgence. There are many factors at work, many changes occurring simultaneously which each present their own challenges. Addressing all of these concurrent societal changes and incorporating the necessary methodological adaptations to each into an organization's practices is a tall order for groups that have followed a very similar framework for nearly three-quarters of a century. Additionally, it is now easier than ever for *self-selection bias* to find its way into a sample since social media and other technologies increasingly condition the general population to quickly reach for the "block" or "ignore" button in response to outreach. The advent of communications tools which allow people to identify who is attempting to contact them before answering means that unexpected messages from unknown parties are less likely to connect with the intended recipient than ever before.

In practice, this has resulted in a precipitous decline in survey response rates. Pew Research Center witnessed response rates drop from 36% in the late 1990s to a quarter of that, 9%, in 2016 remote polls such as calls to landlines and wireless phones.[19] Survey interviews conducted in-person by organizations such as the General Social Survey (GSS) have maintained higher participation and completion rates over the years but have still experienced a drop in the 21st century.[20] From 1975 until 2000, the GSS maintained an average response rate of approximately 76.9%. From 2000 through 2014, this survey has seen an 8.5% decline in response rates. This drop in response rates has been observed across industries and is not limited to public opinion research. The National Survey on Drug Use and Health saw its household screening interviews decline from 93% participation to under 80% from 2000 to 2015.[21][22] The National Immunization Survey's combined response rate fell from 87.1% in 1995 to 34.9% in 2015.[23][24]

Even with the legitimacy of the U.S. Census Bureau to support it, the Current Population Survey has also experienced a drop in response from 93% in 2000 to 86.6% in 2015. Some parts of the survey, such as the Annual Social and Economic Supplement, saw a proportionally greater decline—from 85.6% response to 76.3%—over the same time period.[25] This is a phenomenon that is not isolated to any specific research organization, industry, topic, or survey medium. While the severity of this effect is not uniform, most people are becoming less willing to respond to survey researchers as time goes on.

Figure 2.1 - General Social Survey Average Response Rates by Decade

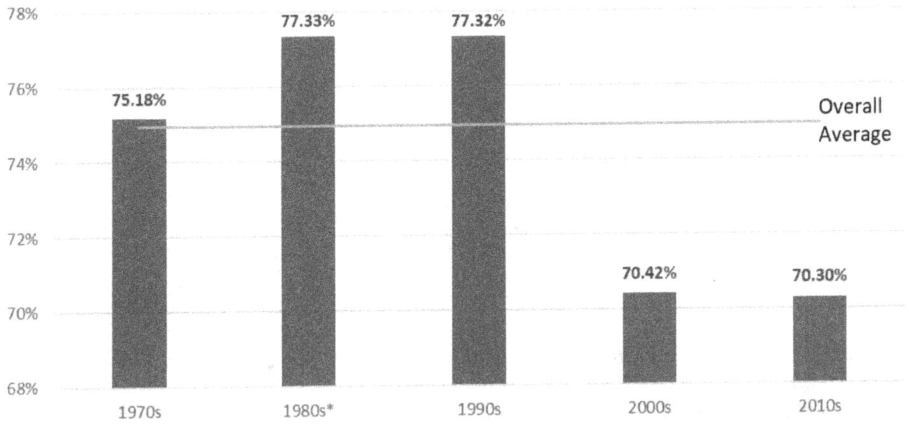

** 1982 and 1987 each had two samples, one containing a* sampling bias, *which are excluded from these averages*

One major source of survey research data that has *not* experienced this response rate decline is the legally mandated American Community Survey. With the force of law behind it, this very long and detailed survey has maintained an average response of over 96% since the year 2000, peaking at 98% in 2009.[26] The low rate of refusal, which since 2000 has varied from 0.8% in 2008 and 2009 to a high of 2% in 2015, shows that mandatory participation can minimize *non-response bias*.

There has been some variation from year to year, but only once, in 2013, did less than 90% (89.9%) of selected recipients provide a complete response to the American Community Survey.[27] The Census attributes this outlier to the lack of follow-up efforts that year due to a government shutdown in which non-essential federal government offices suspended operations.[28] The only other year with a sub-95% response rate was 2004, which the Census similarly attributed to funding issues.

Figure 2.2 – Assorted Survey Response Rates

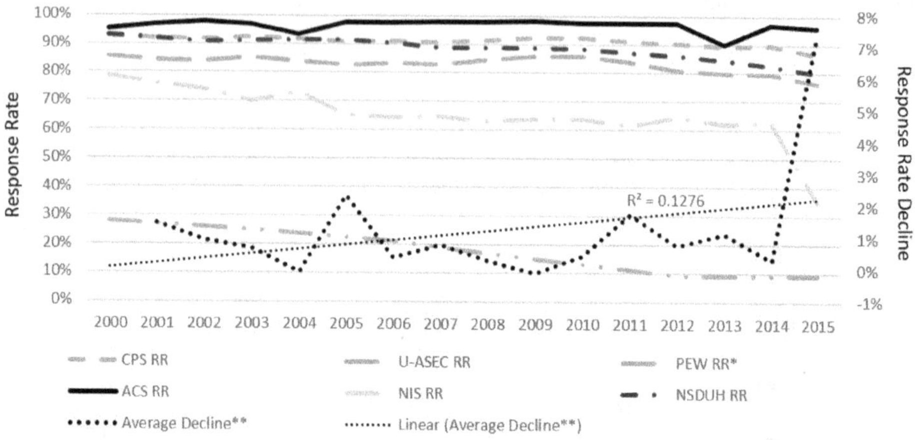

** Pew only provides response rate data at 3-year intervals. Data for missing years interpolated from real data*
*** Average Decline does not include data from surveys to which a response is required by law*

Since few surveys, even those conducted by government bodies, have mandatory participation enforced by fines for missed questions or false responses,[29] the response rate problem is difficult to solve without creating moral and ethical problems.

For the four non-compulsory surveys mentioned above, the response rate decline from 2000 to 2015 was around 1.2% per year. The data does not give any indication that the trend is slowing; the average decline in the most recent five-year period examined (2.3% from 2011-2015) was more than double that of the first five-year period (1.1% from 2001-2005).

This issue is not limited to the United States. Surveys conducted in the United Kingdom have seen similar response rate declines.[30] In a meta-analysis of a dozen studies conducted in Great Britain from the start of the new millennium to 2015, only a single one of the surveys examined saw an increase in response rate. The overall average fell from 67% at the start of the timeframe to 57.5% at the end. 28This approximately 0.679% annual rate of decline is roughly 55% of the drop magnitude witnessed in the United States over the same time period, but provides evidence that this is not a uniquely American phenomenon.

Additional efforts are needed to keep response rates higher, and some organizations have put over 20% additional work into ensuring that respondents are represented accurately.[31] However, there is a diminishing rate of return on additional follow-up efforts. A meta-analysis by Keith Bolling at Kantar Public UK showed that few additional gains are made after the 6th attempt. Additionally, there is every reason to believe that respondents are likely to see repeated communication attempts as a nuisance, which makes it more likely that they will block or ignore future outreach efforts.

This trend has not gone unnoticed. The National Academy of Sciences (NAS) acknowledged that "response rates continue on a long term downward path"[32] in a 2013 examination of the issue titled *Nonresponse in Social Science Surveys: A Research Agenda.* However, while social science researchers have previously documented this drop in response rates, investigations into the reason behind them have failed to pinpoint the cause. The NAS called attention to this in its 2013 study by expressing their concern "that solid evidence about the reasons for the decline is still elusive."[33]

New Social Norms Pose New Research Challenges

The shift towards living a more digital life is certainly a contributing factor. In a realm with ubiquitous filters, people can much more easily remove unwanted intrusions into their daily awareness. There is a good reason for this: the rise of the internet has taken the competition for people's attentions global.

The progression towards a more digital life has occurred in tandem with new developments in AdTech that have increased public skepticism towards external influences. Online advertisements are now able to follow a person around the internet through a process called retargeting, usually carried out through cookies and without explicit consent.

This practice has raised some concerns among privacy advocates, and the practice has faced regulation within the European Union.[34] The EU currently requires people to expressly opt-in to the use of cookies, with varying implementations for each member country. However, the use of cookies is still widespread. One of the side effects of cookies-based retargeting's broad utilization is a phenomenon known as advertising fatigue.

Facebook defines advertising fatigue as "[w]hen everyone in your target audience has already seen your ad many times, it becomes more expensive to achieve desirable results."[35] More broadly, over-tasking human awareness with frequent interruptions and distractions substantially reduces peoples' overall functionality;[36] populations which have been inundated for extended periods are already operating at a base capacity of 60% at best.[37] As audiences become saturated with ads, it becomes increasingly expensive and difficult to reach them, capture their focus, and engage them by any means.

The marked increase in demands on our attentions means that information filters are necessary for people to keep from getting lost and distracted. Once people become accustomed to applying these filters to one part of their lives, it gets easier to do so in other aspects as well. This means that when people start blocking perceived nuisances on Facebook and Twitter, they also become more likely to ignore unexpected phone calls or emails from people they don't know.

The *sampling bias* created by the rise of blocking technologies is immense, as respondents effectively have to opt in to communications from researchers or they won't be seen at all. Being able to reach target populations now requires narrowcasting through their preferred channels, even while doing so inherently creates the same additional biases present in using third party generated lists. Attempts to compensate for *self-selection bias* by narrowcasting recruitment efforts can serve to increase the level of *sampling bias*, just as efforts to minimize *sampling bias* by using traditional broadcasted techniques in 21st century first world societies have contributed to a rise in *self-selection bias*.

There are three main steps for assembling a representative sample: identification, recruitment, and collection. Each step creates the possibility that the integrity and accuracy of the final research results will be compromised.

One way market researchers—though generally not reputable political pollsters—attempt to identify and reach people is by purchasing their contact information from third parties. While people generally dislike having their information sold,[38] this approach can be a decent way to reach general or specific audiences. Purchased lists are far from ideal, though, and there are three major problems with this tactic.

First, it may result in blocks from some of those on the lists. Sometimes, people may block incoming messages that are not from the organization to which they originally supplied their contact information. For example, a user of Google's Gmail service can create an alias for their email address by adding a "+" followed by a string of characters before the "@" sign. A Gmail user with the primary email address "hello@gmail.com" can use "hello+c1@gmail.com" when providing their email to outside organizations if they suspect that their email address may be sold. Emails sent to "hello+c1@gmail.com" will still arrive at the "hello@gmail.com" inbox, and the user can create a filter which rejects emails sent to "hello+c1@gmail.com" unless they were sent by the company to which the alias was originally provided. Some filters may then blacklist the sender's entire email domain permanently.

Second, buying contact lists is functionally identical to the *Literary Digest*'s sampling strategy for its straw polls conducted from 1916-1936 and is subject to the same flaws. Unless the purchased list represents the entire population to be studied, both a *sampling bias* and *self-selection bias* are likely in the final sample. If the reason behind buying contact information is to improve the quality of research results, the presence of these biases can work to counter any benefit from doing so. Addressing this issue requires respondents, once identified, to join a research organization's group of panelists and commit to ongoing participation in a broad range of surveys.

Third, buying contact information may not be always legal and can bring about potentially bankrupting penalties. Each email found to be in violation of the United States Controlling the Assault of Non-Solicited Pornography and Marketing (CAN-SPAM), Act can result in fines of up to $40,654 per email according to the Federal Trade Commission's compliance guide.[39] An email found to be in violation and sent to a 1,000-person list can thus yield a penalty as high as $40.654 million.

The Canadian Radio-television and Telecommunications Commission (CRTC) "has a range of enforcement tools available, from warnings to penalties (up to $1 million for individuals and $10 million for businesses)" for violations of CASL, Canada's anti-spam legislation.[40] This legislation "applies to emails, text and instant messages, and any similar messages sent to electronic addresses."[41] In order to be in compliance with CASL, researchers generally must obtain express consent in the form of an opt-in from the recipient.[42] Additionally, there are "no specific exemptions for survey or market research communications built into CASL,"[43] which means that researchers targeting Canadian audiences need to be especially careful that their actions are not considered commercial activity.

Within the European Union, Article 13 of Directive 2002/58/EC requires that recipients of electronic messaging opt-in.[44] As with the EU Cookie Directive,[45] implementation of this requirement varies somewhat within each of the member nations.[46] Overall, however, it requires that all digital communications be requested in advance by the recipient. Consequentially, the use of purchased contact lists is not an ideal solution to the problem of reaching target populations.

Because sold contact lists often lead to unwanted solicitations, people are less inclined than ever to respond to unexpected outreach attempts from unknown sources. As such, reaching someone by purchasing their contact information naturally lowers their receptiveness and likelihood of participation. A 100% delivery rate to an email list is rare, as is identification of a reachable sample that's 100% representative of the population; this is where *sampling bias* occurs. Additionally, even if the population is correctly identified, the different rates at which individuals are reachable causes problems.

People who spend most of their time in the digital realm live their lives largely in echo chambers.[47] These chambers are consciously chosen and are actively curated by the people within them. These people are generally skeptical of anything that comes from outside their selective spheres. Therefore, penetrating these chambers is in some regards the only way to include such people in a broader representative sample. Failing to include them would create a *sampling bias* every bit as much as relying on assorted membership lists does. Because broadcast messages reach fewer and fewer, narrowcasting is the only way to ensure they are a part of the sampled population.

Attempting to narrowcast to a wide variety of groups in order to appropriately sample a broader population is fraught with several issues. Most important is that narrowcasting by nature creates a *sampling bias,* a problem that can only be overcome through large samples taken from a wide variety of groups. Acquiring appropriately large samples can be expensive. Finding the appropriate groups for whom pollsters should create outreach campaigns also takes time, meaning the respondents must generally be reached in advance.

This is how the Washington Post SurveyMonkey poll was conducted in the leadup to the U.S. 2016 general election.[48] Gathering an audience in advance of a survey presents its own unknowns, however, such as whether respondents will still be available when the survey is deployed and whether they will self-select to participate at that time.

When sample sizes are in the neighborhood of 1,000 respondents, it's not cost effective to develop all the narrowcast recruiting materials and deploy them as is required to ensure a representative sample, especially if the sample is not reusable. Reusing such samples would be the only way to make this cost effective for most research clients, but it is still subject to biases. A sample group that's appropriate for one study may be significantly biased for another, and non-response can still mean that the process needs to be repeated anyway. Gathering a large, representative, and reusable survey sample requires massive investments, which are unlikely to pay off at a time when response rates are in continual decline. A large and motivated team equipped with sufficient funding may overcome these issues, but the outcome is unlikely to be cost effective. Continually making requests of individuals' time creates advertising fatigue, as people tire of seeing the same requests for more than three days.[49]

The unequally-distributed rise in blocking technologies as well as sampling via third party contact lists combine to substantially magnify the biases each individual phenomenon presents. Addressing social shifts by shoehorning new tactics onto older methodologies will bring about an increase in bias. The population of respondents itself is changing; people now live their lives fundamentally differently than in the previous century and are subject to a different set of influences.

When a problem is misdiagnosed, the solutions pursued are unlikely to have the desired results. Even without funding barriers, it is difficult to see a representative sample through from initial identification to data collection, regardless of how effective researchers are in eliminating initial *sampling bias.* Identifying a scientifically sound sample does little to prevent problems that arise in the next step of the process: engaging the members of that sample to solicit their participation. This point is where most *self-selection bias* presents itself.

Cognitive Changes and Pressures Negatively Affect Data Collection

When respondents must opt in to participate, this yields significant loss. Just as marketers must entice readers to click their emails with carefully-crafted messages, researchers must design surveys that encourage respondents to take them. This challenge is made all the more difficult by the fact that that the average human attention span is getting shorter.[50][51]

The average human's short-term attention span shrunk by nearly a third between 2000 and 2015. On average, humans now hold the dubious distinction of having a shorter attention span than a goldfish. With these unprecedented changes in how people relate to the world, it's no surprise that survey completion and response rates are so low. They are competing not only for a potential respondent's time, but also for his or her focus. Decreasing attention spans also pose a problem during the survey itself. Researchers must hold a person's attention for the recommended 20 minute completion time of an average survey.[52] The difficulty posed by this obstacle is evidenced by the fact that a relatively small number of people follow through after initially agreeing to participate in research. Completing a survey requires a continual refocusing on the task by the respondent. If some of the survey questions are substantially more difficult than others and take much longer to complete, respondents may lose interest and abandon the survey.

This problem, too, is getting worse. The severity of the decline implies that this *self-selection bias* may pose a greater challenge to poll accuracy than *sampling bias* does. From the late-1990s to the mid-2010s, Pew Research Center's contact rate fell by 31.1% while the completion rate for those successfully contacted fell by 67.4%.[53] In combination, these changes resulted in an overall response rate 75% lower at the end of this time frame than at the start.

The attention span problem wasn't as severe in the past since interviews generally involve an interpersonal connection between the interviewer and the respondent. In cases where the level of interpersonal interaction has remained higher, such as the GSS,[54] we see a much higher survey completion rate than with less personal formats.[55][56] When some public opinion surveys exceed 60 questions in length,[57] it is unsurprising that increasing numbers of respondents fail to complete them.

Longer surveys, designed to gather significant quantities of information, must somehow entice respondents to complete them lest they get bored and switch to something else. Some surveys attempt to compensate for this by changing subjects, but this can introduce bias into later responses through a process known as response priming, where later answers are affected by earlier ones.[58] This affects all surveys and particularly longer ones, which is why most reputable polls have always asked the Presidential approval question first.[59][60]

It easier for people to maintain focus—or to continually refocus—on a conversation with another person. Social pressure to not appear rude and consideration for the interviewers' feelings can help respondents stay engaged. On the screen, respondents don't receive the same relief from continual focus or nudges to re-engage with the material as when another person asks questions. Nobody feels remorse for abruptly abandoning a machine that requires their time, attention, and information. It's much easier to stop clicking answers on an online questionnaire than to hang up on a person with whom you have already engaged in a discussion and have established a basic level of rapport.

While more data is collected and the respondent pool is less structurally prone to bias when interviews are conducted by a live person, there is some indication that data quality can suffer when respondents provide information to another person rather than to a computerized system.[61] One factor which is more pronounced in person-to-person data collection is the Bradley Effect, sometimes called the Wilder Effect. Named for former Los Angeles Mayor Tom Bradley, this phenomenon focuses on racism as an electoral motivator – it occurs when a white candidate is running against a non-white candidate, and some white survey respondents who are racist attempt to hide their racism by telling pollsters they support the non-white candidate when in fact they cast votes for the white one.[62]

This phenomenon has been subject to several criticisms. The polls from where the effect's name originates, conducted on the 1982 election for Governor of California, were subject to a number of flawed practices.[63] One of these was the same timing problem which led to Gallup's blown call in the 1948 Presidential race between Harry Truman and Thomas Dewey as well as a failure to account for an unexpectedly large number of absentee ballots cast. The elections of Barack Obama also led researchers to discount its effects.[6465]

Although the Bradley Effect has largely been written off by social scientists, the term has evolved to essentially cover all cases in which respondents lie or otherwise deliberately provide false data to pollsters. The concept continues to live on because the general principle of survey respondents misinforming interviewers has seemingly manifested in other forms.

The Shy Tory Factor is one of those manifestations, one which focuses on political parties and philosophies in general rather than specific individuals. This phenomenon was first discovered in Great Britain, where it was found that Conservative voters may refuse to answer pollsters honestly, indicating that they supported the Tory party less than they did. This effect has also been found to understate support for the Republican Party in the United States.[66]

As a result, candidates and issues favored by the right in each of these nations have historically performed better than opinion polls indicate that they should. This makes sense to some extent—it stands to reason that when respondents are already disinclined to trust pollsters, there is little incentive for them to provide honest answers.

The pervasive nature of echo chambers and the *confirmation bias* that accompanies them means that those predisposed to believing that their views will not be accurately represented in research findings can circulate amongst themselves evidence of instances where they can accurately claim this to be the case, continually reinforcing this belief. The confluence of these phenomena serves to amply the effects of the Shy Tory Factor to the point where the data collected may consistently misrepresent reality.

However, due to the already questionable nature of polls, it is possible that the Shy Tory Factor as it is observed is in truth a manifestation of compounded *sampling bias* and *self-selection bias*.[67] This is difficult to reconcile with the fact that the effect seems to be more pronounced in surveys where the respondents have higher levels of personal contact with the research team, but is worth considering.[68]

This results in somewhat of a "balloon effect," as cracking down on one part of a problem without addressing the underlying issue leads to manifestations of the same issue in other areas. Each way in which survey researchers attempt to compensate for rising bias and inaccuracy in one portion of their operations has the unfortunate effect of increasing other integrity issues. Failure to identify the root cause of the problems means that attempts to address them will be largely unsuccessful and often counterproductive.

Efforts to reduce *self-selection bias* can be shown to increase the levels of *sampling bias* within a respondent panel. Actions taken to minimize *sampling bias* are executed in ways which result in a rise in *self-selection bias*. When researchers attempt to address both problems head-on simultaneously, the inability to fully eliminate them leads to compounding errors that offset any potential gains. Additionally, the integrity of collected data may be compromised through effects such as the Shy Tory Factor as a consequence of the evolving ways in which people interact socially.

The affected industries are largely unaware of how deep the problem runs, when they even acknowledge that it exists. Respected institutions seem to recognize the symptoms of what amounts to a cancer in the discipline, but they then ascribe them to the equivalent of the flu or a common cold. The British Polling Council & Market Research Society's Report of the Inquiry into the 2015 British general election opinion polls evidences one such misdiagnosis:

> In this report to the British Polling Council and the Market Research Society we have considered a broad range of evidence in order to assess what caused the polls – collectively and individually – to produce inaccurate estimates of the national vote shares in 2015. Our conclusion is that the primary cause of the polling miss was unrepresentative samples. The methods the pollsters used to collect samples of voters systematically over-represented Labour supporters and under-represented Conservative supporters. The statistical adjustment procedures applied to the raw data did not mitigate this basic problem to any notable degree.[69]

For the most part, social science researchers are dimly aware that something is amiss given the major events that have not gone as predicted, but the problem is largely considered to be a surface level issue. Continual tweaking of and tinkering with established practices is seen as the cure for the problems, when in truth they are merely bandages. Successfully addressing the full scope of historical changes requires either morally-dubious legal mandates, which would only partially address the underlying problems, or more realistically, a significant overhaul of the ways target populations are sampled and surveyed.

Chapter 3 – The Survey Format Itself Invites Unreliability

Unlike the hard sciences, which can compare their data to objective reality and execute hypothesis testing under controlled laboratory conditions, no two surveys are ever performed under identical circumstances. This means that there is almost no way to verify or control for data. The samples that are collected vary with each research project. The mindsets of respondent shift regularly, and the "question and answer" format survey research necessarily entails means no study can be free of bias.

Researchers in the hard physical sciences researchers have the benefit of real-world hypothesis testing, which is not subject to the same biases present in sampling human respondents and is repeatable under conditions that can replicated. This means that other researchers can independently verify findings much more easily and with lower thresholds for margins of error and statistical significance.

The laws of physics are not generally subject to change; any given particle, chemical, or other natural body will largely respond in known ways to given stimuli. This is far less true in the social sciences, where the threshold for a statistically significant relationship is a mere fraction of what physical sciences require. Dr. Christopher L. Heffner, who holds a Doctorate of Psychology and a Ph.D. in clinical psychology,[1] states that "In the social sciences, a correlation of 0.30 may be considered significant."[2] This stands in contrast to the hard sciences, which have much higher thresholds for such a designation.[3] This contrasts with Dr. Bruce Ratner, whose Ph.D. is in statistics and states that correlations "between 0 and 0.3 (0 and -0.3) indicate a weak (negative) linear relationship"[4] while those "between 0.7 and 1.0 (-0.7 and -1.0) indicate a strong positive (negative) linear relationship."[5]

The ways in which we study human interactions are still in their infancy and are only now beginning to transition from their nascent qualitative formats to more rigorous quantitative methods. While recent developments now allow for truly quantified data collection, most attempts to quantify survey research data have consisted of forcing natively qualitative information into a quantifiable format.

The benefits of such quantified data are limited in several fashions—including by law, social custom, and personal preferences—but they can still provide researchers with significant advantages if collected properly. *Sampling bias* and *self-selection bias* can still present, as discussed in Chapter 2, but the greatest benefit they offer are modest improvements in the quality of collected data.

As long as survey research employs qualitative methodologies that collect data based on a waterfall approach, findings therefrom will continue to diverge from objective reality. One major reason for this is because information loss and distortion which occurs at the data collection stage is difficult to identify and quantify. Doing so would require the respondent to effectively rewrite the survey questions in their own words and then collaborate with the research team to determine where any discrepancies between understanding and intent may lie. If the respondent pool is small enough and the researchers dedicated enough, this exercise can greatly improve data accuracy.

However, this would need to be done for every question in the survey by every respondent. This can be very impractical given the demands on all party's time and the standard size of a survey respondent panel. For longer surveys, this can be an insurmountable hurdle to clear even with a smaller panel; the back and forth process can take up to several months to complete with a single respondent.

Length, Response Priming, and Question Order Affects Answers

Questionnaires, the staple of the survey industry, are by their nature subject to levels of bias and inaccuracy that increase with every subsequent question. This effect is called "priming," or *question order bias*, which is defined in the Encyclopedia of Survey Research Methods as "a psychological process in which exposure to a stimulus activates a concept in memory that is then given increased weight in subsequent judgment tasks."[6] This phenomenon can have the effect of altering the response to each question that follows from what it would have been had that question been asked independently. Marc D. Weinher offers an example of such priming in *A Natural Experiment: Inadvertent Priming of Party Identification in a Split-Sample Survey*, from the Bloustein School of Planning and Public Policy at Rutgers University in New Jersey:

> Republican Party identification can be inflated by priming with typically conservative issue concerns, such as the public economics of disaster recovery and rebuilding, and the role of the state in regulating development. At the

> same time, Democratic Party identification is immune to such priming but can be inflated by priming exposure to traditional liberal and more affective concerns, here personal experiences prior to, during, and immediately following Superstorm Sandy.[7]

Any given question alters a respondent's mindset by creating cognitive anchors, which leads to biases for subsequent questions. Priming people to think a certain way by inducing certain emotions is an inherent problem with the question-and-answer format used in survey research. Since the effect is cumulative, answers to questions at the end of longer surveys may be significantly distorted.

Response priming is the reason why the presidential approval question is almost always asked first in political polls. Placing that question after a series of other ones about specific policies gives additional weight to those policies specifically mentioned in the mind of the respondent.

As a thought experiment, consider a hypothetical survey about Richard Nixon seeking to gauge how positively or negatively he is remembered by those born after his death in 1994. This survey has three questions:

A. Do you approve or disapprove of former President Richard Nixon's job performance?
B. Do you approve or disapprove of former President Richard Nixon's actions during the Watergate scandal?
C. Do you approve or disapprove of former President Richard Nixon's actions to end the Vietnam War?

Leaving the questions in the order above would provide a clean answer to Nixon's overall job performance, as would flipping the positions of the Watergate and Vietnam questions. Any other question order would likely result in tainted responses to the job performance question due to the anchoring effect of response priming.

On one hand, asking question B first and placing question A in the middle would elevate awareness of the scandal[8] which resulted in Nixon's resignation[9] and would therefore give more weight to his negatives when the respondent then considers whether they generally approve or disapprove of his overall performance.

Inverting that order by placing question C at the top, A in the middle, and B at the bottom would produce the opposite results due to the same effect. By giving weight to the sentiment which propelled Nixon's electoral success prior to asking about his performance, we should see higher overall levels of approval. Such an ordering would also tend to lower the level to which respondents disapproved of Nixon's Watergate behavior–if primed to regard the 37th President in a more positive light, his actions may seem less significant.

Response priming is a well-known issue to which there is no silver bullet. Most manifestations of this phenomenon are not as clear-cut as in the Richard Nixon example; researchers cannot always predict what cognitive anchors their questions create. The fact that not everyone has the same reactions to a question means that no two samples will experience the effects of response priming identically.

Asking the same set of questions from the hypothetical Nixon survey about former President Obama, for example, and substituting Watergate with Benghazi or the IRS targeting scandals would be unlikely to yield the same weighting effects. Respondents are more likely to have different opinions on Benghazi than about Watergate, which is notorious for resulting in the only Presidential resignation in American history.

This effect can be somewhat reduced by randomizing the order in which questions are presented. While any legitimate political poll will pose the general approval question first, respondents may be presented the following questions in a completely different order. Randomization does not eliminate response priming in the data from any one respondent, but is employed to reduce any cumulative effect in the overall sample.

In the Nixon survey, if one third of respondents are given the original A-B-C question order, one third are given the B-A-C order, and the remaining third see C-A-B, the effects of response priming theoretically should balance themselves out. This does not mean they are eliminated, but rather that the aggregate net effects result in data equivalent to what it would have been if there had not been response priming present.

In practice, since no respondent sample is homogenous, the effects are minimized but still present. The greater the number of questions asked, the more cognitive bias any given response set will contain as a consequence of priming. Question order randomization can lessen the impact of this bias, but it cannot remove bias from the data set entirely and must be done in a calculated manner so as to not cause other problems throughout the survey.

The use of this data hygiene tactic can be jarring to participants if a questionnaire covers multiple subjects and question location is randomized without regard for topic. David L. Vannette, Ph.D., addresses such problems in "Biased Data Are Bad Data: How to Think About Question Order":

> While randomization can help reduce bias introduced by question order effects, it is not a perfect solution. Some questions need to be asked in a particular order to make sense, and other questions, including branched questions, need to be asked in a specific order to be effective..*[sic]* For these types of questions it is best not to attempt randomization and simply ask the questions in order.[10]

The issue of cognitive anchoring also presents itself within individual questions, particularly multiple-choice ones, producing an effect known as *response-order bias*. Vicki Eveland, Associate Professor of Marketing at the Mercer University Stetson School of Business and Economics, and William Sekely, Associate Professor of Management and Marketing at the University of Dayton, acknowledge the problem and yet state that "researchers have long been aware that position or response-order bias may influence an individual's answer to a multiple choice question, but the issue has received limited empirical examination. Only a few studies have examined and documented response-order bias as it relates to survey questions."[11]

Eveland and Sekely suggest that this bias is less attributable to emotional anchoring when it appears within questions. Instead, they write, it is related to two other psychological phenomena known as the *primacy effect* and the *recency effect.* The *primacy effect* is a form of bias in which items at the start of a list are more likely to be selected than others, and the *recency effect* is the inverse, a bias in which items at the end of a list are more likely to be chosen.

The longer the list of choices, the more powerful these effects. Additionally, in "Effect of Response Position and Number of Responses on Responses Selection" Eveland and Sekely note that "the more general the content of a question and the more vague a response it requires, the greater the possibility of order effects."[12]

In an effort to combat *response-order bias*, the order in which answer choices are presented is sometimes also randomized. As when randomizing question order, however, there are many cases in which some answer choices logically need to remain in a specific location, such as an "Other" option at the end of a list.

This randomizing tactic does not truly eliminate *response-order bias*. The primacy and recency effects still have an impact, but the aggregate net impact of these effects on the entire data set of all survey respondents is reduced. Data for any one given response is biased, but the group of responses contains biases theoretically balance themselves out if the randomization is executed correctly.

Another method sometimes used to test for internal consistency is to present reciprocal questions in various sections. When using this technique, pollsters ask essentially-identical questions which should have identical responses but flipping the sentiment orientation from positive to negative, and vice versa. This allows researchers to check whether a respondent's views were influenced over the course of the survey to the point where their answers are no longer "clean."

A standard format for these types of questions is to initially ask "Do you support X?" with a "Yes/No" response option. At another point in the survey, a question asking "Do you oppose X?" appears, with the same answer choices. These questions are best spaced sufficiently far apart so that the respondent doesn't make a connection between the two questions and responds independently to each.

A scale ranging from "not at all" to "support/oppose strongly" may be used as well, but keeping the response options limited in order to avoid *response-order bias* in these questions is essential. Use of a scale rather than a binary response can sometimes make this check less effective because the format does not always allow positive and negative answer choices to simply be inverted. The use of a scale may introduce too many variables when switching from one form of the question to its reciprocal. This is why a simple "Yes/No" answer format works best for these consistency checks.

If a scale is used, then keeping the question wording the same is a better way of measuring the impact of priming biases. However, this increases the likelihood that the respondent will realize something is up, which often creates even more problems in the data and invalidates the results of the test.

Ideally, a respondent who answered "Yes" to the "support" question will answer "No" to the inverted "oppose" version. This theoretically indicates that the respondent has maintained general internal consistency within their responses to the survey. There is always the possibility that the respondent simply picked the "correct" answer randomly or through chance, but as with most techniques employed to improve data quality, this approach does not eliminate bad data; it helps the total aggregated response set more closely reflect reality.

While the response priming effect is among the chief reasons respondents don't always answer the reciprocal question "correctly," there are several other reasons why this may occur. For instance, it's possible that respondents may not be paying close enough attention to the task at hand. In longer surveys, there may be a number of confounding variables which have accumulated to change a response, and these variables can be hard to identify individually. According to Stephen Ansolabehere and Brian Schaffner, "Distractions are common, affecting at least half of all respondents in a 30 minute interval, and... add substantially to the completion time of surveys".[13]

Decreasing attention spans have made distractibility a more pertinent issue in survey research than it has been at any other point in the discipline's history. In some cases, a respondent may take weeks to complete a survey.[14] This is yet another problem which can possibly invalidate the data collected from that respondent; intruding thoughts, distractions, and long breaks can affect the content of responses.[15] Ansolabehere and Schaffner examined the frequency of such distractions in their article "Distractions: The Incidence and Consequences of Interruptions for Survey Respondents," noting that longer surveys mean more distractions are likely to occur:

> At the end of each of the surveys we asked people whether they engaged in any of 9 activies*[sic]* while completing the survey. We sort the distractions into two types – those that are imposed from the outside and those that the individual seeks out. Dealing with a child,

> talking to another adult, and answering a phone call are all events that call our attention. Watching TV, looking at other websites, taking a break, reading email, sending texts, and doing chores are all activities that the respondent would initiate, and might be motivated by the person's lack of interest in the task at hand...
>
> We are struck by their frequency: ***15 to 20 percent of respondents report watching TV while doing a survey, and almost the same percent report talking to another adult*** *[emphasis added].* The next most common distractions tend to be taking a break and making or answering a phone call. Some of the surveys also show very high percentages of people who look at email during the survey.[16]

While there has not been much research conducted as to whether interruptions and distractions during surveys degrade response quality, it is safe to say that an individual returning to complete a survey two weeks after they start will have likely experienced some external stimulus which could affect their responses.

Ansolabehere and Schaffner postulate that response quality degradation would be detectable in two ways: interruptions with this deleterious effect may "reduce the correlations between items before and after a distraction"[17] as well as potentially "affect the extent to which respondents answer factual questions correctly during the survey."[18] The first marker relies on the response priming effect by determining if its strength was diminished by a distraction, while the second is harder to pin down, as the effects "might occur in either direction."[19]

Reciprocal questions can aid researchers in determining the presence of the first marker in longer surveys, but they are not perfect solution. Additionally, they are subject to a diminishing rate of return the more they are used. Reciprocal questions can also be used to test for cases involving factual knowledge, but doing so properly requires that researchers increase the number of reciprocal questions, which in turn decreases their effectiveness.

In November 2016, some who argued about whether or not the presidential election results should be accepted abruptly changed their minds after the election,[2021] showing how external events can significantly change one's perspective. A survey respondent asked whether election results should be respected under any circumstance on November 7th, 2016 who waited three days to respond may have given a completely different answer than they would have beforehand. If this question was in the middle of a survey to which respondent had already answered the first half of the questions, the entire response set is likely to have been compromised.

Ansolabehere and Schaffner claim that there is no compelling evidence that response quality is affected by interruptions or distractions,[22] but the example of the election shows us how response quality may suffer as a result of certain circumstances. Few such interruptions would have such a level of prominence as to be a clearly-identifiable cause, but interruptions can nonetheless influence responses without the knowledge of the research team. Because this can be difficult to test for and since incorporating those tests into the survey can degrade the survey's overall quality, this is a fairly uncommon practice.

Reciprocal or identical questions can annoy respondents as they may feel like they have already answered the question being asked, which they often effectively have. The more robust survey questions designed to test for internal consistency are, the greater the likelihood that they will be noticed by the respondent, which degrades their reliability.

If such a question appears too close to its reciprocal or in the middle of a completely unrelated section, the benefits of this tactic may be negated. Reciprocals which appear too close together may prompt the respondent to go back and review their previous response to ensure they align. This can be a good thing if it keeps the respondent focused on the survey and on providing quality responses. However, it may distract the respondent and push them to scour the survey for other instances of such questions. It can be mentally taxing as well if the respondent spends large amounts of time hunting for a reciprocal question, preventing them from staying focused on completing the survey as a whole.

The Impact of Wording Choices

In addition to question order, word choice in questions and answers also plays a substantial role in determining what sort of response is likely to be given. Leading questions are another issue with the question-and-answer format that can be all but impossible to fully avoid. The Legal Information Institute at the

Cornell Law School defines leading questions as "[a] type of questioning in that the form of the question suggests the answer."[23]

Consider, for example, the following questions:

- "Do you support eliminating state income taxes and raising state sales taxes to make up the shortfall?"
- "Do you support eliminating state income taxes and raising state sales taxes to 10% from 5% to make up the shortfall?"
- "Do you support eliminating state income taxes and raising state sales taxes to make up the projected $10 billion shortfall?"

All of the above questions may describe the exact same plan, but the wording used can significantly affect responses. To prevent support being either overrepresented or understated, researchers may ask each of these versions and compare the responses, randomized to reduce the effects of *question order bias*, but this only minimizes the impact of the problem rather than eliminating it. Leading questions have such widely-acknowledged effect that they are largely disallowed within courts of law,[24] except on cross-examination of witnesses. The profoundly altered responses given to leading questions when compared to "clean" versions of the same questions yield research findings which do not conform to reality.

It is not always obvious that a given word choice will have a leading effect. For example, asking someone if they saw "the" stimulus in question has been shown to generate a greater level of positive response than asking that person if they saw "a" stimulus.[25] Using "the" presupposes the existence of the stimulus in a way "a" does not.

When even word article choice can have an impact on responses, consider complex questions such as "Do you agree or disagree with the following statement: 'He has obstructed the administration of justice, by refusing his assent to laws for establishing judiciary powers.'"[26] It seems unlikely that questions such as this one, which was asked as the 55th of 61 questions in a survey conducted by Public Policy Polling, are collecting the data the researchers originally sought.

This question contains numerous charged words, does not provide for a subject nor is one given in a section header, and uses words in ways which leave the respondent wondering what the question is asking. This question actually requires the invocation of response priming for it to be answered at all; since the pronoun "he" is never defined, each respondent must substitute their own noun in order for the question to make sense. All that survey-takers know from the wording is that the intended subject is male.

A related issue is the fact that the same word often has different meanings to different people. This can be easy to see when we look at different countries which nominally speak the same language. For example, the American use of the word "trunk" to describe what is referred to in Great Britain as a "boot" illustrates regional differences in how wording is interpreted.[27] The same goes for how Americans use the word "pissed" to mean "angry" while in the England the term means "drunk."[28]

The issues caused by different understandings of the same word can be subtle yet profound. For example, if a survey question seeks to determine whether respondents had been recently physically assaulted by asking, "Has anyone committed an act of violence against you in the last month?" it will likely produce a greater rate of affirmative responses than it otherwise would have if the term "violence" was clearly defined.

As of this writing, the American Psychological Association defines violence as "an extreme form of aggression, such as assault, rape or murder."[29] However, there is also a line of thinking that "[i]f words can cause stress, and if prolonged stress can cause physical harm, then it seems that speech—at least certain types of speech—can be a form of violence."[30] This viewpoint has been codified by the Cambridge Dictionary, which currently defines violence as "actions or words that are intended to hurt people."[31] This definition requires violence to be directed at people, exempts unintended actions, and includes speech with offensive intent rather than just acts with a physical component.

According to a Pew report citing FBI statistics, violent crime rates are low enough that it could be reasonable to assume that in a random sample of 1,000 respondents pulled from the general population of the United States, only a single person will have been physically assaulted at most.[32] However, depending on the definition of "violence" used by those answering the question, the findings from the survey may indicate that substantial portions of the population have been physically victimized when in reality respondents were reporting arguments with family or strangers on the internet as acts of violence.

Asymmetric distribution of knowledge and information continues to pose problems even when the researchers are aware that it exists. In many cases, researchers may be attempting to determine support for a proposal or a hypothetical scenario, in which case they must sometimes provide the respondent some information about the subject when asking the question.

In the hypothetical Richard Nixon survey discussed earlier in this chapter, some of the target respondents may not be aware that Watergate occurred during the Nixon Administration, or they may not have been aware that he was elected in 1968 in part due to his campaign promise which stated: "I pledge to you that we shall have an honorable end to the war in Vietnam."[33]

The questions posed in that hypothetical survey assume a level of knowledge on behalf of the respondent. Although this information is part of the history curriculum in most American schools, inattentive students, international students, or others not aware of this information may not recall the Watergate scandal or the end of the Vietnam war, in which case using these terms may confuse the respondent.

Successful survey research efforts depend upon an identical collective understanding of the words used in questionnaires. If the researchers have a different definition of a term than the respondent pool and fails to realize this, their findings may not be reflective of reality. This problem can be addressed by including definitions for key terms used within any given survey, but given the waterfall approach the discipline employs—a method in which a survey is entirely drafted in advance of deployment—identifying the words which are likely to pose definitional problems in advance effectively relies on luck and random chance.

Properly building the question wording such that respondents will not have different responses can be extremely difficult in a world where definitions of terms in common use are subject to significant degrees of interpretation. The waterfall approach does not allow for iterative testing of collected response data quality. This means that problems caused by word selection often go undetected until the final analysis, if they are discovered at all.

An agree/disagree question which is phrased “Those in poverty have shorter lifespans” is largely the same in meaning as one worded “The poor die sooner.” However, the same sample population may have very different responses depending on which wording they see, even if this is the only variation within the survey.

Wording A/B testing can identify how certain words induce different responses, but since there is no true objective wording to measure against, there is no way to know what the true value is for the data being sought. The nature of survey research also makes conducting such tests in a controlled manner more difficult than in other sciences; the mental processes and level of knowledge will vary from one individual to the next, often introducing confounding variables that may affect the results. Ideally, researchers would run both versions past the same sample, possibly within the same survey, though the *question order bias* this would create poses additional concerns to data cleanliness.

Sufficient information must be presented to respondents, but leading phrases should be avoided. Conscious or unconscious bias on the part of the research team can make this problem more difficult to root out. Researchers tend to be more educated than the general population and thus are predisposed to make assumptions about their study populations which may not be true.

Public Policy Polling provides us another real-world example of this issue. It asked, "If your member of Congress voted for the health care bill currently being considered by Congress, would that make you more or less likely to vote for them in the next election, or would it not make a difference either way?" [34] If the respondent does not follow the goings-on of Washington DC politics closely, they might not have been aware that a health care bill was under consideration at the time of the survey. The researchers likely knew which health care bill they were referencing at the time and drafted the question accordingly, but there is no guarantee that the sample which received the survey had the same understanding of the question.

Retrospectively, we cannot know which health care bill this question addressed without knowing more about the survey, as there have been many different health care bills in the last decade alone. Without ample metadata, the response data collected by this survey is relatively useless to researchers, even setting aside the issues with the question itself and any potential problems with the sample. Avoiding leading questions or biased wording requires great care. The wording of questions, as well as what they include and what they leave out, affects the response. Sufficient context must be provided without giving too many superfluous details to secure accurate responses that have not been contextualized to lead the respondent to answer a certain way.[35]

The need to ensure respondents have some understanding of the topics on which they are being surveyed often requires the use of more words in the question. This in turn increases the likelihood that the question is leading and can potentially cross the line into "push polling," which the Marketing Research Association refers to as "deceptive persuasion calls," or "deceptive advocacy techniques." Additionally, it notes that "researchers also refer to 'push polling' as 'political telemarketing.'"[36]

Such polls are not legitimate, although they often masquerade as being genuine. Unfortunately, they are occasionally conducted by researchers generally considered reputable, who themselves may not realize they are engaging in push polling. This in turn can further damage public opinion regarding polls in general.[37]

Combating the problems of bias created by word choice and lack of respondent knowledge requires a high level of precision within each question. In the case of legislation, which is often multi-faceted and complex, it can thus be very difficult to determine true levels of popular support for any given law. This means that attempts to determine levels of support for any given proposal, real or hypothetical, must be broken down into much smaller segments and examined individually.

Appropriately addressing this problem through traditional means requires asking a lot more questions; this leads to substantially greater levels of *question order bias* in the final results of the study. The balloon effect, in which combating one form of bias necessarily creates additional levels of another type of bias elsewhere, can thus be seen within efforts to combat question-based bias.

Scales, Neutrality, and Being Forced to Choose a Side

If we set aside the issues of questions and response wording and ordering in order to focus on the collected data, other problems are revealed as well. Shoehorning respondents into specific for/against categories creates a problem somewhat similar to the one posed by poor question wording.

Questions which are presented in an agree/disagree format often provide little context. This can be seen in the popular survey question, "Do you feel that things in this country are generally going in the right direction today, or do you feel that things have pretty seriously gotten off on the wrong track?"[38] This question tells us very little about why people think the way they do. According to Gallup, a majority of Americans have been "dissatisfied with the way things are going in the United States" since January 2004,[39] but it does not answer the question of why. Follow-up questions can provide a little additional insight but have never told researchers what the "right direction" and "wrong track" are in the minds of respondents. They don't reveal what needs to be done to get the country moving in the "right direction. At best, follow-ups provide targets for blame.

Additionally, a purely binary response format doesn't tell us how strongly held a respondent's beliefs are. Most surveys combat this problem by measuring levels of agreement using the Likert scale, a rating scale through which "[r]espondents may be offered a choice of five to seven or even nine pre-coded responses with the neutral point being neither agree nor disagree."[40] Likert scales provide several advantages. They collect data in more quantified formats, which are much more easily analyzed than free-text or other purely qualitative responses. Researchers also learn much more about the responses since intensity, not just direction, is provided.

Likert scales come with issues, though – if they are used repeatedly or in groups, respondents who have agreed with several questions in a row may continue to indicate they agree to maintain the pattern. This can apply to other patterns beyond straight responses of a single type, such as alternating responses between "agree" and "strongly agree". According to ChangingMinds.org, "[respondents] may also deliberately break the pattern, disagreeing with a statement with which they might otherwise have agreed."[41]

Not all Likert scales have an odd number of choices; some professionals and others with experience in the field will only use even-numbered scales which do not contain a neutral midpoint, or "don't know" option.[42] One major reason advocates for even numbered scales do so is that odd-numbered scales tend to over-represent neutral stances;[43] respondents tend to use that as a default position, which is referred to as *central tendency bias*.

This is the same phenomenon which states that guessing the middle option in a multiple-choice test question is most likely to yield a correct answer if the test-taker has no idea as to the correct response. There are also concerns as to what a mid-point answer truly represents. Respondents may use it to mean "neither agree nor disagree", "undecided", "don't know", or "no opinion."[44]

Additionally, a respondent may end up over-thinking the question and misrepresenting their stance on subjects where they either don't feel particularly strongly or haven't put much thought into the subject before. This can skew the collected data in unpredictable ways which are difficult to test for across respondent pools. This is also where the Bradley Effect and Shy Tory Factor, if present in a dataset, are generally theorized to hide. Respondents who experience *social desirability bias,* defined as "The tendency of research subjects to give socially desirable responses instead of choosing responses that are reflective of their true feelings" by Pamela Grimm at Kent State University,[45] can indicate they are neutral towards something on which they actually have stronger opinions. This issue is generally more prominent in surveys conducted in person or by some other interpersonal method, but it may still present itself in less personal formats such as online questionnaires.

Even-numbered scales, on the other hand, can pressure people into taking a side on subjects where they truly are neutral. James Brown at the University of Hawai'i has found that some respondents may be "so prone to selecting the neutral answer that they circle the space between the 2 and the 3" in a four option scale.[46] On a four-point scale, some respondents may be forced into providing an inaccurate answer, which by definition degrades the quality of the response set as a whole.

New Social Structures Require New Research Methodologies

Survey research faces many problems. Any one of the many issues this practice faces can be nominally addressed, but at a cost. In some cases, this cost comes in the form of a substantial financial investment, but the issues run deeper than anything that can be addressed by cash infusions. Pouring money into one aspect of data integrity issues can yield progress on that point, but this necessarily creates other problems if researchers adhere to the same general principles in their solutions which gave rise to the initial problems.

One of the core problems with survey research is the fact that surveys are rooted in the question-and-answer format. The act of asking a question necessarily affects the response in ways that can be impossible to measure, especially when doing so requires asking even more questions. This is a closely related phenomenon to the Observer Effect, where the act of measuring a particle's behavior changes it, as famously demonstrated in the Double Slit Experiment.[47]

In many cases, the way in which a situation is presented to a person affects their response. There are a great many ways in which a question could be constructed, and each one may elicit different responses. Since no question can objectively measure a respondent's position on a topic, questionnaires can only approximate the respondents' true stances.

The adaptations made within the survey research field and the tools adopted to facilitate them are still centered on the same flawed methodological approaches which made them necessary at all. Tweaking existing measurement tools only moves the source of data problems from one place to another. This allows the experts and professionals whose paychecks depend on solving these issues to claim they have made progress and gives them some supporting evidence to which they can point, but in reality the status quo has been largely maintained.

Polling and survey research must account for psychological effects due to the fact that they are examinations of the human mind. Methodologies and practices which walk into the issues presented by known psychological factors under the assumption that they can be addressed though survey structure will never fully excise the biases these phenomena create within the data.

Chapter 4 -
There are Insufficient Motivations to Improve

Despite the significant problems polling and survey research faces, there is not a sufficient impetus to drive real change within the industry. Those who hire pollsters seem willing to continually forgive and forget the numerous blown calls; each time a major election has not gone as polls predict, there is only a brief period of questioning. Then, another poll comes out with results that conform closely enough to what those who commissioned it believe reality is or should be, at which point that questioning largely stops.

This phenomenon is very similar to what is known as the Gell-Mann Amnesia effect, a term coined by Dr. Michael Crichton in a 2002 speech called "Why Speculate?" This term describes research conducted by Murray Gell-Mann. This effect states that people will read something in the media that, because they have particular subject-matter expertise in that area, they know or recognize to be false. After turning to another story, they completely forget how inaccurate the last article they read was and take everything read in the next one at face value. Crichton noted the ways in which this amnesia effect differs between the media and other aspects of life:

> In ordinary life, if somebody consistently exaggerates or lies to you, you soon discount everything they say. In court, there is the legal doctrine of falsus in uno, falsus in omnibus, which means untruthful in one part, untruthful in all.
>
> But when it comes to the media, we believe against evidence that it is probably worth our time to read other parts of the paper. When, in fact, it almost certainly isn't. The only possible explanation for our behavior is amnesia.[1]

Similarly, polls which consistently fail to accurately predict reality in high-profile cases continue to be taken at face value. Researchers may be benefitting from this effect in part because most people are exposed to poll findings by way of media outlets, but regardless of the cause, the effect is clearly observable.

In the Georgia 6th Congressional District special election run-off, Democratic candidate Jon Ossoff received exactly 600 more votes than the Democratic candidate in that district had received during the general election six months prior.[2] Republican candidate Karen Handel received 66,289 votes less than the Republican candidate in the general election,[3] who vacated the seat shortly after winning re-election to serve in the Trump administration. The most expensive U.S. House race in history[4] was unable to move the needle for the Democratic candidate at all.

While the race was closer than the previous, this was only the case because nearly a third of voters who had voted for the Republican candidate in the general election stayed home during this race. Every poll conducted between the original special election and the run-off missed the mark, with all but one overstating Ossoff's final vote percentage even though it remained within 0.1% of what he attained in the first phase of the special election two months prior.[5] Every poll understated Handel's percentage of the vote by at least one full point.[6]

This race makes for an excellent case study and should have been a relatively easier one for the polls to get right. The level of funds available[7] to pay for top notch polling, the concise geographic nature of the race, the high level of awareness, and the fact that the run-off outcome was so similar to the first special election mean many of the variables we generally cannot control for in opinion and survey research remained in a relatively stable equilibrium during the period in question. Nonetheless, the polling projections were still troublesome.

While this serves as an excellent example of how pervasive the polling discipline's problems are, it also highlights another issue: there is not enough incentive for the industry to make the right calls. The high-profile mistakes of the 2016 general election were still fresh in mind, yet money still poured in to conduct the same sorts of polls. The same missed outcomes, even in a much more controlled environment, should not come as a surprise considering all the problems with the practice itself.

The Georgia case was a particularly damning indictment of polling and opinion research accuracy, but as with the results of the general election, it also had no effect. In the time since, money has kept flowing into polling: polls seriously examining rapper Kid Rock's viability as a candidate for U.S. Senator from

Michigan were conducted, with questionable findings.[8][9][10] Billionaire Facebook CEO Mark Zuckerberg hired a prominent pollster from Hillary Clinton's 2016 electoral campaign who oversaw substantial failures in that field.[11][12] As recently as six weeks after the Georgia 6th run-off, claims that "Democrats stand to win big in the 2018 midterm elections, according to a new poll" started cropping back up again in the news media.[13]

The recent lackluster industry track record has not resulted in any financial pressure to change or improve, as the money keeps flowing. Flawed polling practices persist throughout nearly every election polled and conducted in 2017, including those held a full year after the 2016 general election, and they have showed no sign of ending since then.

Similarly, the race for Governor of Virginia was one of the most polled races in the latter half of 2017. 38 polls examining the status of this race were conducted during the 20 week period between the Georgia 6th District Special Election Runoff on June 20th, 2017 and Virginia's gubernatorial election on November 7th.

Table 4.1 – 2017 Virginia Gubernatorial Race Final Week Polls

Polling Firm	Date	Size	MoE	Northam (D)	Gillespie (R)	Hyra (L)
Monmouth[14]	11/2 - 11/5	713	3.7	47	45	3
FOX News[15]	11/2 - 11/5	1,239	2.5	48	43	2
The Polling Company[16]	11/2 - 11/5	800	3.5	45	44	3
Emerson[17]	11/2 - 11/4	810	3.4	49	46	1
Quinnipiac[18]	10/30 - 11/5	1056	3.9	51	42	3
Rasmussen Reports[19]	10/31 - 11/3	875	3.5	45	45	2
Christopher Newport U.[20]	10/29 - 11/4	839	3.5	51	45	2
Trafalgar Group[21]	10/31 - 11/2	1,200	2.8	49	48	1
NY Times/Siena[22]	10/29 - 11/2	985	3	43	40	2
Gravis[23]	10/30 - 11/3	1,143	2.9	48	43	3
The Polling Company[24]	10/30 - 11/2	800	3.5	43	45	2
Roanoke College[25]	10/29 - 11/2	781	3.5	47	47	3
Suffolk[26]	10/30 - 11/1	500	4.4	47	43	2
Final Outcome[27]	11/7	2.6m	*	53.9	45	1.1

While most inaccurate polls have generally erred by predicting outcomes which fall outside of the actual result, either by identifying the wrong winner or overstating their margin of victory, in Virginia's case the polls had the opposite problem. They grossly understated the level of support for Ralph Northam. Only two of the 13 polls, or about 15.4%, conducted in the final week identified Northam's final vote totals within their margins of error for that metric, both of which were on the low side.[28][29]

Despite repeated evidence of polling failures following the November 2016 election, low-quality polling data continued to make major headlines a year later, as 2017 drew to a close. The December 2017 special election for Senator from the state of Alabama saw relevant polls published with more variation than any other that year. There were three polls released in the few days before the election that were over 19 points apart, including one which predicted a tie. This poll ended up being the only poll conducted in the final week to correctly identify both major party candidates' vote percentages as well as the spread within that poll's margin of error.

Table 4.2 – 2017 Alabama Senate Special Election Final Week Polls

Poll Results				Divergence from Election Results			Sample Size
Moore (R)	Jones (D)	MoE	Spread	Moore (R)	Jones (D)	Spread	
40	50	3	Jones +10	5.4	--	2.5	1,127[30]
53	44	3.9	Moore +9	0.7	2	2.7	600[31]
46	46	4.2	Tie	--	--	--	546[32]
51	46	2.6	Moore +5	0	1.3	1.3	1,419[33]
49	45	2.8	Moore +4	--	2.1	--	1,254[34]
50	43	2	Moore +7	--	4.9	4.5	3,200[35]
48	44	2.7	Jones + 4	1.7	--	--	1,276[36]

Note: "--" indicates a result within the margin of error. A divergence of 0 means the result was roughly equal to the bounds of the margin of error

The only final week Alabama Senate race poll which could claim accuracy on every metric—defined as both candidates' vote percentages and the spread between them—was also the poll with the largest margin of error, at 4.2%, and the lowest sample size, at just 546 respondents. Every other poll missed the mark on at least one of these metrics, and some polls missed them all.

Should the one "accurate" poll have had a margin of error equal to any other final week polls, Jones's vote percentage would have fallen outside that margin. Considering some of these polls had response rates as low as 3%, it should come as no surprise that only the polls with the widest error margins can lay claim to accuracy. Collectively, these seven polls were less accurate than random chance even within their margins of error, as less than 50% of the 21 metrics they examined turned out to be accurate within those margins.

Just as politicians can suffer from record low approval ratings yet are continually re-elected, pollsters' clients keep committing themselves to the same groups and practices which have increasingly failed in the first decades of the 21st century. Congressional representatives and senators who keep their jobs despite their track records have about as much of a reason to change as researchers who keep their jobs despite theirs.

As with any business, the primary incentive for opinion researchers and pollsters is turning a profit. If turning a profit is decoupled from producing accurate research, there is no reason to expect accuracy. What we are seeing now are the consequences of what is, in effect, a broad acceptance of low quality research. Findings which reflect what people expect or want to hear are rewarded with additional contracts, publicity, and a lack of questioning or examination. This does not give pollsters many reasons to change or improve.

High-priced firms with worsening records continue to be hired for work which they are no longer well-equipped to perform. The researchers who work at such institutions remain employed in similar, if not identical, capacities. Without any external pressure upon the industry to be more accurate, it's no surprise they have failed to do so. If necessity is the mother of invention, a lack of necessity for change means no change will occur.

Why Be Right?

The accuracy of election polling can be objectively shown at some point, but the same cannot be said for other manifestations of opinion surveys. Corporations attempting to sell a product have every bit as many confounding variables affecting their research efforts as political campaigns do, if not more, but there is no objective check on the extent to which a population favors a product.

This lack of an objective product favorability check is in part due to pricing concerns and awareness levels. This differs from elections, which are very publicly known and have no price tag associated with making one's voice heard. Elections additionally benefit from a public push to participate because of the sense that one is doing a civic duty, an idea not present in any given market for a particular product.

Since the incentive for researchers is not to be right but to keep the money coming, there is a lot of what amounts to fraud within the practice. Some studies are commissioned not with the objective of determining reality, but rather to manufacture evidence contrary thereto. Prominent individuals and groups will coordinate with groups that have an inherent bias on a topic to produce research which supports their position. In such cases, these results are produced regardless of whether those efforts are grounded in solid science.

When researchers at the University of Washington took to examining the effects of incremental minimum wage increases in Seattle,[37] their findings regarding the increment from $11 per hour to $13 per hour showed that the shift "reduced hours worked in low-wage jobs by around 9 percent, while hourly wages in such jobs increased by around 3 percent. Consequently, total payroll fell for such jobs, implying that the minimum wage ordinance lowered low-wage employees' earnings by an average of $125 per month in 2016."[38]

This finding did not reflect the story which the Seattle Mayor and City Council wanted to tell. Having promised that passage of the minimum wage increase would "inspire people all over the nation"[39] and "serve as a model for the rest of the nation to follow,"[40] a study which showed low-wage earners taking home $1,500 less in 2016 than in 2015 ran counter to that narrative.

In what Seattle Weekly reporter Daniel Person called "an object lesson in how quickly data can get weaponized,"[41] the Seattle Mayor's Office reached out to University of California, Berkeley researchers to rush a counter-study in coordination with organizations that supported minimum wage ordinances.[42] When political collusion to push for a narrative is the genesis of a research study, and when the results are consequentially known in advance, there is no incentive for the findings to correspond with reality. On the contrary, it was clear from the outset that the incentive was to produce a report which reflected favorably on the minimum wage hike.

There may have been methodological issues with the University of Washington study, or "anti-minimum wage editorializing" as alleged by Seattle City Councilmember Kshama Sawant,[43] but the appropriate response to this is not to commission another study specifically to be more favorable to your cause in coordination with groups that have already publicly taken a stand on the issue. The only ones served by such approaches to research are political ideologues, but the public misses out on valuable insights into how policies are unfolding.

This in turn alters their perceptions on the issue being studied and creates even more issues with follow-up research on public opinion. If people are basing their responses to research surveys upon works performed under the guise of legitimate research which are in actuality political advocacy efforts, research efforts become more about shaping reality instead of identifying it.

If research efforts with politically motivated findings result in more money for pollsters than actual efforts do, we can expect the problems to get worse. The decoupling of funding and accuracy only serves to further prevent the practice from identifying its problems and adapting to address them.

When it comes to opinion research, being wrong does not mean one's work won't continue to be cited and held in high enough regard that one can continue operating in the same manner. Some smaller firms, such as Research 2000, may not benefit as much from this effect and have even been sued by their customers for the problems they contained,[44] but those lawsuits generally rely on comparisons to other work that is also riddled with problems, regardless of how highly-regarded it may be.

Research efforts which predict less shocking results don't call for as much additional follow-up research. An accurate poll of the 2016 Georgia special election run-off likely should have shown support for Ossoff holding steady right around 48.1%, the vote percentage he earned in both election phases two months apart, but this finding would have done little to invite additional funding.

A poll, or any research effort for that matter, with a surprising finding begets more inquiry into the topic in order to confirm the original effort. This concept is known as reproducibility, which is defined by Jeffrey Leek and Roger Peng at Johns Hopkins University as "the ability to recompute data analytic results given an observed dataset and knowledge of the data analysis pipeline."[45] Replicating research findings is a cornerstone of good science, yet doing so within the social sciences is exceptionally difficult, as they explain in "Reproducible research can still be wrong: Adopting a prevention approach":

> The replicability of a study is the chance that an independent experiment targeting the same scientific question will produce a consistent result (1). Concerns among scientists about both have gained significant traction recently

> due in part to a statistical argument that suggested most published scientific results may be false positives (2). At the same time, there have been some very public failings of reproducibility across a range of disciplines from cancer genomics (3) to economics (4), and the data for many publications have not been made publicly available, raising doubts about the quality of data analyses. Popular press articles have raised questions about the reproducibility of all scientific research (5), and the US Congress has convened hearings focused on the transparency of scientific research (6). The result is that much of the scientific enterprise has been called into question, putting funding and hard won scientific truths at risk.[46]

Replicating findings is particularly difficult when conducting research into psychological processes. When a study's results indicate significant shifts, more money is typically poured into the studies in efforts to replicate the findings. Shock findings are monetarily rewarded, which to most people is little surprise.

If reproducing surprising results is a more lucrative venture than improving initial polling accuracy so that results are more accurate the first time around, why be right? Not only are the incentives not there, but it is particularly easy for survey researchers to claim that while they weren't accurate, they were close enough that clients should continue to pay for their services.

The Definition of "Wrong"

One factor which is intrinsic to survey research and probability sampling, or any method of sampling that utilizes some form of random selection,[47] is what is known as the margin of error. This factor makes it hard to definitively state that findings are wrong; more often, they are presented as simply imprecise. Probability samples using the standard 95% confidence level generally have a margin of error roughly equal to the inverse of the square root of the sample size.[48] The confidence level tells us how sure we are that the true average lies within the margin of error.

For example, take a simple random sample of 836 registered voters. If 45% of these individuals state they intend to vote for candidate A, we can be 95% sure that between 41.6% and 48.4% will actually do so. Stated another way, candidate A's stated support should fall between 41.6% and 48.4% 19 out of 20 times this study was conducted. This is the case because the margin of error for that sample at a 95% confidence level is approximately 3.4%.

Changing the confidence level to 99% increases the margin of error by about 32% of what it would have been at the 95% level. A shift to 90% confidence decreases the margin of error from what it would be at the 95% level by around 20%. Consequently, for a standard probability sample of 1,000 respondents, the margin of error is about 3.1% at a 95% confidence level, 2.6% at a 90% confidence level, and around 4.1% at a 99% confidence level.

A political poll which claims to have a specific margin of error but does not provide the confidence level leaves out a lot of information that is necessary to properly analyze and report on the poll's accuracy. Additionally, the stated margin of error is rarely if ever the true margin of error. Election polling involving two candidates which states that one has a lead with a specified margin of error has a true margin of error that is double that amount.

If in our above example with a simple random sample of 836 registered voters wherein 45% state they will vote for candidate A, assuming there are only two candidates in the race and nobody claims not to know whom they support such that the other 55% state they will vote for candidate B, the real margin of error for that poll at a 95% confidence level is 6.8%. While this poll would report candidate B with a 10-point margin over candidate A, in reality this poll states with 95% confidence that candidate B's lead over candidate A will be between about 3 and 17 points.

In closer races, this means election polls can claim to be accurate while having next to no predictive power. If in our example, the candidates instead polled at 48% and 52%, the candidate supported by 48% may actually have a lead of nearly 3 points.

Someone who sees a candidate reported to have a 4-point lead with a 3.4% stated margin of error would feel quite safe in claiming that candidate was all but assured to win, when in fact the poll itself indicates that may not be the case. Nonetheless, the poll slyly hides that fact unless the candidate reported to be behind ends up pulling out a win. Andrew Mercer elaborates on the ways in which margins of error can be misleading, especially when used in the media, in "5 key things to know about the margin of error in election polls":

> News reports about polling will often say that a candidate's lead is "outside the margin of error" to indicate that a candidate's lead is greater than what we would expect from sampling error, or that a race is "a statistical tie" if it's too close to call. It is not enough for one candidate to be ahead by more than the margin of error that is reported for individual candidates... To determine whether or not the race is too close to call, we need to calculate a new margin of error for the difference between the two candidates' levels of support. The size of this margin is generally about twice that of the margin for an individual candidate. The larger margin of error is due to the fact that if the Republican share is too high by chance, it follows that the Democratic share is likely too low, and vice versa.
>
> For Poll A, the 3-percentage-point margin of error for each candidate individually becomes approximately a 6-point margin of error for the difference between the two. This means that although we have observed a 5-point lead for the Republican, we could reasonably expect their true position relative to the Democrat to lie somewhere between –1 and +11 percentage points. The Republican would need to be ahead by 6 percentage points or more for us to be confident that the lead is not simply the result of sampling error.[49]

The existence of large margins of error mean researchers don't need to get it right—they just need to be close enough that they can claim to have been right within the broad margins allotted by their statistical methods. Additionally, larger confidence levels provide another out by allowing researchers to claim that instances in which findings didn't conform to reality were the one-in-ten or one-in-twenty case in which results would fall outside of predicted margins.

Combined with the multitude of issues researchers face in sampling, the use of smaller sample sizes is incentivized. These smaller samples necessarily have greater margins of error, which in turn makes the research findings harder to assail or label incorrect even though by default they are more likely to diverge from reality. The fact that confidence levels are almost never publicly reported for election polls or other opinion research compounds the problem by depriving third parties of an avenue by which to conduct independent analysis.

Few who commission such research have a comprehensive understanding of this issue, leading to widespread confusion as to what results actually mean. This problem also allows diminishing research quality to go unnoticed for extended periods. Since these methods have been the industry norm for decades, arguments about broad margins can appeal to those who have not examined the issue in great detail.

There is no standard rule for determining how large of a sample any given research survey or poll must have. Consequentially, in many cases the research team works backwards to derive how large of a sample is needed based on the desired margin of error,[50] but particular subsets of a population may have much larger margins of error.

An article by the American Association for Public Opinion Research touches on this issue by mentioning that if a 1,000 person sample "includes, for example, 200 Hispanics, the overall results based on the subsample of Latinos is plus or minus 6.9 percentage points."[51] In order to compensate for this and be able to report on sub-groups with lower margins of error "the pollster needs to have enough women, for example, in the overall sample to ensure a reasonable margin [of] error among just the women. And the same goes for young adults, retirees, rich people, poor people, etc.," according to Robert Niles.[52]

This means sample sizes greater than 1,000 respondents are uncommon but do occur in some circumstances. Out of about 260 polls conducted for the 2016 Presidential election, about a third had samples of less than 1,000, and nearly half had between 1,000 and 2,000 respondents. Roughly 18% were above the 2,000 respondents mark, but the use of such large samples only served to highlight how far from objective reality polling results have become.

During the 2016 general election, NBC News conducted 17 polls regarding the election results in conjunction with SurveyMonkey, an online survey hosting platform. All but one of these polls had sample sizes in excess of 10,000 with the one outlier being a mere 5.6% smaller than that figure (9,436). The margin of error for each of these polls was less than 1.5 points,[53] which puts these organizations in a bind: the final result for all but two of these polls was outside of the full doubled margin of error. Worse, the two closest polls were the ones conducted the earliest in the election cycle, four months prior to election day.

Figure 4.3 - 2016 General Election Polls by Sample Size

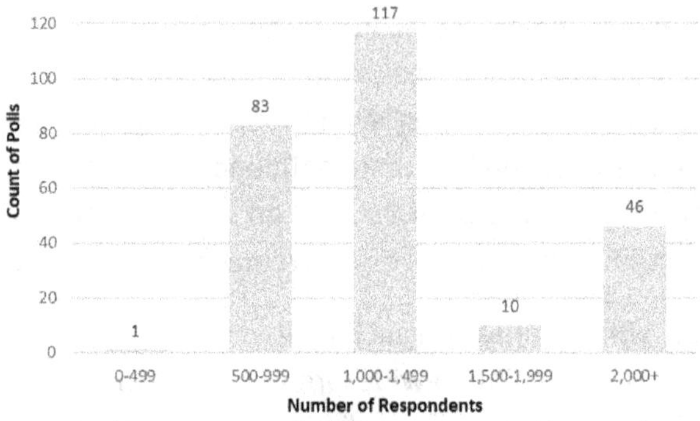

Table 4.4 – NBC/SurveyMonkey 2016 General Election Polls

Start of Poll	End of Poll	Sample Size	Margin of Error	Finding	Population
10/31/2016	11/6/2016	70,194	1	Clinton +7	LV[54]
10/24/2016	10/30/2016	40,816	1	Clinton +7	LV[55]
10/17/2016	10/23/2016	32,255	1	Clinton +6	LV[56]
10/10/2016	10/16/2016	24,804	1	Clinton +8	LV[57]
10/3/2016	10/9/2016	23,329	1	Clinton +7	LV[58]
9/26/2016	10/2/2016	26,925	1	Clinton +6	LV[59]
9/19/2016	9/25/2016	13,598	1.1	Clinton +7	LV[60]
9/12/2016	9/18/2016	13,320	1.2	Clinton +5	LV[61]
9/5/2016	9/11/2016	16,220	1.1	Clinton +4	RV[62]
8/29/2016	9/4/2016	32,226	1	Clinton +6	RV[63]
8/22/2016	8/28/2016	24,104	1	Clinton +6	RV[64]
8/15/2016	8/21/2016	17,459	1.1	Clinton +8	RV[65]
8/8/2016	8/14/2016	15,179	1.2	Clinton +9	RV[66]
8/1/2016	8/7/2016	11,480	1.2	Clinton +10	RV[67]
7/25/2016	7/31/2016	12,742	1.2	Clinton +8	RV[68]
7/18/2016	7/24/2016	12,931	1.2	Clinton +1	RV[69]
7/11/2016	7/17/2016	9,436	1.4	Clinton +1	RV[70]

If larger sample sizes don't necessarily result in better data but rather highlight methodological problems, there is very little incentive to narrow that margin of error, especially when the popularly-accepted margin is large enough to give researchers an out for bad methodologies. Smaller sample sizes are cheaper and provide much more wiggle-room when called out for inaccuracy.

In some cases, researchers will bridge this gap by using larger sample sizes while also maintaining a large margin of error, but this raises other questions. When we see a poll with a sample size of 2,935 which reports a 4.5 margin of error and also states it used a 95% confidence level,[71] there is very little way to properly assess its accuracy. If "wrong" is defined as cases in which the real-world outcome is outside a total margin of error, a poll which allows for a 9% variability from the published results makes it almost impossible to label it as such.

While margins of error on the order of 3% or more are unacceptable in most other industries, this is not the case for survey research and public opinion polling. A 3% margin of error when calculating anticipated revenues can mean the difference between a profitable company and bankruptcy. The oil and gas industry, where companies like Exxon take in hundreds of billions in annual revenues,[72] often posts profit margins on those revenues as low as 2% over a 12-month period.[73][74] A speedometer with a 3% error level could mean the difference between a legal speed and a traffic ticket. The highest stated margin of error in any Georgia 6th special election run-off poll was 4.9%,[75] meaning the true margin for a candidate's lead was nearly 10%. Imagine what the consequences could be for a person who was going 10% faster than the speedometer on their car stated.

Larger margins of error are considered normal in the polling industry, but often this means the presented findings are almost worthless. Two polls can have nearly diametrically opposite published results yet still claim to be accurate.

Between July 25th to 27th of 2017, Target-Insyght and the Trafalgar Group conducted simultaneous polls examining the candidates for an upcoming race for U.S. Senator from Michigan to be held in 2018. Both polls found Robert Ritchie, also known as "Kid Rock," to be the Republican frontrunner in the race against incumbent Democrat Debbie Stabenow, but the similarities between the two effectively end there.

The Target-Insyght poll found that Stabenow polled ahead of Kid Rock by 8 points, with a margin of error equal to 3.5 points.[76] The Trafalgar Group poll, which had a margin of error of 3.1, claimed that Kid Rock was ahead of Stabenow by 3 points.[77] These two survey research efforts differed in their findings by 11 points.[78] On the surface, it seems that one or both of these polls must be wrong, but due to the wide margins of error and the fact that those margins must be doubled when examining a candidate's lead, both of these polls can claim to be accurate and even "right."

In the case of Target-Insyght, the margin of error means that Stabenow's true lead over Kid Rock should be anywhere between 1 point and 15 points. The Trafalgar poll's findings range from about a 9-point lead for Kid Rock to around a 3-point lead for Stabenow. This would imply that the current true positioning in a Stabenow-versus-Kid Rock election at that time was somewhere between +1 and +3 for Stabenow, but finding any overlap between the two surveys requires going to the extremes for both surveys, and to the casual observer would appear impossible.

In another example, two polls were conducted between November 9th-11th 2017 which examined the Alabama special election for U.S. Senate. One poll showed Republican candidate Roy Moore with a 10 point lead,[79] while the other showed that his Democratic opponent Doug Jones had a 4 point lead.[80] This 14-point differential between the two polls conducted over the exact same period of time seems on the surface to be highly implausible, but the uncertainty provided by small sample sizes of 600 and 575 respondents push the margins of error up to 3.9 and 4.1 points respectively. This means that both polls could lay claim to accuracy so long as they were within 16 points of each other.

The problems involved in sampling, as evidenced here by low response rates for some of these polls on the order of 2%,[81] in addition to known issues with actual data collection, make these findings somewhat dubious. However, even if we assume that both of these polls' findings are "accurate" and technically "right," the fact that this can be claimed when the published findings are so far apart demonstrates that there is no incentive for the industry to aim for greater precision. This is especially true when we consider that polls with large samples and small margins of error, such as the NBC News/SurveyMonkey polls during the 2016 general election, can still be very far off base.

Incentives Matter

Throughout most aspects of our lives, there is every incentive to minimize error. The consequences of being wrong are felt rather acutely. That structure has been shown to be an effective motivator to foster improvement at the individual and societal levels.[82]

Political polls, as well as most other forms of survey research, are not subject to such incentives. In fact, researchers in these fields typically have incentives to do the opposite: they are encouraged to take steps which increase the margins of error so as to create a buffer zone. This way, they cannot be faulted for making incorrect predictions. This does little to inform leaders of what actions they should take to improve the organization's metrics, as precision matters every bit as much as accuracy in these circumstances.

While precision and accuracy are two distinctly different concepts, they are closely related; in most situations, having one without the other does little good. A piece of artillery firing upon an enemy military installation which overshoots by 50 yards, then adjusts such that the next bombardment falls 50 yards short, was accurate. From a statistical standpoint, both attacks were direct hits because the target fell exactly in between the bounds of both strikes, even though they were sufficiently imprecise that neither actually hit the target. Conversely, if both bombardments hit the exact same point 50 yards past the target, the overall attack was very precise because it was consistent, but it was not accurate because the intended target was outside the bounds of the attack. Without both accuracy and precision, efforts are largely a waste of resources.

In the polling industry, there is much emphasis placed on being accurate, but little attention is given to precision. Therefore, researchers can achieve higher levels accuracy by allowing for substantially greater levels of imprecision than would normally be accepted.

In most cases, the only metric for a poll's success is acceptance of the findings and continued funding. The difficulties researchers face in getting it right, and the lack of adequate incentives to do so, are what allow for push polling and politically-oriented "research" to thrive.

Activists who pose as legitimate researchers themselves do not face any immediate fallout for engaging in these practices unless evidence of collusion with intent to mislead is discovered. This was the case when the Seattle Mayor's

Office and City Council attempted to preempt the University of Washington report that showed a $2 increase in Seattle's minimum wage on average resulted in lower take-home pay for low wage workers. Because there is rarely a consequence, individuals have no incentive not to engage in such actions. However, this form of research as political activism further dilutes the value of all survey research findings. Future research which builds off findings from this pseudo-research starts from a point of bias that can be hard to eradicate after work has begun.

The fact that only one objective measure exists causes additional problems. If political pollsters get the election right, the entire industry becomes largely unassailable. This gives cover to less scrupulous individuals who use survey research efforts to create the appearance of support for a cause. It also means that legitimate researchers feel as though they need not examine their practices and methodologies at least until the next election, as they produced a result which was close enough.

Unfortunately, it appears that even when survey researchers make the wrong calls in election after election, they are still revered as viable. Media citations of incorrect findings continue, pollsters who produce demonstrably false research keep their jobs, funds for additional work continue to come in, and the same methodologies continue to reign supreme.

Imagine working for a company which only conducted performance reviews every two to four years, and which then only looked at one aspect of your performance. Such a review would not be very effective in multiple respects. It's important to receive ongoing feedback if one's performance is to improve, and there would be little incentive to perform well in areas that you knew would not be reviewed.

Elections are the only objective accountability check on the entire survey research industry. Major elections are the only calls the discipline truly needs to get right. In most cases, the accountability checks therefore only occur every two years, with a full comprehensive examination once every four. However, even in these cases, research findings only need to be accurate within the final weeks leading up to the date of the election for their continued funding to be assured. Truthfully, so long as the results of the final polls conducted align with the outcome at the ballot box within the broad margins of error they provide, the polls are considered accurate regardless of what they said beforehand.

Chapter 5 – Band-Aids are Cheap While True Fixes are Expensive

Occasionally, it briefly appears as though researchers have recognized the need for change in the industry. Some researchers made attempts to branch out into new methods during the 2016 races by trying out non-probability samples and employing Big Data. These efforts may have looked to fix a larger problem, but they were poorly executed because they originated from a traditional mindset. The novel solutions the discipline needs cannot simply be bolted on to existing practices; they need to be built from the ground up.

Even when serious problems regarding the collection of survey research data are recognized, the core assumptions go unquestioned. The premise that stated preferences equate to reality is a core tenant of opinion polling, and it has remained so even when revealed preferences have been shown to diverge from what those polled have stated on many occasions. The core of the practice, it appears, is flawed in a way which dooms question-and-answer research unless this problem is addressed, which seems unlikely without taking the draconian step of criminalizing inaccurate survey responses.

Upon realizing there were problems in the findings from data collected during the lead-up to the 2016 general election, several organizations attempted to identify the problem, but they did so without looking at its core. In fact, the efforts undertaken to review these initial findings employed the same problematic approaches that led to the disconnect between survey results and election outcomes in the first place.

There were many post-mortem discussions which examined Trump's unexpected victory. Few of these examinations bothered to look at the efficacy of the polling and research done throughout the campaigns; most of these studies either glossed over the issue or dove head-first into making the same mistakes.

Without fail, these investigations continued to operate under the assumption that polls and survey research findings should be held in high regard. In fact, this sort of data was usually at the core of the follow up analysis, making it highly unlikely that the findings would be any more accurate than they had initially been.

Organizations such as the political action committee Priorities USA have continued to engage researchers that use the same flawed reliance on polls and focus groups to examine the motivations of voters who switched from supporting Obama in 2012 to Trump in 2016.[1] Considering this same group relied heavily on this polling to direct its efforts in during the 2016 election, including the decision to cease spending in states where Hillary Clinton was polling with a strong lead but ended up losing,[2] one would think such organizations would have developed a measure of skepticism regarding public opinion research.

It is possible for these retrospective efforts to produce enough information to explain why voters behaved the way they did, but they are just as likely to create red herrings[3] as they are to generate useful insights. Geoffrey Skelley, of the University of Virginia Center for Politics, provides some insight into this issue in his 2017 publication Just How Many Obama 2012-Trump 2016 Voters Were There? Mr. Skelley discusses how responses to questions regarding previous behaviors become less reliable over time:

> Bias toward current political preferences can affect responses, as can simple forgetfulness — as much as it may surprise hardcore politicos, many Americans don't necessarily remember their voter information with precision. While four years doesn't seem like a very long time, one Dutch study found that the probability of someone consistently recalling their vote fell by about six percentage points over 3.5 years. Moreover, voters may remember a previous winner better than a loser, and thus some people who voted for the prior loser may not remember if they voted, while others will misremember voting for the winner.[4]

At present, there is little way to tell the difference between reliable and erroneous responses; since objective reality checks generally only occur years apart and memory is unreliable, it's very hard to tell what is useful information and what is random noise. Nevertheless, many are still desperately hungry for some insights into what the public is thinking. People and organizations desperate for answers continue to invest in the same sort of research that has failed in the past.

The problems with traditional tactics cannot be eliminated simply by expanding the scope of such tactics, as the Voter Study Group attempted to do.[5] Increasing the sample size and collecting more response data from each participant "allows analysts to dig more deeply into smaller groups of the American electorate than most other surveys" but does little to addresses the numerous biases present in modern survey research efforts.[6] Additionally, a larger sample does not mean that sub-groups of the population contained within that sample are substantially more representative than those in a smaller sample. Looking at smaller groups within a sample greatly increases the level of error for that meta-sample.

With each day that passes, researchers become increasingly set in their methods. People are creatures of habit, and those habits are strengthened each time they are indulged. When those habits are damaging, ceasing them sooner rather than later is essential. As the body of research that has used these approaches grows, future works which are based on those previous efforts will decrease in accuracy. Worsening quality baseline research will not produce higher quality subsequent research any more than flawed data will produce a valid study.

Getting It Right Is No Longer Worthwhile

Survey research is hard to get right. This has always been true to some extent, and it should come as no surprise. Getting people to do something, especially when they don't receive compensation, is no easy task. As we progress through time into an increasingly digital world, each step in the survey research process is becoming more and more difficult.

The onset of digital communication methods has streamlined some parts of the process, but it cannot offset many of the other difficulties that continue to grow in strength. This isn't to say that all the problems with traditional survey research methodologies cannot be addressed; they can, but the costs of doing so often makes the entire process no longer economically viable.

First, the researchers must have a lot of time to tackle the issues. In many cases, the information sought is time-sensitive so excess time is considered a luxury, but it is a necessary component to ensuring quality response data. This is the case because in addition to the time it takes to identify the respondents, collect the data, and produce the analysis, that data must be vetted and verified. Confirming the data and ensuring that the responses are properly understood can take months. Should it turn out that any of the questions or terms were misunderstood by respondents, the entire data collection process may need to be repeated, which may even require re-deploying an updated version of the survey.

Second, personal relationships between the researchers and the respondents must be cultivated. Respondents are more likely to provide responses if they have a personal connection to those who requested them. In such cases, respondents are also much more likely to work with researchers over the extended timeframes necessary to ensure data quality. This process generally must be started well in advance of survey deployment.

Third, the respondent size must be proportional to the size of the research team. Most surveys have hundreds or thousands of respondents; this is too many people for a survey team to track individually. British anthropologist and evolutionary biologist Robin Dunbar claims that a person can only maintain about 150 social connections,[7] and since a personal connection to the respondent is necessary to ensure quality data collection, the number of respondents cannot exceed the research team's capacity for making personal connections.

Fourth, respondents must have incentives to provide high-quality responses. The establishment of personal connections provides this incentive in the form of social pressure, but this factor alone is insufficient in part due to the increased possibility of *social desirability bias.* Additional incentives are needed, which usually takes the form of exchanging something of value in return for the data. Money or other property need not change hands, but some form of incentive beyond social obligation must exist.

Finally, the researchers need to have a connection to the material. Simply being paid to do the work is not a strong enough motivator for high-quality research, especially considering all the additional effort that must be made to get it right.

Without a personal investment, it is unlikely that the team will be able to hit the mark on every point that requires proper execution.

Few organizations can make the investments needed to get high quality response data. The national association examined in Chapter 1 —which spends months providing technical assistance to respondents and builds connections between researchers and state contacts prior to survey deployment, and thoroughly reviews data for quality assurance—is a splendid example of a group that does make the investment. Their dedication to quality is why their findings and reports are considered to be the "gold standard" for their industry, but this organization is an outlier from the industry's norm.

This national association invests enormous amounts of time into their annual surveys to guarantee accuracy. They have spent years developing relationships with their respondent panels, which allows them to collect reliable data each year. The fact that their surveys only require a single respondent from each state helps keep the researcher/respondent ratio low enough that their small team can maintain those relationships even when the specific state respondent changes.

The respondents have strong incentives to provide accurate response data too, as the reports these surveys inform are widely cited by national and local news outlets, and they are sometimes used to advocate for new laws and regulatory standards. They help determine legislative priorities and often generate media inquiries, allowing respondents to gain exposure for themselves and advocate for their views. Both the respondents and the researchers are also dedicated to the purpose these efforts serve: ensuring affordable access to safe, quality educational programs. Their personal connections to this mission mean that researchers and respondents have the drive to see research through to completion at high quality standards, regardless of the obstacles.

When a survey research effort lacks any one of these five factors, the quality of the data is imperiled. All five are necessary for the final dataset to produce the objective measures these types of research efforts are generally assumed to represent. However, in most cases, there is barely even a semblance of such factors present.

Many researchers fail to have the proportionally-small sample size necessary to enable quality survey research. The average sample in a 2016 general election poll was 2,543, which drops to 1,236 if we remove the outlying samples from the NBC News/SurveyMonkey polls. Even if everyone on the research teams used all of their 150 social connections for these polls, that team would need more than eight people who were doing nothing but vetting data. Considering these polls are usually conducted and results released over the course of less than a week, it's easy to see why this isn't a viable option in many circumstances, unless very large research teams conducted the work.

In absence of these five aforementioned factors, the other only effective traditional methodological approach for gathering quality data is using the force of law to compel an accurate, quality response from populations sampled from groups in which they are required to participate. When people face legal penalties for non-response or for providing bad data, many of the requirements for a quality dataset can be achieved. Studies by the U.S. Census Bureau claim that removing the "YOUR RESPONSE IS REQUIRED BY LAW" messaging from the American Community Survey lowers response rate by 5.4% and increases the overall cost to execute the survey "by roughly $9.5 million."[8] Similar work also suggests that transitioning to a fully voluntary survey would substantially affect data quality, increasing by over 2,400% the population affected by poor response rates.[9]

This legal mandate approach is highly effective. The requirement makes it much easier for interviewers to collect data at a lower cost and with much higher completion rates. However, this tactic is fraught with moral and ethical dilemmas, which occasionally bring the American Community Survey under fire. In 2012, there was an attempt to kill the survey,[10] and in 2015 the House Appropriations Committee pushed to remove the legal requirement.[11]

It would be hard to apply this controversial legal mandate in broader circumstances. It already has been called "a program that intrudes on people's lives, just like the Environmental Protection Agency or the bank regulators,"[12] and expanding its use would raise many concerns. If used to directly benefit private organizations, survey efforts would create additional perverse incentives.

Logistical concerns aside, this would cause an explosion of privacy issues. Scores of new laws and regulations controlling question wording and allowed subject matter would inevitably follow, greatly restricting the flexibility of the industry and probably ensuring some material could never be examined. The issue of push polling would likely be exacerbated as well. Organizations to which a survey response is required by law would be ripe for political advocacy disguised as research. However, inaccurate findings would likely still affect the quality of such studies, as *sampling bias* would still exist. Additionally, such measures would eliminate competition and remove client choice, as only firms which could guarantee high response rates would stay in business.

The societal changes which are driving problems in the polling industry can be addressed by only very few organizations: those which can invest extraordinary efforts over several years to ensure top-notch, quality survey research data is collected. Most firms' business models preclude the conditions under which survey research can be effectively executed such that high quality, accurate findings can be assured.

Respondent samples are not representative of the population, and the data collected from those respondents is itself riddled with a broad array of problems. These flawed inputs mean the outputs will also be flawed. This is what is known in computer science as the GiGo principle, which stands for "Garbage In, Garbage Out."[13] A dataset filled with biases and errors will not (and arguably cannot) produce findings which accurately correspond to objective reality. Alterations of the collected data can partially compensate for this issue but cannot overcome it.

In most cases, the conditions and effort required to produce accurate, precise findings aren't worth the effort. Low-quality work is widely accepted, rarely faces true accuracy checks, and is still cited despite clearly-incorrect predictions. By and large, low-quality research has become the standard.

Adjustments are "Good Enough"

One reason that low-quality research has become rather commonplace in the 21st century is that it has become a relatively customary practice for researchers to paper over problems by massaging inputs that they know to be flawed, bringing them more in line with what researchers would have expected without the identified biases.[14] One of the primary ways in which data is adjusted during the analysis process is known as weighting, which is defined by Research and Marketing Strategies as "adjusting data results to either overcome sampling bias or to give more or less significance to factors based on their estimated relevance to the question at hand."[15] Professor Jelke Bethlehem, from the University of Amsterdam, elaborates on how weighting works:

> Ideally, a selected sample is a miniature of the population it came from. This should be reflected in the sample being representative with respect to all variables measured in the survey. Unfortunately, this is usually not the case. One of the problems is non-response. It may cause some groups to be over- or under-represented. Another problem is self-selection (in an online survey). If such problems occur, no reliable conclusions can be drawn from the observed survey data, unless something has been done to correct for the lack of representativity.
>
> A commonly applied correction technique is weighting adjustment. It assigns an adjustment weight to each survey respondent. Persons in under-represented get a weight larger than 1, and those in over-represented groups get a weight smaller than 1. In the computation of means, totals and percentages, not just the values of the variables are used, but the weighted values.[16]

In theory, weighting allows researchers to compensate for issues which present themselves during the sampling process. As an example, let us consider a survey of ten respondents that asks for their favorite color. Eight respondents answer with red, and the other two choose green. In this case, the findings would indicate that red is the favorite color of 80% of the population. However, if examining the data shows that eight respondents in the sample were female and the other two male, while the population is an even 50/50 split, research analysts would likely assign weights of .625 (50% / 80%) to the female responses and 2.5 (50% / 20%) to male responses in order to bring their representation in the sample into alignment with their prevalence in the study population.

As a result, if the females in the sample all preferred red while the males all preferred green, the weighted study findings would show that half the population likes green while the other half likes red. There are several problems with this approach. Among other things, it increases the standard error of the response findings.[17]

Weighting, like other forms of data adjustments or changes, can help to hide the issues which work their way into the inputs and minimize their impact on the outputs. However, as with most ways in which researchers compensate for problems, they simply reduce the visibility of problems while doing little to solve them. This practice gives the illusion that problems have been addressed or even eliminated, although this is far from the truth. In efforts with smaller samples, weighting may even serve to exacerbate errors and other forms of bias by assigning them greater value.

Table 5.1 – Favorite Color by Sex Weighting Example 1

Favorite Color	Sex	Weight
Red	Female	.625
Red	Female	.625
Green	Male	2.5
Red	Female	.625
Red	Female	.625
Red	Female	.625
Red	Female	.625
Green	Male	2.5
Red	Female	.625
Red	Female	.625

By its nature, weighting entails a lot of assumptions which do not necessarily hold up to scrutiny. It embeds the presumption that researchers somehow know the actual proportion of various groups within the study population such that deviations from those proportions within the sample can be detected. It also presupposes that each group behaves as a block with identical characteristics, rather than as individuals. This could be described as a form of scientific stereotyping, since it suggests that individuals have behaviors identical to the groups to which researchers have assigned them.

In our example above, males comprised 20% of the sample group and 50% of the overall population, meaning that males were substantially underrepresented. Therefore, their responses were given a weighting factor of 2.5 to compensate. This is not uncommon, in magnitude or in frequency of occurrence; weighting factors as high as 8 were used for many years, though they have generally been limited to 4 since the mid-1980s.[18]

These are not minor adjustments that are being made! In such cases, major revisions to the sample data are undertaken to give the findings the appearance of proportional representation, but researchers are increasing the levels of error in the data by doing so. It is a well-intentioned technique designed to correct for some inevitable errors, but it can cause more problems than it prevents.

Let's say the researchers who sampled ten people to determine their favorite colors ran the study again with a new random sample pulled from the same population. This time, a sample of 8 people are selected instead of 10. When this group is surveyed, the results are substantially different from the first group: four respondents pick green as a favorite color, one chooses red, and another three select blue. When looking at the sex of the respondents, the researchers notice that seven of the eight in this sample were male, with only one female.

Table 5.2 – Favorite Color by Sex Weighting Example 2

Favorite Color	Sex	Weight
Green	Male	.5714
Green	Male	.5714
Blue	Male	.5714
Blue	Male	.5714
Blue	Male	.5714
Green	Male	.5714
Green	Male	.5714
Red	Female	4

The findings from this second study and those from the first are both equally considered valid. However, the first study made it appear that green and red were the only colors preferred by the population. Due to sampling and weighting errors, it completely missed the fact that blue is also a common preference for some. Additionally, in the second sample, a single data point was used to represent the entire population block of females. A larger sample would have reduced the magnitude of this error, but this example shows how weighting can misrepresent the data and increase error while theoretically accounting for *sampling bias* in both cases. Weighting trades precision in the hopes of increasing accuracy, yet it can actually detract from both.

Data adjustment practices are widely accepted despite their unsound nature,[19] but adjusting poor inputs cannot yield high-quality outputs. This is the statistical version of alchemists attempting to turn scrap metal into gold.

If the proportional representation of each sub-group within a population is known in advance, then allowing sampling error in the form of *sampling bias* and *self-selection bias* but then attempting to massage those errors out post-data collection is a lazy approach. However, it's much easier than continually re-sampling until the respondent panel is representative of the population; it saves time and money, and the results are touted as though they have equal legitimacy.

If the proportions of each group's representations are not known in advance, then weighting is inappropriate, as the values by which the data should be weighted cannot be determined. Using old, outdated, or otherwise incorrect benchmarks for the overall population's makeup is another problem that sometimes appears in data analysis, as the adjustments will inherently be made incorrectly and will introduce more significant errors into the findings.

Making adjustments to data is a seductive way to address some of the well-known systemic issues that researchers face, especially because it has worked somewhat effectively in the past. This approach has been shown to work well enough on a macroscopic level; it's seemed to get close enough to reality in a large number of cases that researchers were able to claim that they made the right call. As a consequence, it became a commonplace tactic to "correct" for certain known errors.

While not every research study employs weighting to proportionally represent samples at the same ratios in which they exist in the larger population, this is a rather widespread phenomenon. Even the American Community Survey introduced weighting in the 2011 data year to address representation of individuals in group quarters, as opposed to household units.[20] Researchscape's "Weighting Survey Results," published in 2016, indicates the prevalence of weighting:

> Of surveys whose results were published in press releases, 43% were weighted, almost always by at least age, gender and geographic region. In such cases, responses are actually weighted differently for each configuration of

age, gender and region. More extensive weighting attempts to bring even more variables into alignment with the target population: race/ethnicity, education and household income. Certain organizations champion unique weighting variables as part of proprietary methods to improve representativeness: for instance, YouGov and news interest; and Mktg Inc. and panel tenure. Most organizations that weight presume that weighting by additional factors produces greater representativeness.[21]

However, this tactic will only become less and less effective over time as we get further and further away from the baselines which are used to make those data alterations. When even the Census Bureau is unable to produce a comprehensive dataset without such adjustments, the core baseline data used to make those adjustments is called into question. Adjusting data by using already-adjusted data as a baseline only increases structural inaccuracies.

By its nature, making data adjustments is suspect. Researchers are isolating specific clusters within the sample, conducting a separate analysis upon that sub-group, and replacing a portion of their final analysis with the findings therefrom. Since smaller samples are less representative, and findings from smaller samples are more prone to error and bias, this practice magnifies the impact of smaller problems in the overall project.

An analysis which cobbles together several analyses of multiple smaller samples does not have the same strength as a single analysis of a larger sample. The application of weighting increases the error of the weighted value. There will be some error regardless of how extensively weighting is employed, but a collection of smaller analyses will have more error than a single larger one, and is more likely to misrepresent each cluster.

Table 5.3 shows that applying weights to demographic groups which are underrepresented in a 1,000-respondent sample in proportion to the U.S. population can substantially increase error.[22] Applying a weighting factor of about 2 to responses from Asian respondents in order to normalize their representation actually increases the margin of error for that group by over 6 percentage points, from an already very high 14.3% to 20.4% at the 95% confidence level.

A margin of error greater than 20% means that any insights gleaned from an analysis of that data is meaningless. If such an examination showed that 60% of Asians supported banning driving on interstate highways while listening to headphones, all you know is that somewhere between 39.6% and 80.4% of Asians will support this proposition in 19 out of 20 studies. Oversampling is one way to avoid this problem, as the error margins are reduced for those sub-groups, but oversampling one group requires undersampling another. This is where large samples can come into play, but this requires a possibly uneconomical greater investment of time and resources for gains that may not be substantial.

Table 5.3 – Weighting to achieve proportional ethnic ratios example

Demographic	Population Ratio	Sample Ratio	Sample	Weight Factor	Error Change
White	0.637	0.714	714	0.892156863	-0.2%
Black	0.122	0.1	100	1.22	0.9%
Asian	0.047	0.023	23	2.043478261	6.1%
Indian	0.007	0.007	7	1	0.0%
Hawaiian	0.002	0.002	2	1	0.0%
Other	0.002	0.002	2	1	0.0%
Two or more	0.019	0.05	50	0.38	-8.6%
Hispanic	0.163	0.102	102	1.598039216	2.0%

If the overall sample in Table 5.3 was doubled from 1,000 to 2,000, a size which only 18% of 2016 general election polls exceeded, the same weighting would still need to be applied for ethnic representation to be normalized with the general population if the distribution ratios were unchanged. In this case, weighting Asian respondents accordingly still increases the margin of error by 4.3%, changing it from 10.1% to 14.4% at the 95% confidence level. This error range of 28.8% is only 25% smaller than it was with a sample of 1,000 respondents.

Many prominent researchers, pollsters, and social scientists use weighting in their studies. The specifics of the practice vary in complexity and are becoming more advanced, such as the with the use of raking, or "sample balancing" to replace standard cell weighting.[23] However, the fundamental concept of adjusting data collected so as to bring it in line with a broader population is not decreasing in popularity. Considering the problems associated with what amounts to compound analyses, it is not the best approach to error reduction, although it can give the appearance of having done so.

Survey research findings and outputs are increasingly filled with issues because the inputs are increasingly prone to error and bias, and addressing the problem in the analysis stage merely sweeps the problem under the rug. If data error is the social science equivalent of an illness, it seems obvious that it's better to avoid contracting the illness than to treat it after the fact. Not smoking in order to avoid lung cancer has outcomes far superior to radiation treatments and chemotherapy. Ensuring proper sampling and data collection yields far better analytical findings than running biased inputs through algorithmic cleaning procedures.

The bad inputs need to be eliminated or sidestepped. They are not a problem that can be solved by compensating for their presence; they need to be removed entirely. Traditional methodologies are less suited to doing this due to the many ongoing societal and technological changes which are occurring in Western nations.

For the most part, these issues go unexamined by the consumers of opinion polls, market research, and other social science surveys. Researchers' work still gets funded and taken seriously even with the problems we see on display. As a result, there is little to no incentive—in fact, there may even be a disincentive—for the established players in the discipline to make or even identify appropriate changes without experiencing some sort of push by an external third party.

What Can Be Done?

Clearly, many things must change if opinion research is to remain a viable science. Minor adjustments will not suffice, nor will attempts to double down by growing the scope of studies until they are too big to fail. A wholesale paradigm shift is the required to remake the industry into a mold that can thrive in the world of Big Data.

If the act of asking a question necessarily changes the response, lengthy questionnaires will never be able to produce objective measures of individual opinions. Since stated preferences only occasionally align with revealed preferences, stated preferences are not an entirely reliable way to measure how people will behave in response to certain stimuli. The information gathered is merely a proxy for that which is sought. The methodological biases inherent in opinion research data collection cannot be addressed in ways that will resolve them to anyone's satisfaction so long as those researchers continue to use surveys. Posing a series of questions to solicit responses from increasingly less representative samples is inherently problematic in ways that cannot be fixed by slight adjustments or by cleaning the data after it has been collected.

Since the problems lie at the source of the data, it is at the source that contamination needs to be prevented. This requires an entirely different approach than has been undertaken in the past. Traditional question-and-answer surveys must be de-emphasized in favor of less bias-prone data collection methods that are more in line with those employed by the hard sciences.

The source of the problem that has caused growing inaccuracies in opinion and other survey research also presents the solution. The onset of the digital age has opened up a wealth of data collection and aggregation opportunities. The 3.5" floppy disk, which first shipped in 1986, was a breakthrough technology that held 1.44 megabytes of data.[24] At the time it was hard for anyone to imagine needing more storage space than this, but by 2020 there will be 20% more data than that generated every second per person.[25]

Information about details that have never previously been examined is now tracked, logged, and indexed in massive databases which are still growing at incredible rates. In May of 2013, ScienceDaily claimed that in the prior two years, the amount of data generated was 900% greater than the sum total of all data that had been generated in human history up to that point.[26]

Table 5.4 – Data Unit Conversions

	Gigabytes	Terabytes	Petabytes	Exabytes	Zettabytes
Gigabytes	1	1,000	1,000,000	1,000,000,000	1,000,000,000,000
Terabytes	0.001	1	1,000	1,000,000	1,000,000,000
Petabytes	0.000001	0.001	1	1,000	1,000,000
Exabytes	0.000000001	0.000001	0.001	1	1,000
Zettabytes	0.000000000001	0.000000001	0.000001	0.001	1

According to IBM, this was true again for the period between 2015 and 2016.[27] Global internet traffic nearly doubled between 2013 and 2018, generating over 50 terabytes, or 50,000 gigabytes, of data every second;[28] data created from internet-connected devices has nearly tripled over the same timeframe to 403 zettabytes per year.

The size of the digital realm more than doubles every two years.[29] People have signed on to the systems which aggregate this data freely, and they often provide much more information to those systems than they ever have in response to survey solicitations. A lot of this data isn't very useful–90% of it is unstructured and hard to use for analytics purposes,[30] but that hasn't stopped companies from using this information to target product advertisements. However, the volumes of data, its largely unstructured state, and the fact that most of the growth comes from hard-to-index videos[31] means it will likely be a while before most of this data can be used by researchers.

In the meantime, large internet companies like Google and Facebook are already looking for new ways to use these copious quantities of data. In order to show advertisements to the appropriate consumers, platforms must determine things about users such as interests, hobbies, gender, and political party preferences, even if that information has not been provided by the user.[32] It is possible that as these platforms' userbases grow and the identification algorithms become more accurate, they may help alleviate some of the issues facing researchers by enabling them to identify and reach more representative samples, but this approach itself faces numerous obstacles.

The use of surveys will still have issues, but this is not to say questionnaires no longer serve any function. For example, they can still be effective in researching novel scenarios where other forms of data may not exist in sufficient quantities to allow for predictive modeling. However, the research industry's emphasis should be on development and deployment of alternative methods to traditional survey research. Some overlap can certainly be useful, if not necessary, for creating new baselines of higher quality data to which traditional survey response data can be compared. Applying both approaches in tandem can help refine both processes as their comparative representativeness to real world outcomes is examined.

Researchers know there are problems, but getting to the root cause requires a rethinking of the problem and the deployment of new methodologies, both of which are difficult for entrenched players at the individual and organizational level to conceive. This is unfortunate, because this re-conceptualization is what the discipline needs in order to remain relevant in today's evolving society.

Since the turn of the millennium we have progressed to a point where information is staggeringly abundant and available, even without the use of duplicity or covert surveillance. Figuring out how to properly harness the wealth of available data poses numerous challenges, but properly executing on this front opens up a vast amount of opportunity for gleaning unprecedented insights.

For most of human history, figuring out what people were thinking or doing has been an arduous process. Mass communication has only been possible since Guglielmo Marconi's creation of the first devices capable of sending and receiving radio transmissions in the late 1890s.[33] Prior to this most people rarely engaged with those outside of their geographically concise social networks,[34] which made examining their interests and needs difficult.

Compounding this issue is the natural disinclination of people to trust and cooperate with those who are socially distant from themselves.[35] When gathering opinion information requires asking complete strangers questions about their behaviors and the inner workings of their thought processes, a great deal of trust is required to have any hope that the results will be accurate. Those charged with leading hundreds of millions of people need accurate assessments of what they want from their leadership in order to do their jobs effectively, which results in a plethora of problems when those being assessed lack the requisite level of trust and prefer instead to maintain their privacy.

In many ways, this has started to change. Individuals freely give out information much more expediently than before, ironically trusting machines with personal information even though such information will be interpreted by someone with whom they've never had personal contact, a topic addressed by the Institute for Cognitive Sciences and Technologies in the article In machines we trust?

> [T]rust can exist only when there is risk, when agents do perceive the possibility of being cheated yet decide to run some risk and trust the partners anyway. In case of technology, users do not decide to be engaged in cooperation despite of the risks perceived: they

> accept to use technology just because they do not see any risk. So the hard technology protected environment kills the possibility of trust: agents will feel safe, not trusting.[36]

Traditional methodologies will continue to have a place in research and will likely retain some predictive power for many years. Even a stopped clock is right twice a day, according to the old saying, and standard practices will occasionally identify an appropriate sample which is surveyed in a manner that produces relatively little bias within the data. However, such cases will occur less and less frequently, a deterioration of quality which has already characterized the early 21st century.

Methodologies developed for an analogue world are insufficient to explain the digital one. As a result, we will see growing imprecision within research findings until such methodologies are set aside in favor of approaches suited for the society that currently exists.

This is nothing new – every discipline has to come to terms with the continually evolving nature of the world we inhabit eventually, and the social sciences are no exception. Isaac Newton revolutionized the study of physics, yet even though his formulas explain much of the world, that doesn't mean those methods are fully correct. Einsteinian physics is far more precise and allows for many of the advancements we enjoy today. Failure to account for relativistic effects, as with Newtonian physics, would make technologies such as the GPS network impossible.[37]

The natural sciences have undergone numerous paradigm shifts over the centuries, each of which has brought a much more comprehensive understanding of the world and have in turn enabled tremendous technological advancements. The social sciences, particularly those which depend on survey research, are ripe for a paradigm shift of their own. Otherwise, opinion research will devolve to the point where accuracy is determined primarily by chance. This is the point at which the discipline dies. When the results of the elections which serve as the industry's accuracy checks are "a surprise to almost everybody in the field of political analysis, ourselves most definitely included," as UVA Center for Politics Director Larry J. Sabato stated,[38] yet such groups continue to commission the same sort of polls and focus groups to examine the situation, it is arguable that this point has already been reached.

The need for a new scientific approach threatens to put a lot of survey researchers out of work though, which gives them little incentive to make necessary adjustments. The era of Big Data has created great opportunities for opinion researchers to learn more than was possible at any other point in history. It is a crucial development that must be properly built into the discipline in order for social science to attain the level of predictive power that the physical sciences have reached.

The impetus for change must come from outside the survey research discipline for it to happen at all. Integrating Big Data appropriately into opinion research efforts requires mindful creation of an environment that fosters the clean and ethical generation of high-quality data, which the industry requires to once again produce findings that correspond to objective reality. Inertia within the practice largely prevents this from happening, meaning that without external influences, the needed changes are unlikely to occur.

Digital data collection methods make quantifying and assigning proper attributes to data much easier, but it is not a panacea. Most new information generated via technology is inappropriate or in unstructured formats; for example, a large majority of the existing data volume consists of videos,[39] but this isn't always the case. It is likely that continual technological advancements will eventually allow for properly indexing this vast quantity of data that has thus far provided little research value, but retroactively using such data for social science purposes would be questionable. Purposefully gathering exclusively high-quality data while excluding biased 'noise' on an ongoing basis is a much better approach.

Chapter 6 –
New Technologies Enables Issues to be Sidestepped

While the technology needed to properly quantify much unstructured data is likely still years away, we can glimpse some of the advances now. Facial recognition technology has advanced to the point where large social networks are able to identify the people in a given picture,[1] and developments such as the Disguised Face Identification[2] system show that the means to quantify visual data will soon reach a point where the quantification process can be reliably automated.

In the meantime, we can see that people structure or index their data voluntarily when its suits them, usually if they receive some value in exchange for doing so. One popular example of this is the use of hashtags, which are defined in the Fifth Edition of the American Heritage Dictionary of the English Language as "a searchable keyword or sequence of characters prefixed with the pound sign (#), included in a tweet or other electronic communication and indicating the subject matter."[3]

Hashtags allow people to spontaneously coordinate individual participation in conversations as they occur across the globe so that all participants know they're talking about the same subject. The use of hashtags also allows researchers to quickly identify trending discussion topics. Further application of text analysis tools can provide greater insights as to what the discussion's participants actually think about the topic.

Voluntary structuring only provides high-quality insights and data when done spontaneously and when there is no perception that it was requested. When individuals perceive themselves as adding structure to data for their own benefit rather than as a request for free labor by a third party, they are incentivized to do so in a high-quality manner so as to receive the maximum benefit from their efforts. Attempts to impose data structuring from the top-down by asking or directing people to follow a recommended pattern are subject to hijacking and misinformation.

There are many examples of such phenomena. When Attack Watch, a website created by then-President Obama's campaign in 2011, publicly asked social media users to report attacks on Obama's record using the #AttackWatch hashtag, their pages were quickly flooded with heavily sarcastic messages that drowned out those who attempted to submit the requested reports.[4] In such instances, additional textual context analysis must be incorporated into data analysis efforts to realize any of the value originally sought. If the hashtag was used ironically or sarcastically 90% of the time, an analysis which cannot account for this may classify the campaign as a resounding success, when in fact it was anything but.

When voluntary structuring is perceived as labor that's requested by an individual or group rather than as a technological feature which individuals choose to use, the issue of trust surfaces. This inhibits the collection quality, sometimes to the point where any information gleaned becomes suspect. In order for large numbers of people to reliably structure their own data, an organic, bottom-up approach is required.

Data is of better quality and cheaper when offered up freely. Removal or minimization of unnecessary superficial human-to-human interaction, which can lead to the sort of skepticism that results in distrust, also improves quality while also making research more cost-effective. High-quality social research by traditional means requires strong interpersonal relationships between researchers and survey respondents because social pressure somewhat compensates for the lack of immediate tangible value in responding.

By contrast, data which is freely provided and voluntarily structured generally provides some form of instant (or near-instant) gratification in exchange. In the case of hashtags used in social media posts, this takes the form of an increased number of likes and shares which fills what Naomh McElhatton, Founder and Director of Digital Education of consultancy firm SMART NI, calls "that need for affirmation constantly."[5]

When researchers have the time and resources necessary to build strong interpersonal relationships, personal contact has the potential to yield better data. However, since this is rarely the case, it is generally better to minimize such contact to the greatest possible degree or eliminate it entirely. *Social desirability bias* is another factor intrinsic to data collection efforts where there is human contact, regardless of how strong interpersonal relationships between individual researchers and respondents may be. It cannot be excised without eliminating any semblance that another human may be reviewing the data and passing judgement upon those who provided it; since people generally feel more secure entrusting their personal information to a technological system than to another person,[6] eliminating the need for and appearance of human contact effectively kills two birds with one stone.

Researchers need to harness the tendencies of individuals to be more open in ways that are structured for research purposes at the point of collection when other people aren't directly asking for information. This is no simple task, but it is necessary in order for opinion research to stay relevant. Successful execution of this strategic pivot will require researcher to build entirely new systems from the ground up. The only other alternative is to continue employing practices which have produced significantly inaccurate results.

Eliminating Questions Eliminates Observer Bias and Interpretation Issues

In order to make accurate predictions and assessments, the opinion research industry must create systems wherein people provide structured data in real time without much effort, cognitive or otherwise. The less cognitive effort that it takes for people to provide data, the better the data quality will be. This is especially the case when there is minimal social component to the process; even though social affirmation can be a strong motivation to provide structured data, the introduction of *social desirability bias* irreparably taints its quality. Therefore, it seems that digital replications of human interactions would be less successful than systems which do not replicate human interaction.

There has been a lot of research on human-computer interaction (HCI). Much of it is focused on making interactions with machines feel more natural,[7] as though one were actually engaging with another human rather than with a collection of silicon processors. Realistic dialogue is one major avenue by which HCI researchers attempt to make engagements with technology feel more human. These advances can provide benefits to many organizations, but social science researchers who need clean data should go in the opposite direction.

A maxim of modern science, as explained by officials with NASA's Glenn Research Center, is that an ideal researcher "causes no unnecessary perturbations to the system being observed."[8] People are only their most authentic selves when they believe they are acting privately and without being observed. Since the mere presence of an observer necessarily changes what is being watched, unobtrusive data collection methods must be used to eliminate the biases created by this phenomenon.

Dialogue necessarily alerts study participants to the presence of an observer, affecting their responses. Direct questions can also cause respondents to engage in "satisficing," a term coined by Nobel Prize winning economist Herbert Simon[9] in 1982 to describe "[a]iming to achieve only satisfactory results because the satisfactory position is familiar, hassle-free, and secure, whereas aiming for the best-achievable result would call for costs, effort, and incurring of risks."[10]

A dialogue also requires that all parties use a more or less common dictionary and possess a similar understanding of phrases used. In most instances where people communicate linguistically, this is not an issue, since people most frequently engage in discussions with those in similar environs to themselves and subsequently have similar vocabularies as well as understandings of those terms.[11][12][13][14][15][16] This is not the case when highly credentialed researchers attempt to engage with broad samples of diverse regions, sometimes with populations in the millions or hundreds of millions.

Even the legal definitions of terms can vary substantially from place to place and change over time. As a result, even words that are thought to be widely understood with a common meaning that carry the force of law conjure up different concepts in different minds. Few people bother to account for these varying definitions when answering a question posed to them by a survey researcher. Consider the term "rape," which was redefined by the FBI in January 2012:

> "Forcible rape" had been defined by the UCR [Uniform Crime Report] SRS [Summary Reporting System] as "the carnal knowledge of a female, forcibly and against her will." That definition, unchanged since 1927, was outdated and narrow. It only included forcible male penile penetration of a female vagina. The new definition is:
>
> > "The penetration, no matter how slight, of the vagina or anus with any body part or object, or oral penetration by a sex organ of another person,

> without the consent of the victim."
>
> For the first time ever, the new definition includes any gender of victim and perpetrator, not just women being raped by men. It also recognizes that rape with an object can be as traumatic as penile/vaginal rape. This definition also includes instances in which the victim is unable to give consent because of temporary or permanent mental or physical incapacity. Furthermore, because many rapes are facilitated by drugs or alcohol, the new definition recognizes that a victim can be incapacitated and thus unable to consent because of ingestion of drugs or alcohol. Similarly, a victim may be legally incapable of consent because of age. The ability of the victim to give consent must be determined in accordance with individual state statutes.[17]

The Justice Department plainly states that the updated FBI definition of rape will vary in applicability from state to state, in that "consent must be determined in accordance with individual state statutes." Consequently, we can see that there exists no single, clear, fully-agreed-upon definition of the word "rape." Even within the Justice Department, the definition varies; the Bureau of Justice Statistics uses an entirely different definition when conducting the National Crime Victimization Survey (NCVS). This discrepancy emerges when examining publications from the Bureau of Justice Statistics:

> NCVS uses the following rape and sexual assault definitions:
>
> Rape is the unlawful penetration of a person against the will of the victim, with use or threatened use of force, or attempting such an act. Rape includes psychological coercion and physical force, and forced sexual intercourse means vaginal, anal, or oral penetration by the

> offender. Rape also includes incidents where penetration is from a foreign object (e.g., a bottle), victimizations against male and female victims, and both heterosexual and homosexual rape. Attempted rape includes verbal threats of rape.
>
> Sexual assault is defined across a wide range of victimizations, separate from rape or attempted rape. These crimes include attacks or attempted attacks generally involving unwanted sexual contact between a victim and offender. Sexual assault may or may not involve force and includes grabbing or fondling.[18]

Presenting people with questions that use legally-charged terms which vary in definition even within the same department of the U.S. Federal Government, and further vary by geographic location "in accordance with individual state statutes" that few are likely to have read, then asking for a response which will necessarily require the respondent to apply their own interpretations/definitions to those terms, is but one example of how researchers need to remove as many subjective interpretations from the equation as possible.

Questions are inherently subjective because they must be interpreted by the person answering the question. Researchers require objective, quantified data rather than a collection of individual interpretations. While some question formats may appear to make quantification possible, such as a "For/Against" question, no two responses are truly comparable when individuals are responding to questions with their own subjective interpretations of the question's meaning. The same core concept, that different people must answer the same question for the data collected to be comparable, is behind the importance of using identical wording when asking the same question at different points in time to measure changes between the two periods.[19] However, because every individual has a different understanding of any given word's definition, the folly of asking questions at all becomes apparent.

When combined with the problems posed by perpetually variable definitions, the issues surrounding analysis of text responses are too great to overcome.

Free-text responses pose the greatest challenges, but "quantified" multiple-choice responses are only marginally better. The former requires respondents to be sufficiently descriptive in order to get their point across, and the responses must go through comprehensive text analysis for translation into usable data, a process which requires a fair amount of time as well as some mind-reading. Multiple-choice responses represent researchers' best guesses as to likely stances or responses and may not actually represent respondents' views at all. Additionally, the problem of wording interpretation is still at play, although here it's the respondents' interpretation of researchers' phrasings that may lead to error.

While researchers cannot structure their opinion data collection such that it includes explicit requests for information if they want accurate results, this is true whether or not such requests are made in the form of a question. Engaging respondents creates a dialogue which inevitably fosters suspicion. This means eliminating the dialogue structure itself from opinion research and replacing it with direct observations of behavior would be beneficial. Revealed opinions, it seems, are far more reliable than stated ones.

Many sources of problems are substantially mitigated by eliminating question-and-answer dialogues in favor of directly identifying thoughts and preferences. This can be accomplished though data generated from observed behaviors, but only if social pressure and suspicion of motives by participants are kept minimal.

Participation must not feel like a research study in which someone wants or needs the information being provided, in which one's peers could eventually gain access to the data involved, or ideally in which any data is being collected at all. This is not to say that informed consent[20] can or should be bypassed, but rather that researchers should fold participation into other mutually-beneficial activities where the collection of research data is incidental and subtle, not the entire point of the engagement.

By avoiding specific requests for a participant's response, error from misinterpretation of wording either on the part of the researcher or the respondent/user is effectively eliminated at best, or drastically reduced at worst. A behavior is a behavior: they are observable, recordable, and quantifiable. While motivations may be subject to debate, once the behavior has been recorded, the fact that it occurred is not.

Motivations can be derived through context and supported or falsified with additional behavioral data far more reliably than can be achieved through questionnaires or dialogues. This means that aggregate behavioral data are capable of providing far greater levels of insight with much higher levels of accuracy and scientific rigor than are achievable via traditional surveys. A poor implementation of such a behavioral approach to opinion research will provide few if any additional benefit over questionnaires, but any concept is only as good as its execution.

Shifting to research approaches based in behavioral data analysis brings a challenge in that, without questions to prompt a response, a major incentive for individuals to provide information disappears. Asking questions is an active form of data collection; researchers prompt respondents to provide data immediately. An approach based in behavioral data is more passive and must be done without the researchers inserting themselves into the participants' lives or by making requests.

Unless a passive data collection system is sufficiently advanced so as to observe and quantify all of a participant's behavior, it must be constructed to encourage those using it to continue doing so on an ongoing basis. People are unlikely to go out of their way to engage a research project from which they derive little benefit, which is why any such effort much be structured as a mutually beneficial exchange. Incentives must exist or respondents will be unlikely to actually provide data, even if for no other reason than because it's not on their minds.

You Get More of What You Reward

It is highly unlikely that individuals will opt to give researchers the data they need freely. People know that data is valuable and are typically willing to trade it, but they generally want something in return.[21] Compensating research subjects to improve response collection is nothing new. Research by Sandra H. Berry, Jennifer S. Pevar, and Megan Zander-Cotugno at the RAND Corporation in Santa Monica, California indicates that a very high percentage of research surveys use incentives, a figure they peg at a little under 83%.[22]

This is fair. Researchers should compensate people for the information anyways, if for no other reason than to leave a better impression upon those with whom they need to have positive relationships. Use of incentives is a basic tenant of operant conditioning, as described by B.F. Skinner,[23] which has been shown to increase responsiveness in numerous fields, including survey research.[24] You get what you pay for, after all, and the more value that can be provided to individuals in exchange for their data, the more information they are likely to offer up. Facebook and Twitter provide value in the form of their online platforms; in exchange, they receive individuals' thoughts and content. The more that can be offered, the better, especially when the incentives closely align with the information researchers seek in exchange. There are many forms incentives can take. Cash payments are sometimes used, but this is rarely ideal. Sandra Berry *et al* claim that the "most popular forms of incentives were cash (31%), gift card/certificate (27%), and check (25%)" while others "offered the more common mugs, bags, water bottles, and in a few cases, copies of the research results" in addition to a few which "offered unusual incentives such a lottery for an iPod, gift certificates, or a health club membership for a year."[25] The effectiveness of these approaches has been demonstrated repeatedly in the past, though contingent on numerous factors. Paul J. Lavrakas elaborates on the effectiveness of incentives in his 2010 appearance at the *"COPAFS Incentive Conference Session II: Use of Incentives – Who, What, Where, When, Why, and How?"*

> There is considerable past research that shows that a cash incentive of a given value is much more effective in raising final response rates if it is given as a noncontingent incentive than if it is given as a contingent (promised) incentive. This follows from Social Exchange theory as discussed by Dillman and others.[1] Other research has shown that lower value noncontingent incentives are able to stimulate higher response rates than somewhat higher value contingent incentives. In essentially all of this research, the incentives were given as "a token of appreciation" for the respondent's cooperation in completing the survey task.
>
> However, it is not known if there is a cost-effective threshold in the amount (value) of a promised incentive (given only to cooperating respondents) that would bring about a cost-

beneficial effect on final response rates compared to a smaller value noncontingent incentive (given to all respondents). Furthermore, in deploying large valued contingent incentives, it is not known whether characterizing (framing) these as "payments for your time" (i.e., payment for services rendered, as in an economic exchange) rather than as merely "tokens of appreciation" (i.e., a courtesy "thank you," as in a social exchange) might not further raise final respondent rates, although Biner and Kidd (1994) reported suggestive results from an unconfounded experimental design to this effect.[26]

Most approaches to incentivizing data collection focus on the entire response set. While one in nine research studies examined by Sandra Berry *et al* offered prepaid incentives, the rest of the studies' incentives were allocated in response to either considering or actually completing the survey in whole or in part. By incentivizing each contribution of a data *point* rather than providing a fixed reward for a data *set*, researchers can address the fact that incentivizing "general" data collection over collection of "specific" data does not improve data quality within a survey.[27]

While effective if done properly, using cash or other financial incentives could potentially turn the research project into an economic exchange. Once incentives become large enough, participants may feel as though they're working a job rather than participating in a social engagement.[28] However, it is rarely economical for researchers to provide financial incentives high enough that participants see them as adequate compensation when approached from that perspective.

Additionally, financial rewards can introduce the risk of fraud, and they threaten to make the exchange process transactional, with participants seeking to maximize their payouts. Use of financial incentives at the individual data-point level can be prohibitively expensive even without instances of fraud, especially when the collection process is ongoing. Research by Mario Callegaro, Reg Baker, Jelke Bethlehem, Anja S. Göritz, Jon A. Krosnick and Paul J. Lavrakas, demonstrates how this is becoming a bigger issue by noting that we are witnessing the rise of "a breed of 'expert' volunteer survey respondents who are solely interested in monetary incentives and therefore cannot be compared with the general population."[29]

Affordable "social engagement" financial incentive levels[30] on the order of cents per data point are likely to seem trivial and possibly insulting, certainly insufficient to induce people to provide data, while "economic engagement" level incentives can add tens of thousands to the costs of a study.

The best approaches limit costs to the research team while maximizing participants' incentive to provide relevant data. Researchers who do this effectively must make use of information provided by users to provide them with relevant information in return, as value can be provided by trading relevant information rather than financially. That way, a single expenditure in the form labor can be leveraged into substantial personalized value that can be difficult if not impossible to obtain elsewhere.

There are numerous examples of this concept put into practice already. One prominent instance of trading information for more information is fitness trackers, which collect health and activity data that fitness trackers provide back to the user in a consumable format. The quality of data varies from one fitness tracking device to the next, but generally the more information an individual user provides, the greater the usable functionality and personalization of the data users receive in exchange. For example, providing such a device access to one's weight and location can substantially increase its ability to provide statistics on how healthy and vigorous a run or hike was, especially if the device is fitted with a heart rate monitor. The more data users give, the more data the device can give back.

This is an effective example of how a non-monetary incentive can be just as effective as cash distributions, possibly even more so in some instances. There are scores of smartphone apps that constantly track their user's location[31] while providing zero financial incentive in exchange; this information needs to be voluntarily turned over by users, either upon installation or after first accessing location-based features within an app. Research indicates that large majorities are in favor of doing this and have been for years.[32] Attempting to buy this data from over 100 million people[33] would likely be prohibitively expensive, yet such information can be obtained without direct monetary outlays by offering other data in return.

Just as fitness trackers collect data in a manner structured for conducting and displaying analysis thereof to their users, opinion researchers would be best served by creating tools which collect subjective interest data in ways that immediately return informational value to the users. It works—non-cash incentives produce results,[34] and with proper application they can be used to facilitate ongoing collection of vital research data while at the same time generating substantial value for users.

An ideal version of such an information exchange would collect the needed data in a format that is properly structured for research and analysis from the outset. This makes it much easier for researchers to provide immediate value, and it encourages users to provide even more information than they would otherwise be inclined to give. Instant gratification is a strong motivator; having to wait days or weeks for copies of research results[35] reduces the effectiveness of an information exchange as an incentive, which anyone who has taken an instant online poll simply because they wanted to see the results immediately will understand.

When researchers are able to structure the value they offer in return for data, can provide that value immediately, use non-monetary incentives, and are able to offer "specific" incentives in response to each data point rather than "general" ones for whole data sets, we can expect to see substantial benefits that eclipse those experienced through more traditional incentive offerings.

Providing discrete bits of relevant, usable, possibly actionable information in exchange for specific related data points results in the collection of data which is far more reliable. When the value received is directly tied to the quality of data provided, especially when the difference between the value received in exchange for less or lower-quality data is measurably lower, people will typically provide more and higher quality data in return for the higher value. Of course, it is important that information of lower value does not come across as punitive but instead functions as an incentive to enhance data quality.

Additionally, when incentives are structured around needed data, there is more instantaneous feedback for participants and more immediate data collection for researchers. Providing substantial value in this manner which would be hard to obtain by other means is especially critical when temporary issues regarding internet connectivity or data processing arise. Few are likely to make a trip to a public library to research a subject when the internet temporarily goes out –

most would either move on to something else or, if it was important, wait for the connection to come back. Ensuring that the value provided in exchange for one's data is highly valuable, important, or both amplifies the effectiveness of an incentive by keeping people interested and invested in the project when issues outside of the researchers' control arise. Furthermore, such methods provide less financial risk for researchers. When the incentive for providing data is information, it is unlikely that individuals will attempt to excessively provide the same data to reap additional incentives, especially if the same data provided results in the same information delivered. This is different from providing *additional* data which improves the quality of the delivered information.

If providing the same data multiple times in a row yields the same value each time, that behavior is disincentivized in favor of providing new data. For example, a user who provides their unchanged weight to a fitness tracker multiple times gleans no new information, so there's no reason to provide this data excessively. However, if they also record their height and therefore provide the tracker with a new data point, then they will receive more usable health information than if they had only provided their weight.

Of course, if the incentive to provide data is that the user receives usable information, then the information that users receive must be correct. Erroneous information not only has zero positive value, but it can have negative value if it prompts action which turns out to be harmful. Researchers using this incentive structure need to ensure that any information provided to users is accurate, provide additional value for each data point provided, and not collect data which isn't directly relevant to their research.

One of the best practices for using incentives, as outlined by Eleanor Singer at the University of Michigan Survey Research Center, is to "spend more money."[36] This is not meant to imply that incentives need to have a higher monetary value attached. Instead, the suggestion is to spend more in the lead-up to data collection, specifically on materials, testing, and staff. This is in line with of the structure of information-based incentives, which require far more groundwork in advance of deployment. Value delivered by trading information requires a lot of up-front investment in initial research, testing, developing formulas, and validation. It also requires ongoing monitoring of the underlying data to make modification as necessary.

While there are substantial costs associated with non-monetary incentives, most of the costs are front-loaded and only incurred once, used to create that initial value to be delivered. This stands in stark contrast to ongoing cash disbursements. While undertaking development from scratch for each research project would be prohibitively expensive, the fact that such efforts result in reusable tools that can be applied to a multitude of projects means the savings that this approach provides substantially outweigh the startup costs.

Large, Quantified, Proper Datasets Bypass Sampling and Selection Bias

A radical overhaul of the data collection process designed to properly address the major problems faced by social science and opinion researchers must do more than eliminate the issues in the data itself. Removing social and linguistic impediments to proper collection of error-free data only fixes part of the problem. Getting the rest of the way to a comprehensive solution also requires dealing with the *sampling bias* and *self-selection bias* which make their way into response sets.

Traditional methods, which rely on intrusive tactics that interrupt people's lives, are not well suited to minimizing the introduction of bias. Other approaches which attempt to use third-party data are often similarly flawed. Data collected for scientific analysis must be done purposefully, privately, and unobtrusively in order to achieve true validity.

Compiling a dataset by gathering information from a multitude of sources—all of which are structured differently and which may not correctly track the information that researchers seek—is an arduous and unreliable task. Making adjustments to normalize the data worsens this problem. This is not purposeful data collection—this is the scientific equivalent of filling potholes. This practice does more than practically invite *sampling bias* into a project; it makes cherry-picking and selective construction of the aggregate dataset to support a predetermined conclusion far easier.

Researchers are not immune to c*onfirmation bias* – they can certainly fall prey to the human tendency for seeking out data which support their preconceived notions, whether subconsciously or deliberately. Scientific investigation is founded on principles, embodied in practices such as double-blind studies, designed to prevent this phenomenon from influencing results. If the conditions allow for *confirmation bias,* the validity of the project is compromised. Even widely-cited researchers that are celebrated in their field have been shown to fall prey to this tendency to cherry-pick and adjust aggregated datasets to fit preconceived notions when a single comprehensive source is unavailable.[37]

There are steps that can be taken to prevent such contamination of data. Researchers must construct the necessary data sets from the ground up to ensure that a single unified dataset exists wherein all data is similarly structured, quantified, controlled, and truly comparable. Such a purposeful approach can be designed so as to be applicable across a broad spectrum of cases to be studied and include a wide array of data collection mechanisms, but it is important that research data be collected by the research team and not acquired from a third party. A fitness tracker can receive updates to a user's weight if that user steps on a scale which shares the measurement with the tracker and this data will be just as valid as if the user added this figure to the fitness tracker manually, but that information cannot be pulled from the user's public Facebook profile.

The data collection process must also be conducted in such a manner that contributors can reasonably maintain an expectation that nothing they provide to researchers via any collection mechanisms will become public knowledge or personally identifiable.[38] Eliminating the sort of dialogue which is created by asking questions and concurrently removing as much of the human element from the process as possible only partially meets this need.

Research subjects must be able to maintain a significant expectation of privacy regarding their data and know that their interactions with the data collectors will be kept confidential or they may not consent to the sort of information trading that makes this a viable research avenue. The need for data collection that is both purposeful and private means that attempts to derive sought-after information by examining public or semi-public data is also not a viable option.

Organizations such as social media companies which offer public or semi-public platforms as an incentive in return for data consequently do not collect any scientifically-valid data. Even the largest among them are incapable of producing accurate, precise research findings; researchers should take care to avoid using data from such sources. Such platforms primarily collect data in the form of tracking public declarations, or declarations which could be made public at some point in the future, by those being examined. In doing, so these platforms are collecting data that are inherently subject to multiple biases, including *social desirability bias*. Social media posts are often directly tied to one's identity, so making taboo statements or posting certain perspectives may have ramifications. Therefore, individuals using social media have incentives to portray themselves in a specific way based on the perceived preferences of their chosen social circles.

As far as samples drawn from social media populations themselves go, there is a fair amount of *self-selection bias* at work which is closely related to the *social desirability bias* contained within the data. Many individuals, even those who nominally use a given public or semi-public platform, will react to perceptions of facing social disapproval for their beliefs or group membership by simply opting not to make statements at all, effectively withdrawing from such platforms. Some views are consequentially likely to be proportionally misrepresented. As Anne Halsall, co-founder and CPO of the company Winnie, noted, "Online representations of self must be carefully designed and maintained; a well-cultivated social media account has taken the place of the well-manicured lawn in signaling wealth, status, and general got-it-togetherness to peers."[39]

The fact that content on publicly visible platforms is subject to so many biases renders it unsuitable for legitimate scientific purposes, regardless of how large the dataset might be. Individuals must consider their information private if bias is to be eliminated, so the submission and collection of data must be largely done in an anonymous fashion. The most effective approach in this regard are data collectors which are divorced from public personas or identifiers that collect data in seamless, non-intrusive ways while providing real, ongoing value to users.

Dropping the questionnaire format and requests for information would help researchers avoid intrusive collective tactics. Deploying collectors in the form of tools that help users with the behaviors on which researchers need data is not only unobtrusive, but it can be supportive and provide the incentives for users to share their information. The ubiquity of mobile communication devices in the 21st century allows researchers to develop these tools so that research subjects either take them everywhere they go or have readily available access to them, ensuring that an effective collector will always be readily available.

There is a deep hunger amidst over half the world population, and nearly the entire population of the developed world,[40] for this type of technological assistance. People wouldn't carry smartphones with them in such high percentages[41] if that weren't the case. The 21st century is a world in which everyone wants "an app for that,"[42] whatever "that" might be from one situation to the next. Researchers would benefit from taking advantage of this development, which has never before been possible.

In order to take this approach, researchers must build very large datasets in which the data are continually refreshed. The volume of data people are willing to provide in exchange for technological services, especially when those services are free of charge, as well as the general ubiquity of these services' penetration means that very large samples can be assembled. If structured correctly, these samples will continuously provide updated, quantified data which is appropriately structured for opinion research analysis.

New modes of data collection, if properly executed, can not only drastically reduce errors or bias in collected data, but can also eliminate a lot of the data cleanup and adjustments that occur during the analysis stage. The sheer volume of aggregated data collected means that it may be possible to conduct analysis without subsequent data adjustments.

The strength of large, properly collected datasets can allow for active proportional sampling. A large dataset may not itself be perfectly representative of a given population, but it is likely to contain representative samples of any given population. Once such a dataset has been assembled, the proper sample for a particular study need only be identified from within that broader dataset.

In cases where specific representation is necessary, researchers can repeatedly randomly sample an existing large set of data until certain parameters are met and study that sample. Since the data has already been collected and researchers in this scenario are only conducting sampling to determine which data to pull, rather than who to attempt to reach, results can be synthesized without worrying about *sampling bias*, *self-selection bias*, or the increased error associated with traditional sample adjustment methods. This sample can even be tagged and repeatedly referenced in the future to examine change over time. It can also be isolated from the larger dataset before again running the sampling process until the same parameters are met in a new sample without using the initial sample group, in order to conduct verification checks.

Moving away from questionnaires and towards direct, incentivized, continuous collection of structured behavioral data can correct for significant levels of error in many areas of opinion and interest research. This is not a perfect solution—using behavioral data to uncover revealed preferences can present issues in determining reasoning or motivations for a given behavior, though these problems are no more severe than those experienced as a result of traditional survey research.

In some specific cases, such as hypothetical scenarios, questionnaire-style supplementation to behavioral data will still be necessary to fill in the gaps, at least for some time. Some questions that survey research attempts to answer, such as whether people see themselves more as a "Type X" or "Type Y" person where X and Y are any two positions on a given spectrum (such as "assertive" or "laid back") or which of two statements they agree with more, can be soundly answered with behavioral data only when copious quantities of such data are available.

Many survey research efforts seek to provide cross-examinations with other data in order to make claims such as "assertive people are more likely to agree with statement X while laid back people are more likely to agree with statement Y." However, in reality, a traditional survey would only truthfully allow the claim to be phrased "*self-described* assertive respondents to our survey are between 48% and 54% more likely to *profess agreement* with statement X than statement Y." Because of the desire to make such claims—as well as the difficulty and time-consuming nature of building a sufficiently robust repository of behavioral data to do so—surveys are likely to persist as a shortcut.

Until significantly greater levels of data collection and analysis are viable, such that individual responses to specific novel stimuli can be predicted with a fair degree of accuracy, there will still be a need for question-and-answer survey research. Mixing the two approaches within any one data collector would be counter-productive however; keeping questionnaire-style collectors separate from behavioral data collection tools is paramount in order to ensure the integrity of the data. Attempting to combine them would eliminate the benefits of non-intrusive technological collectors by reintroducing the biases they were deployed to avoid.

Nearly the entire adult populations of Western nations use internet-enabled services that collect and distribute data in some form or another.[43] Even many individuals in developing countries—which have largely skipped the landline era of telecommunications and gone straight to implementing cellular networks—are now connected to the digital world.[44] Leveraging this medium to generate the data that researchers need can be a highly effective solution to the problems posed by traditional social science research methodologies.

The major sources of data integrity issues at each step in the survey questionnaire approach process—from initial conception of the study through publication of findings— can be greatly reduced or entirely eliminated. There are sure to be new, unexpected challenges to implementing effective alternatives which will need to be addressed as they arise, but this is no reason not to start developing and deploying new behavioral based approaches.

All of this potential benefit assumes that the research team or teams conducting such work are sufficiently trusted not to compromise data privacy through duplicitous means. Violating this maxim means findings from behavioral data will be no better than those reached through traditional surveys.

Dislodging the strong hold surveys have achieved, especially now that technology has made conducting surveys almost frictionless, will take some time. If you have an internet connection and either a contact list or a few extra dollars lying around, you can conduct a survey in minutes.[45][46][47] However, just because it's easy doesn't mean it's an effective way to gather usable information that corresponds to the world at large. But the choice between the quick, easy path and the long, hard path frequently faced throughout human history often results in many taking the former road, even when it's counterproductive in the long run.

Chapter 7 - Privacy and Proper Incentives Yield Superior Results

A switch from the question-and answer-format of data collection to behavioral data collection tools requires strong incentives for people to provide that data, but those incentives need to be both affordable and manageable for the research team. Financial incentives can get pricey, especially when payment is given for each datapoint. Considering a mobile device can generate an average of over 40 data points per month,[1] collectors with 100,000 users could easily cost over $10,000,000 per year at a quarter per data point.

Regardless, continual incentivization is needed for continual data collection to be possible. While cash or its equivalents are one valid means to induce such collection, a financial approach would need to be well-tailored so as to not bankrupt the project.

Offering "market value" for individual response data, effectively buying it from people, keeps costs in the value range for social exchanges but isn't particularly viable. While any individual data point need not cost very much, with whole profiles often priced at under a dollar,[2] it can quickly add up for researchers attempting to construct a very large dataset. This is especially the case for more robust profiles; including physical location or digital communication histories can run over $50 per year.[3]

Affordability is not the only necessary consideration though; care must be taken to ensure that incentives themselves do not introduce bias into the collected data.[4] Reduction (and preferably elimination) of bias is a key factor in producing quality research results with predictive power that correspond to reality. Improving response or engagement rates by sacrificing objective validity is not a viable or scientifically sound approach. James S. Cole, Ph.D., Shimon A. Sarraf, and Xiaolin Wang explain both the necessity and challenges of incentivization in "Does use of survey incentives degrade data quality?":

> Theories such as Leverage-Salience Theory and Social Exchange Theory provide causal explanations as to why survey incentives might be effective at increasing response rates,

> however little empirical information exists about the impact these incentives have on data quality… Though response rates are generally recognized as the data quality indicator, it may be imprudent to use incentives for bolstering response at the expense of other data quality indicators. At the very least, incentive users should be fully aware of any potential tradeoffs, if they do exist.[5]

Trades of information are an ideal alternative, and they are certainly a more cost-effective approach. The primary benefit of offering informational instead of financial incentives though is that in addition to being much more affordable, sources of bias which can be introduced through the use of the latter form[6] are kept to a minimum.

Buying data from people, either directly or indirectly, or even the perception that data is bought may make respondents suspicious of the data's purpose. This line of thinking results in an *observer effect* that necessarily changes the data, similar to how people alter their behavior when they know they are on camera.[7] While this alteration may in some cases be the result of *social desirability bias*, the *observer effect* in play here need not skew the data in a socially desirable direction; it may simply be the case that a suspicious individual provides less accurate, more random data without regard to how it would reflect on them personally.

It also introduces some *self-selection bias*, as people opt out of providing the data that researchers need. When researchers offer information, this phenomenon is eliminated. It changes the thought processes occurring in respondents minds such that consideration of who is watching or benefiting from the exchange doesn't typically arise.

Research by Linda Molm, Nobuyuki Takahashi, and Gretchen Peterson supports the notion that offering information freely "without explicit negotiations or binding agreements" can produce "stronger trust and affective commitment than negotiated exchange[s]."[8] With an ideal implementation, it is possible that the engagement between researchers and respondents is not even perceived as an exchange but rather as an explicit offer of value by the research team. Such a structure may even be perceived as more altruistic; participants may perceive themselves as simply accessing an information storehouse which the researchers have made freely available, which is effectively true when this is done effectively.

The existing model, in which researchers offer incentives once for participants who achieve a certain milestone, is not compatible with data collection efforts of an ongoing nature. A shift away from one-off surveys towards continuous, ongoing data collection means that incentive models designed to get people to complete long questionnaires which take over 45 minutes to finish[9] will not function.

The traditional approach must be revisited and revised to facilitate a change in research methodologies. Incentives cannot be a one-time deal – anything offered must be something that can be continually provided, built up towards, or added to over time to ensure that participants keep coming back to provide more data. They need to be designed to provide value for participants which is realized upon each engagement with a data collection mechanism. Implementations also need to account for the shortening human attention span;[10] they must ensure that participants don't simply forget that the collector exists and remind users of the ongoing value associated with participation.

As has been previously mentioned, some research projects will offer respondents access to selected research findings when those results are not confidential,[11] but these motivators are not entirely helpful, as they often do not impact the respondent directly. A survey which collects information regarding respondents' use of financial institutions and offers in exchange the results which indicate the extent to which the respondent pool maintains various types of accounts at select institutions is not likely to be a very enticing incentive for participation. Research projects which offer information as an incentive in exchange for the information they collect must make sure that, like any other type of incentive, what they are offering is something that will have real value and will be useful to each respondent.

Offering information of value to each individual respondent is not difficult, especially in an age where personalization of data delivery is rarely perceived as invasive. It is in many ways the status quo, though not universally so. In cases where information delivered to respondents is subject to change or variation due to any number of factors, periodically notifying participants regarding changes particularly applicable to participants can effectively serve this need to provide them with a unique value in return for participation.

This is especially so if any factors are related to changes in personal situations, individual information, or external factors over which individual respondents have little control. In fact, this is optimal: if data delivered to a research project participant is both personally relevant and subject to change as a result of changing circumstances about which they might not have even known, this serves as a powerful incentive for continued participation. However, doing this only in line with a participant's predetermined wishes, and without introducing external biases, is crucial to ensure there is no violation of trust and to minimize perturbations of their lives.

As an example, consider a hypothetical research project undertaken to identify people's use of financial instruments. Imagine that this project found that residents of Alaska were unlikely to be interested in taking out Certificates of Deposit (CDs), measured by offering rate information and other related data while asking participants to rank CDs relative to other financial instruments.

If financial institutions wanted to change that by temporarily offering special CD rates in that state, the data collector could notify Alaskans while providing that updated rate information, and could measure whether interest in taking out Certificates of Deposit changed as a result. The collector may then additionally notify those Alaskans as the expiration date approaches and again measure any change in consumer interest. By structuring information as an incentive in this manner, the research team has provided value to participants at multiple points in time while collecting the data needed by the financial institutions, who are their clients, to determine whether the rate shift had an effect on likelihood to use that particular product.

Formats which optimize value for all parties are generally data-driven. Identifying relevant data protects the data that researchers receive from biases, protects the research team and its funders from financial overexertion, and creates incentives for timely engagement.

Automating Incentive Delivery Streamlines Continuous Collection

When using traditional surveys, it is relatively easy for researchers to deliver incentives, as they are generally disbursed at predetermined milestones.[12] The commonly-employed approach of cash payments or their equivalents is among the most straightforward models of incentive distribution. However, in an ongoing behavioral data collection scenario, the specific moments when incentives should be delivered will naturally vary from participant to participant.

For the incentive delivery process to be effective in an ongoing collection scenario, it must be automated in a manner that intelligently determines when appropriate moments for distribution arise. Consequently, incentives must be provided continuously to each individual participant without need for direct input or action from the research team itself. Using information-based incentives makes this challenge much simpler.

The traditional use of incentives is primarily geared towards increasing the level of participation, both to collect more data and to reduce bias. The vast majority of research projects examined in a study by the RAND Corporation indicated that increasing response rate was the main reason they offered incentives, with nearly three-quarters (73.2%) claiming this was the case.[13] Additionally, 52.9% said reducing non-response bias was another very important reason they did so.[14] Although a third (36.6%) also mentioned they wanted to reward their respondents for participating,[15] no other factors were deemed important by more than a fifth of researchers surveyed. Automation of value delivery in the form of nudges or notifications can accomplish these goals by inducing participants to act and provide the data sought.

When researchers are tracking activity data, participants must be incentivized and stimulated time and again to provide such data. Without incentives that remain at the forefront of participants' minds, many will not engage with the collectors deployed by the research team if for no other reason than because they don't think to do so. The vast amount of competition for each person's attention[16] means that without incentives that successfully grab attention, data collection efforts are likely to suffer.

The advent of the digital age and ubiquitous computing technology allows researchers to build systems that determine when external, real world events are likely to affect a research participant based on their prior engagement with the researcher team's data collectors. This, in effect, enables delivery of a stimulus to participants simply by informing them of relevant real world events and providing related data for participants to review. The way in which participants respond can then be recorded. By providing value in the form of actionable information, research participants can be induced to supply data without a sense of "being watched" which could trigger *observer effects*.[17] This, it seems, would result in cleaner data with less bias.

For example, fitness trackers which notify their wearers of lengthy inactive periods induce that person to get up and move around, thus providing new data to the fitness tracker. In a great many instances,[18] these trackers log the information that they display to their users and allow them to store that information in the cloud,[19] often by transmitting it to external data warehouses which are maintained by their creators.

The nuances of this approach vary from company to company, and certain implementations of cloud functionality can create *observer effects* including *social desirability bias*, but the concept of providing people with relevant pushes has been demonstrated to work in a variety of circumstances. The myriad of privacy concerns surrounding the security of user data[20] does create the possibly that some may opt out, though these concerns can reasonably be addressed by ensuring anonymity of users. So long as researchers don't require personal identifying information (PII) with the data gathered, privacy concerns can be addressed in a fairly straightforward manner.

Ample research on the proper way to deliver such notifications and nudges has been conducted, which itself provides a substantial boon to opinion researchers who seek to adopt a similar proactive, less invasive approach.

The information gleaned from fitness trackers is only one piece of the broader pie—weather updates, sales calls, social pings, sports announcements, time sensitive offers, and location based deals have all been thoroughly studied and reveal ways to generate unobtrusive notifications which drive engagement without turning off users.[21] Suraj Dubey provides advice useful to researchers and other notification-sending companies about how to use mobile push notifications effectively in "11 Types of Compelling Mobile Push Notifications That Delight Users":

> Here are 3 key qualities that keep users happy to receive your notifications. They should be:
>
> - Highly personalized
> - Timely
> - Very relevant

> …
>
> The most effective notifications marry user data with external and user inputted data to send highly relevant, timely notifications.
>
> A good rule of thumb when deciding between using a push notification and other less intrusive and immediate communication channel is: "Will this change how users act or feel in the next 24 hours?"[22]

This form of automated incentivization can serve to meet all the data collection needs of researchers while leaving a positive impression upon those using the collector. The lack of an explicit negotiated exchange in such a scenario further builds trust between participants and the research team.[23] This in turn can push individual participants to promote a collector's benefits to friends or family, which grows the sample of usable data.

According to Localytics, a leading mobile engagement platform which "processes 120 billion data points monthly", individuals "who complete between 1 and 3 sessions in an app have an average [push notification] opt in rate of 35%" which "doubles to 70% when users complete between 4 and 6 sessions in an app."[24] Structuring the collector and these nudges such that they coincide with participants' interests means that automated systems can deliver timely nudges that participants not only engage with, but actually appreciate and in turn actively seek out. Research by Localytics supports this, indicating that "users are more likely to respond to a message with information that directly affects them" and "are 3x more likely to complete a conversion event if the message incorporates some kind of personalization."[25]

A collector that is sufficiently helpful to the population it seeks to examine can very effectively incentivize the sort of engagement which provides researchers with the data they need. This is particularly so when those notifications are personalized, delivered in a timely manner, and relevant to the user's specific situation.

Nudges which fail to meet the criteria for keeping users happy risk having the opposite impact; they may turn people off. If this occurs, the population may cease participation or ignore delivered stimuli, devaluing the aggregate collected data in the process by depriving researchers of time-series information. Ineffective nudges may also tear down the trust that researchers work hard to build. If former participants disparage the data collection platform, they may sway others within their social circles from engaging with the team's collectors. In "The Inside View: How Consumers Really Feel About Push Notifications", Caitlin O'Connell warns of the stigma surrounding push notifications and the importance of personalization:

> Push messages have a reputation for being unwelcome. When you consider the fact that over 35% of push notifications are generic "broadcast" blasts to all users, it's easy to see that a lack of relevancy plays a major role in this perception.
>
> Sending the same push message to every user should not be part of an app's marketing strategy, especially considering our last post proved that personalized push is a better strategy than broadcast marketing. For instance, there is a 3X improvement in conversion rates when push notifications are personalized to user preferences.[26]

When implemented properly, this form of automation can substantially support continual data collection both by helping to foster the necessary conditions and by providing real and unique value to participants. Using notifications which are individually relevant and timely to deliver incentives helps mitigate respondent concerns over researcher trustworthiness and data security,[27][28] especially when personal identifiers are either not collected or not required.

Researchers should acknowledge that respondents are more likely to take an action that they see as benefitting themselves than they are to act with the goal of helping an anonymous third party. Accommodating this facet of human nature by emphasizing the direct benefits of participation through unique offerings and incentives can lead the target population to the conclusion that using a particular data collection tool is in their best interests.

Charging for and basing compensation around time and materials is commonplace, but is not always the best approach for research project incentives. For researchers attempting to extract value from a substantial number of individual members of large populations it can not only be prohibitively expensive when using financial incentives, it can also be rather impractical. In many cases, the research subjects in a continuous data collection model only invest a few moments of their time during any given engagement and are not consuming much if anything in the way of materials, nor are they exerting much energy to do so.

Since compensation which is based on time and materials is unlikely to yield much benefit for those participating in the research project where little of either are required, alternatives with a different focus can be far more enticing. There is a philosophy which states that people should be paid for the value they provide rather than strictly for their time.[29] By adopting this approach for research project incentives, much more value can be delivered to both the researchers and to the participants. Providing participants value delivered by an automated mechanism in response to specific engagement of the sort researchers seek follows this model of compensation which emphasizes value created over time spent.

Tying incentives for participants to the value they deliver for the research team should improve data quality in the same way that paying workers for the value they deliver, rather than by the hour, improves their productivity and the overall quality of the final product. This is why large tech companies often offer stock-based compensation – employees with a stake in the well-being of their employer and the quality of its products are invested in the final results. By creating a structure wherein research subjects actively seek to provide information so that they can receive informational value in return, *self-selection bias* can be short circuited. People opt not to respond to surveys because they do not perceive it to be in their interest to do so. Turning this around by demonstrating to individuals that it is in their best interests to participate means that in many cases, the research subjects sought by the team will be more apt to adopt and engage with the collection tools.

Selective, Responsive, Data Incentivization Can Produce Great Results

Using technology to marry user data with relevant real world events then deliver timely personalized notifications generates engagement with the applications that do so.[30][31] Researchers can appropriate this phenomenon to effectively stimulate project participants who are using the team's collectors in ways that result in the generation of high quality data. Since the user data need not include personal identifiers, the measurement errors caused by *observer effects* and *social desirability bias* can be kept to a statistically insignificant level.

Delivery of relevant information does not necessitate disclosure of one's identity, merely that individuals provide collectors with enough information to determine what is relevant. Exclusively using data inputted by the user without calling upon data from outside systems that monitor them in other ways has two substantial beneficial effects.

First, it increases trust, as the data that users provide is clearly being kept anonymous and not "matched" with or traded in exchange for additional data from third parties.[32] This is especially important for researchers who need clean behavioral data for their analyses; by ensuring and demonstrating anonymity for participants, the entire dataset is much more reflective of reality. Combined with the trust-building which results from the social exchange of offering information freely,[33] the high levels of resulting trust can yield very representative data.

Secondly, since the information-based incentives provided to users depends solely on the data they input, users will naturally input more data since third party sources aren't bridging any gaps by filling things in for them. This means all data in the set is gathered through similar mechanisms and possibly a single collector, so researchers will have a more comprehensive dataset at their disposal. Data is intrinsically comparable when it comes from sources which collect it purely in identically natively quantified formats, rendering transformation and cleaning techniques unnecessary. This is a significant step in the elimination of biases that can be introduced and error that results from using large datasets aggregated from various sources.[34]

The data generated by such properly-constructed and deployed collectors is far more valuable than the sort collected by traditional surveys. All the information gathered is structured in the same manner. It grows over time while older data is regularly refreshed. This combination of factors allows for rapid multivariate analysis and nearly real-time updates. As a result, researchers can calculate the impact of a given stimulus on target populations with a high degree of precision.

Since this approach does not involve asking research participants any questions, potential issues that would arise from misinterpretations are drastically reduced. Additionally, any possible *observer effects* are minimized further still by broadly divorcing the collector from any apparent human interaction. In their work *Risk and Trust in Social Exchange: An Experimental Test of a Classic Proposition*, Linda D. Molm, Nobuyuki Takahashi, and Gretchen Peterson also suggest the benefits that this approach provides by avoiding negotiated financial exchanges and building trust:

> Whether trust actually develops depends on the partner's behavior and the information it conveys about the partner's trustworthiness. In support of these predictions, our results show that reciprocal acts of individual giving produce significantly higher levels of trust than the joint negotiation of binding agreements, even when exchanges of equivalent value, in equivalent structures of power and opportunity, are compared. And, when the risk of reciprocal exchange provides the opportunity to demonstrate trustworthiness, actors' behaviors-their commitments to one another and the equality or inequality of their exchanges-strongly influence the level of trust that develops.[35]

The only known significant downside to of this approach, other than difficulty in collecting individual preference data related to hypothetical scenarios, is the lack of assurance which results from entering into an explicitly negotiated exchange where a violation by either party can be prosecuted in a court of law, especially when there are financial considerations involved.[36] Trust and assurance, while related, are difficult to secure simultaneously due to how one implies the other is either not present or required.

For example, a person who asks a friend to help them move in return for pizza and beer trusts that the friend will show up on moving day but has no assurance this will occur. Few would ask a friend to sign a contract obligating that person to help in exchange for food and drink. However, when opening a bank account, few people would trust the bank not to charge fees simply because they promised they would not. Explicit contracts detailing agreed upon fees are expected, and violations of that agreement by the bank can result in potentially ruinous lawsuits.

Adopting an information-trading approach to research where no money changes hands largely relies on mutual trust and lacks the assurances of a formal negotiated agreement. Presenting users with detailed terms, although they may or may not read them,[37] helps with this issue somewhat but cannot come close to achieving the levels of assurance that come from a negotiated economic exchange.

Researchers intent on doing more to reassure users can address this issue by incorporating components of an economic exchange into the collectors, but they should still be certain to expressly divorce the economic exchange from the data collection process itself. Any economic exchange must not be connected to information-based incentive delivery or be augmented using data that's supplied by or gathered from participants.

Certain implementations of an economic component could risk negatively impacting data quality, although they generally do not involve ongoing incentive delivery. Advertisements, for example, can create a breach of trust[38] if they involve employing user data that's gathered by or supplied to the collector in order to tailor ads to those users, even if the research team at no point shares any data with advertisers. Using static, contextual advertising more akin to a billboard along the side of the road rather than smarter, individually targeted ads similar to those which follow people around the internet can avoid this risk, but the mere presence of any advertising can potentially have such results regardless.

Some additional engagement incentives which augment assurance can be created by implementing freemium aspects of the platform which enable users to make purchases which unlock additional functionality. People are generally inclined to use something they paid for more than something they got free of charge,[39] which is among the reasons why collection platforms that are freely-distributed use incentives to drive engagement. However, a collector which users must pay for from the outset is much less likely to be initially adopted,[40] and it results in biases within the collected data. Freemium models combine the positive aspects of these two phenomena so long as original functionality is not hindered over time to drive adoption of the freemium aspects, which would negate the advantages of this approach to data collection entirely.

Regardless of whether any economic component is incorporated into such tools, aptly timed engagement nudges in the form of notifications that provide a real value to participants have an effect similar to a virtuous cycle. Each additional engagement improves the participant's perspectives and sentiment on the project, specifically towards the collector. In a scenario which meets these conditions, ongoing future re-engagement is all the more likely.

Building and deploying data collectors which are looked upon favorably by users is highly beneficial. For researchers to fully grasp all the nuances of what they are observing, vast amounts of data are required to help eliminate spurious variables and relationships,[41] or those which appear to be correlated but aren't actually causational.

Only when the effects of third variables that create a correlation between two others are detected and addressed can researchers conduct thorough and accurate analyses of their findings; without knowing whether there are additional intervening factors which create an observed correlation, researchers cannot know for sure what caused the observed response to a given stimuli. This problem often leads to misattribution of cause and effect, such as in the supposed case of "ice cream consumption causing drowning deaths."[42] Such cases can result in suggested courses of action or policy prescriptions which will likely be ineffective in creating the desired impact.

Since an ongoing approach of continuous incentivization and subsequent data collection yields much more comprehensive datasets without the issues associated with traditional collection methods, it is clearly a superior option. As in many cases, though, better tactics are not necessarily easier ones. It takes much more time and effort to build a collector that meets these standards than it does to throw together a survey. However, for a research organization with sufficient competency in programming, software engineering, user interface design, and psychological principles in addition to the analytical acumen needed to process the information, the benefits of adopting this approach are substantial.

Competition for people's time and attention is fierce. Attempting to aggressively grab too much time from what any given individual can spare may have the opposite effect; it can lead to opt-outs and oversaturating users such that they start to tune out even without fully disengaging from the collector. However, in general, people are willing to engage with properly developed tools, and they will do so continuously when all the conditions necessary for the creation of a virtuous cycle exist.

This phenomenon means that a competent team can independently and purposefully build large datasets which enable them to overcome the problems opinion researchers face as part of the transition to a digital-primary world. The relatively unique structure, format, and distribution of incentives combined with the continuous nature of the data collection process itself synthesize to create an approach to social science research far more rooted in agile methodologies rather than in waterfall approaches.

As detailed by the project managers and software developers at VersionOne, an agile approach "accelerates the delivery of initial business value, and through a process of continuous planning and feedback, is able to ensure that value is continuing to be maximized"[43] throughout delivery as a result of its use. The benefits of adopting an agile methodology over traditional waterfall-based concepts are numerous.

Since quantified behavioral data is being collected, and continually so, the value that can be delivered to research clients using this approach is substantially greater to that provided by traditional methodologies. Addressing questions raised by clients after the fact, drilling deeper into the findings, slightly tweaking parameters or incentives to optimize ongoing collection, and many other options not generally possible in traditional methods open up when an agile approach is implemented.

Figure 7.1 – Agile vs. Traditional Value Propositions

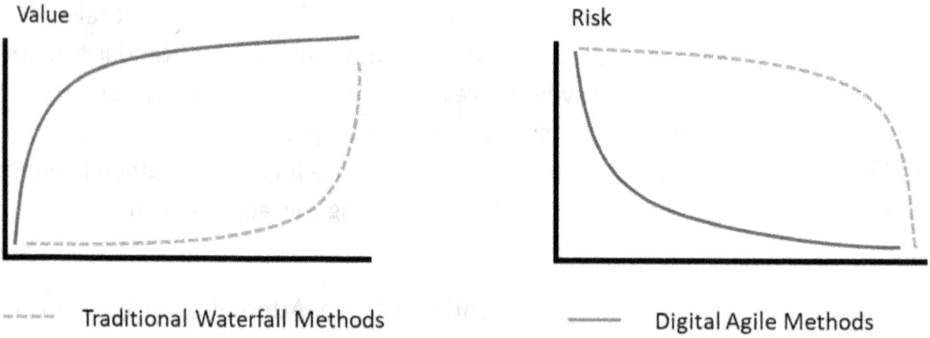

Proper execution of a digital-primary data collection regime requires that any collectors be "firewalled" from the rest of the digital realm. This can complicate the development process and require more resources than would otherwise be necessary were such a collector designed as a direct-revenue-generation tool rather than primarily as a data collection tool, but it is necessary to keep data clean.

When data is being collected for social science research, it's important that users are given no reason to worry that their individual information could publicized. Since no amount of data security is infallible, the process must be fully anonymous. Additionally, this maxim must be clearly adhered to in ways which are plainly visible throughout every possible engagement with the collection tools.

Once the data collection and incentive delivery mechanisms are properly constructed, researchers gain access to a new trove of data which provides insight into peoples' true preferences and interests. It does so without the need for surreptitious practices or secret surveillance, an authenticity now possible for the first time in human history. Access to this information, legally and ethically collected *en masse*, allows for unprecedented advances in each of the social sciences.

Truly accurate public opinion data cannot come through survey questionnaires. Stated preferences, stances, and interests far too frequently contradict those that individuals actually hold, yet reported preferences are the only sort traditionally collected in the vast majority of cases. With the proper alignment of incentives, the use of tools focused on behavior rather than statements, the assurance of anonymity, and the full quantification of each data point collected, social science research can take large strides towards becoming a rigorous discipline with predictive power on par with that of the natural sciences.

Chapter 8 - Collecting Good Data and Avoiding Noise is Imperative

Observing our behaviors, even those that primarily occur digitally, can help social science researchers obtain information that has been largely unavailable in the past. Since the ability to record authentic human behavior in a fashion suitable for research purposes is relatively new in our history, there are a lot of inappropriate applications thereof which end up degrading the quality of collected information. Additionally, it too often infringes upon the rights, customs, and sensibilities of those from whom data is sought.

The process of observing human behavior in a manner which does not perturb those being observed or impart a sense of being watched allows for insights into revealed preferences. Revealed preferences are far more accurate predictors of future outcomes and responses to stimuli than can be generated from solicited stated preferences. However, it is ideal to have a central repository of both.[1]

The social sciences have largely gathered stated preferences in the past and consequently, in building such a central repository, less examination and development is needed to deploy more robust means to collect stated preference data compared to the need to build behavioral data based systems from the ground up; the quality of the former can be improved by building off successful implementations of the latter.

Researchers who attempt to build large, comprehensive, and sound datasets are better-served by aggregating quantified, behavioral-revealed preference data before examining natively qualitative, stated preference data, which is typically obtained through questions or volunteered statements. This is not to say this data should not be sought out, but rather that it should be a secondary goal, especially considering the quality issues generally associated with survey data.

Once robust collectors of quantitative data have been deployed, proven their trustworthiness, and achieved generally high engagement, qualitative data collection can be incorporated carefully into the existing processes. This can be executed by deploying new, additional collectors linked to (yet independent from) the original quantitative versions, or by augmenting the originals such that they themselves gather the data. Separate, yet linked, collectors are ideal if engagement can be assured, but either process risks reintroducing the biases that quantitative, agile, behavioral collectors are effective at eradicating.

Digital data collectors can effectively do for social science the equivalent of what particle accelerators and atom smashers do for physics, or what the microscope does for biology and health sciences. They can serve to gather information which gives us a refined, granular look at what's happening beneath the surface, and by doing so they can expand the frontiers of human knowledge. Of course, it's important to still keep in mind that people are not objects, and they shouldn't be treated as such.

The volume of information out there is mind-bogglingly huge and can help illuminate nearly every aspect of human existence, but just because data exists and can be obtained doesn't mean it should be aggressively sought. While practices of harvesting people's interests and histories to provide more relevant content by very large organizations such as Google[2] and Facebook are normalizing collection of personal data, individuals are by and large reluctant to provide it and are hesitant to turn over this information. Alyssa Darmanin, Senior Mobility UX Design Specialist at Volkswagen Group of America, suggests that there is nearly-universal resistance to requests for personal data even when these requests come from technology:

> Technology today is no longer a nice to have. Society relies heavily on scientific knowledge for practical purposes. The expectation that a digital experience "just works" is a significant social norm. In UX (user experience) design, we explore the journey people take on as they interact with technology, and execute on the paths that induce positive emotions. A user flow has the potential to be disrupted in any number of ways, causing friction for users in satisfying their mission. A common example of this type of interruption is seen when a user is forced to sign up for an account or provide an e-mail address in exchange for making a purchase online. In the real-world, people are used to preserving control over disclosing their personal information, and certainly don't serve up these

> details before purchasing in-store—that long established societal norm should be considered for digital experiences as well. Why should your users bother to give you something before you give them a reason to? You'd better have a good rational.[3]

When a data collection tool is clearly or blatantly attempting to aggregate as much data as possible from those who engage with it, especially when this is done in ways which provide few measurable benefits, the result is the introduction of error and bias. At each point of friction where a data collection attempt is actively initiated, as opposed to occurring passively as a consequence of the collector's functionality, *self-selection bias* appears when users opt out.

Actively hunting for specific data points can skew findings and eliminate the benefits of incentivized continuous collection. Allowing information to flow naturally resulting from organic engagement with a collector rather than pushing people to provide data without an obvious immediate benefit is the only way the scientific benefits of this data collection model are realized.

Pushing users to engage with a collector may be a good way to immediately and directly improve engagement metrics,[4] but it comes at a cost. If improving these metrics in the short term is the only objective, it can (and often will) work. However, not only will this end up creating churn which results in bias (as opt-outs are unlikely to be randomly distributed throughout the participant base) but those who remain will be more suspicious of, and more likely to ignore,[5] further attempts to drive engagement. All subsequent data gathered will thus have an increased level of bias, which will grow each time engagement with a collector is inorganically pushed.

For firms focused on generating profits that result from user engagement, pushing user engagement is a viable strategy, even if it's often annoying to them. These organizations don't necessarily care whether their population of users is properly representative of the general population, and they can generally afford this loss of data quality if it produces revenue as a result. This is another reason researchers cannot trust data from such third parties.

In contrast, the data needed for rigorous social science research needs to be collected in a relatively passive manner in order to avoid breaches of integrity. Datasets compromised by a plethora of biases, which result when collectors annoy or aggravate their users, are not viable. A few additional data points might be gathered, but if those data points are not sound, then they are worse than useless. Bias-infused data causes active damage to the integrity of any findings for which that corrupt data was used.

Any collector pushes for user engagement must be pushes that users opted-into, and can choose to disable, in order to avoid the issues associated with aggressively hunting data. When users opt in, they are expecting the engagement pushes. They requested and want them. Offering to enhance this functionality (which should only be done within the collector and not as a push to engage itself) in return for any small pieces of data required to do so, such as accessing a user's current location in order to only notify them of geographically-relevant data, falls within the bounds of appropriate collection protocol because it does not create a nuisance for users.

Properly constructing collection mechanisms can achieve most of what aggressive data-hunting will, but it achieves this aim without compromising the dataset's integrity. While it is likely that not every bit of data sought will be part of the database, nearly everything that is truly needed to conduct high-end research and build accurate predictive models can be obtained simply by using collectors which filter out bad data.

Since not all data is worthy of inclusion in any given database to begin with, collectors should be designed to only gather data which meets the criteria for value and quality. Not all data are created equal,[6] and collecting the appropriate data for the task at hand is of the utmost importance. Junk data can sometimes be easily identified,[7] but oftentimes it can be hard to diagnose as such. Anyone who has encountered a troll on the internet has witnessed instances of junk portrayed as a worthwhile contribution.

Sometimes actionable intelligence can only be delineated through aggregation of substantial quantities of relevant data. This is more common in cases where any given data point contains relatively little information, such as a single, isolated swipe on a dating app. By itself, that data point tells researchers little about what motivated that swipe; a much larger dataset of high-quality swipe data would be needed to generate this information if the service wants to serve up better matches.

In other cases, only a few high-quality data points are needed to generate actionable intelligence due to the larger amount of information that these data points contain. An internet search for "my infant won't stop crying" immediately provides actionable intelligence by identifying the individual who conducted the search as a new parent, and one who needs help with at least some aspects of parenting.

This specific case provides great actionable intelligence for advertisers, but not so much for social science researchers. This data point is qualitative by design. While quantified information can be extracted from it, the process of doing so necessarily involves assigning values which are arguably disputable. A sales team may notice if assigned values turn out to be incorrect if the individual's behavior does not align with expectations, but a social science researcher who isn't trying to drive or change that individual's behavior is unlikely to ever become aware of such problems and compensate, thus introducing error into the dataset each time such information is quantified.

Collectors that automatically send continuous updates and additional data points to a central repository can, once sufficient quantities are achieved, supplant a lot of the actionable intelligence sought by surveys and do so in a much more robust manner. Quantifying information that was previously only gathered qualitatively can yield better insights into how and why people respond to a given stimulus. It can be informative from the larger population level all the way down to the individual actor level. Furthermore, it can stand up to hypothesis-testing in ways that traditional survey research methodologies can never hope to achieve.

While ensuring that data is only collected when true value can be delivered in return for that information helps keep data corruption to a minimum, this is not the only reason to employ this practice. The amount of information available for collection, dissemination, or analysis is astounding. More importantly, it dwarfs the ability of our brains and computers to process all of it in all of the ways necessary to provide maximum actionable value. To produce rigorous, high-quality social science research, data collectors must stay on target by aggregating only relevant information as well as properly structuring and segmenting gathered data.

A Vast Ocean of Data

Not only are there unprecedented levels of data now available, but ever more data is generated every day in ever more formats. Each individual digital platform generates its own proprietary data, effectively creating a new reservoir of information that's often only marginally connected to those of other platforms. The value of a data point therefore varies from one platform to the next, with much data collected bordering on worthlessness when assessed in conjunction with other platforms and formats.

A single download of a peer-reviewed study PDF file generates a similar volume of data as a swipe on a dating app, though the data in each case is formatted and structured very differently. Consequently, each of these data points has a different value to researchers. For example, the PDF download is much more likely to indicate true interest in a subject than is a match on the dating app Tinder, where many users are known to simply swipe right and approve every possible match presented.[8]

The majority of data created nowadays is made for social reasons.[9] However, since data generated for the purposes of social engagement is not viable for research purposes, finding the valuable bits and bytes can pose problems which require purpose-built collection tools to address. Creating systems which attract valuable knowledge while filtering out or rejecting junk data is the only real way to extract anything useful from the expanses of information.

This is analogous to the existence of enormous amounts of gold in the world's oceans. The National Ocean Service within the United States Department of Commerce's National Oceanic and Atmospheric Administration (NOAA) estimates that ocean waters hold "nearly 20 million tons" of gold.[10] At the price of roughly $1,250 that an ounce gold has averaged in the 10 years since 2008,[11] one ton is worth about $36.5 million, making oceanic gold worth a staggering $750 trillion in total, nearly ten times the gross domestic product of all the world's nations combined as of 2017 according to estimates by the International Monetary Fund (IMF).[12]

As with valuable data mixed in with comparatively worthless information, however, the issue with oceanic gold is getting to it. The National Ocean Service points out that "[g]old in the ocean is so dilute that its concentration is on the order of parts per trillion. Each liter of seawater contains, on average, about 13 billionths of a gram of gold."[13] Finding and extracting that gold poses challenges reminiscent of the issues associated with gathering the relevant, valuable data. Scientists must develop tools that attract the particles sought while rejecting those that are not.

Gold isn't the only valuable resource in the oceans—the water itself is also very valuable, though not fully useful in its raw form. Clean, fresh water can be extracted from the oceans through desalination.[14] This is a much easier task than extracting gold from the oceans. Similarly, while social data like that on Facebook or Twitter is not viable for research, it does have value for marketing and advertising purposes.

These platforms do not work to extract actionable intelligence, the "gold" of the digital oceans. Rather, their primary collection utility is more analogous to desalination plants. They identify possible new customers for advertisers by scooping up copious amounts of data which are then processed to extract the marginally-valuable tidbits. Any apparent "gold," or scientifically-valid social insight, they do produce is likely to actually be the data equivalent of pyrite, or "fool's gold", because these methods lack the properties which make their data robust and scientifically valuable.

There is a vast amount of data out there, a body of information which doubles in size roughly every two years.[15] While this information provides a lot of raw material which can be distilled to produce sales leads, only a tiny fraction of this data is good, usable, and valuable for elevating social science research to a truly rigorous and quantitative discipline. For casual researchers who don't care to have rigorous findings that align with true values observed in the real world, or for activists posing as scientists, this does not present a real problem. For leaders making decisions on how to chart their organization's future actions, though, this can present a grave issue.

Suctioning up enormous quantities of information into a massive data warehouse for processing won't produce the ideal actionable intelligence that researchers seek and leaders require. While that golden data would likely be present within those warehouses, it would exist in such minute quantities as to be effectively worthless because the costs involved in separating the sought-after data from the rest of the information would eclipse the value generated from doing so.

While this approach is indeed possible, it is far more effective to simply go directly to the people who both generate the data and are the subjects thereof though collectors which only collect that specific information. By filtering out everything except that valuable data, and by using incentives which attract it, far less data will be generated though it will, byte for byte, contain far more value.

Filtration and Standards

The data generated from large public repositories like social media giants, in which one's identity is openly tied to every piece of information (and is effectively publically-available), is much akin to the data generated by focus groups. Indeed, research conducted using publically-available information is effectively the Big Data equivalent of aggregating a very large collection of focus groups. The same issues, such as misrepresentation of viewpoints,[16] are generally present in both.

Error and bias cannot be eliminated from a dataset by aggregating a series of similarly-tainted sets. This isn't a case of mixing a very acidic fluid with a very basic fluid in equal amounts to produce one with a neutral pH;[17] combining multiple piles of garbage only gives you a bigger pile of garbage to sift through. It doesn't change the properties of that garbage to make it any more useful. At best, what results from such aggregation is an average which may very well not be representative of the broader population, such as in cases with bimodal data distribution.[18] In such instances, findings which are at all representative of the study population most likely achieved that status by random chance.

Everything done in the digital realm leaves an electronic record with unique properties and a specific set of attributes. Filtering out the junk and only collecting actionable intelligence data is merely a matter of properly constructing the collection tools. Structuring data for research purposes is much easier when the data collection tools themselves filter out non-useful pieces of information by allowing only that which already serves an identified scientific need or purpose.

Since the availability of this sort of information is relatively new in human history, properly identifying and sorting out the good, valuable data from the mostly-worthless noise is an evolving practice. However, ensuring that only quality data makes its way into a dataset is a crucial step towards building robust models that are reproducible and that can make accurate, verifiable predictions.

Since people have by and large signed on to turning over their personal data in exchange for modern conveniences, researchers don't typically need to even ask questions any more. They can completely filter out lower quality qualitative textual responses to textual collectors, and in many cases need not rely on visual or auditory data which can be difficult to properly quantify and structure. These formats all lack several attributes associated with data in a scientifically rigorous dataset: objective measurability, internal comparability, pertinence to the subject matter, and static meaning. While some of these properties may arguably be present in some text-based information, it is uncommon that such data possesses all of them. Additionally, some data thought to be scientifically rigorous and quantified may actually lack these features and not be as robust as sometimes believed.

For a data point to be objectively measurable,[19] it must have an intrinsic unit value assigned to it. If something cannot be measured and expressed quantitatively prior to any analysis, algorithms, or adjustments, then it is not viable for inclusion in any dataset that's meant to produce rigorous and objective scientific analysis. A person's vote is objectively measurable; whether a person's vote was good or evil is not. That is a subjective determination.

The idea of comparability is rather straightforward—it refers to the requirement that each data point can be objectively examined in relation to other data points from other datasets. Internal comparability[20] is a closely-related concept where this principle applies within a single dataset. To get an idea of what a dataset which lacks internal comparability looks like, imagine a file which contains a list of peoples' "favorites" including favorite color and favorite song. A list of favorite colors or of favorite songs would have internal comparability, as the data therein could be quantified and ranked, but a list of favorites alone is purely qualitative.

A marketing team attempting personalize an appeal to potential customers may be interested in both their favorite songs and colors, but the list would need to be internally comparable in order for their efforts to be effective. "Would this population be more likely to respond positively to red or blue?" makes much more sense and can be answered far more definitively than "would this population be more likely to respond positively to green or *The Star-Spangled Banner*?" The former can be compared to one another while the latter cannot in any meaningful way.

The need for pertinence[21] to the subject matter is relatively clear; the data must have a clear relation to what is being studied. Unless perhaps the researcher is also an astrologer, it makes no sense to include an individual's time of birth in an examination of what their ideal time of day for working out should be. In such a case, other behavioral data on a person's circadian rhythms, heart rate fluctuations, and daily routine would all potentially be pertinent. A person's views on financial policies likely would not.

Whether or not a data point has a static meaning is closely related to its objective measurability. Anyone with a basic understanding of the data who examines the same data point at any given point in time should agree on its values and be able to understand it in the same manner as any other scientifically literate individual, and these values should never change. This is opposed to a dynamic meaning, where the true parameters and values of a data point may be subjectively interpreted and debated.

Dynamism and subjectivity in data are not limited to formats such as free-text; these qualities may appear even in nominally quantitative information, such as responses to a question like "Would you support or oppose banning the sale of assault weapons?"[22] In such cases, replies in either the affirmative or negative cannot definitively shed light on how the respondent would support the core proposition if the hypothetical scenario presented were to occur, leaving the results open to interpretation. Questions regarding hypothetical scenarios will nearly always lack static meaning unless all possible variable details and terms are first explicitly defined. If any two researchers examining the data collected do not agree on what was collected, the meaning of the data is not static.

Datasets used for scientific research must not be allowed to contain data points which lack objective measurability, internal comparability, pertinence to the subject matter, and static meaning. It is an unfortunate fact that traditional data collection methods are riddled with subjective data which can by dynamically interpreted in many different ways. The data produced are oftentimes not comparable to other data on the same topic within the same dataset; in many cases, they are not even truly objectively measurable. Yet this sort of data has repeatedly been used to produce widely-circulated analyses which have not held up to real world observations.

When researchers know what types of data can provide the insights they need as well as where to get it, then building collectors that adequately filter out the junk becomes an issue of time, money, and skill. Creating sets of high-quality data can be accomplished within these constraints in a straightforward manner without violating any laws or anyone's rights, including privacy rights, in ways which were not technically possible prior to the onset of the information age.

Additional Granularity Enables Greater Precision

The more finely one examines the data on any given subject matter, the more perturbations and variations appear, even when the data looks rather uniform from a distance. Oceans visible from space vary in depth with the tides in ways that are only apparent from a much closer viewpoint. Similarly, broad policies or omnibus legislation that are generally supported often contain specific clauses which many find objectionable but accept as a part of a larger package. Very solid, dense objects turn out to be 99.9999999999996% empty space when examined at the atomic level.[23]

Each of these phenomena are only revealed when looked at on a much closer level than that which allows the entire scope to be seen all at once, and the same is true of human behavioral data. Individual reactions in response to a given stimulus vary from person to person in ways that are not readily apparent when broad behavioral observations are generalized.

This reality means that many common and accepted practices, such as taking a straight average of collected data's values, the most basic form of generalization, can present findings which are actually not representative of true reality at all. Consider mass shooters, for example; the average age of perpetrators who committed these crimes within the 35-year stretch between 1982 and 2017 generally ranged from 30 to 35 depending on the methodology and definitions used, yet comparatively few mass shootings are perpetrated by those in their 30s. A graph of mass shooters' ages more closely resembles an M-shape bimodal data distribution rather than the normal distribution epitomized by an inverted-U shaped bell curve.

Far more mass shooters are in their twenties or forties than are in their thirties. Yet broad generalizations created by averages inappropriately imply that those in their thirties are most likely to commit mass shootings while saying nothing of those in their twenties and forties.

The issue is exacerbated by changes in definitions over time; for example, the Investigative Assistance for Violent Crimes Act of 2012, approved in January of 2013, lowered the threshold for a mass killing from four killings in a single incident to three.[24] Although these data points are quantified behavioral metrics, such definitional shifts can risk "breaking" the dataset by compromising its internal comparability.[25] It potentially invalidates the data as a viable source for legitimate social science purposes. In this specific instance, the changes were expansionary and, especially because the dataset is particularly granular, it is possible to examine the information in a way which maintains time-series integrity. The expansionary nature of these changes also enable inquiring minds to see how such changes affected the contents of the dataset.

Table 8.1 – Age Ranges of U.S. Mass Shooters from 1982 Through 2017 and 2013 Through 2017

Age Range	1982-2017		2013-2017	
	Number of Shooters**	Number of Shooters*	Number of Shooters**	Number of Shooters*
Under 10	0	0	0	0
10 to 19	10	10	1	1
20 to 29	28	31	13	16
30 to 39	14	20	1	7
40 to 49	25	27	5	7
50 to 59	6	7	0	1
60+	3	3	2	2
Average	***30.92631579***	***35.62105263***	***34.38235294***	***32.86363636***

Source: Mother Jones, US Mass Shootings, 1982-2017: Data From Mother Jones' Investigation[26]
Note: Dataset excludes "shootings stemming from more conventional crimes such as armed robbery or gang violence."[27]
** In 2013 "President Barack Obama lowered [the mass shooting threshold] to three or more victims killed"*[28] *from the former threshold of four or more victims killed. Mother Jones' dataset thus "include[s] attacks dating from January 2013 [onward] in which three or more victims died."*[29]
*** To present figures which all use the same definitions of "mass shooting," these counts use the original definition throughout.*

When people act upon generalized explanations of the past as though they will be effective predictors of the future, they invite counterproductive action. A more granular view of the issue has many benefits, including greater precision and predictive power. Surveys often fail to account for this or are unable to address it due to the waterfall methodological approach, which precludes researchers from gathering data from their sample which they did not anticipate needing in advance.

The process of weighting tends to exacerbate this issue.[30] Assuming that individual humans all act identically and that their behaviors are in line with certain subcategories of the population into which they fall is a fallacy similar to averaging sea levels. It can be an effective method for quickly generating rough approximations where a very high degree of precision isn't necessary, but is far less powerful for examining human behavior than explanations and predictions of variations at the individual level are. This phenomenon is not even limited to variations between individuals reacting to the same stimuli –[31] the same person can and often will have different reactions to the same stimuli at different points in time[32] as a result of external events or repeated exposure through a process known as habituation.[33]

Additionally, the finer details of individual behavior which vary and cluster can have substantial real-world implications for leaders. A nation with a population of which only 0.1% exercises regularly may not able to support many gyms. If the 0.1% that does exercise is evenly distributed throughout the nation, they may opt to use their own equipment. However, if that entire 0.1% is clustered in two concise geographic areas, those two locations may be able to support large exercise facilities profitably.

Furthermore, the individuals in those two regions may exercise completely differently. The grouping located in one area may prefer cardio-heavy routines, while the other may primarily wish to engage in weight training. If the total available cardio equipment and weight equipment are equally dispersed across those two areas, profitability will suffer lower returns than if the gym equipment distribution reflects the fitness interests of their respective populations.

Specific details are far more subject to variation than are more broad classifications, and they change more frequently. The tides produce far more change in sea levels than centuries of melting glacial ice do, and they will continue to produce substantial variations in sea levels should all that ice melt. Imagine builders in a coastal city worrying about rising sea levels from climate change but failing to account for a low tide when surveying waterfront land for new home construction projects. If those running the project are expecting a sea level change of at worst 2 feet over the next 100 years,[34] they would be rather distraught to find such an area near San Francisco over five underwater after purchasing the formerly waterfront land when they come to examine the space again at high tide.[35]

Short-term variations often impact trends, and this is true within individuals as well as on a broader social level. For example, an individual who considers themselves a political Independent but whose attitudes on specific issues start to change in the direction of an established major party will retain their identity as an Independent for some time even after their views have changed to align more with a partisan ideology. It is only after time that the individual will likely declare a change in their ideological allegiance. During the interim, these variations mean this person may be more openly supportive of given proposals (or vice versa) than their broader classification as an Independent indicates. If such fluctuation at a more granular level is substantial, analyses which rely on coarse clustering will have far less predictive power.

Tracking and quantifying multiple layers of interest and behavior is a much more agile approach. It can give broader context without requiring question-and-answer format data solicitation, and it allows for continuous refinement of existing data's level of detail. When researchers can drill down into the fine specifics of a very large, internally comparable, time-series dataset, this opens up the possibility of much more accurate, precise predictions.

Knowing an individual's political party affiliation may greatly help broadly determining their choice of candidates on Election Day, but is less effective as a predictor of whether they will turn out to vote. Whether a voter goes to the polls can be effectively predicted through behaviors marked by two specific genetic configurations,[36] specifically those genes which regulate monoamine oxidase A (MAOA) and presynaptic serotonin transport (5HTT).

Neither traditional surveys nor digital data collectors are likely to have access to information regarding their users' genetic makeup. However, research by James Fowler and Christopher Dawes at the University of California–San Diego indicates that "two genes we study, 5HTT and MAOA, influence social behavior via their impact on the serotonin metabolism and research within political science has identified prosociality as a significant determinant of turnout, thereby establishing a potential causal chain leading from these genes to observed political behavior."[37] This means that there are other layers of social behavioral data which could be collected and examined to compute likelihood of any given individual participating in an election more effectively than asking them questions.

Additionally, a candidate of a party who sharply differs from that party's membership on a substantial number of issues may not garner a high voter turnout. This is especially the case when negative ratings of specific political parties are particularly high, as they have been in the latter half of the 2010s.[38]

This can be hard to predict from coarse data alone and requires the sort of granularity that questionnaires are unlikely to gather.

After Election Day, support for individual proposals can vary substantially with those more granular variations as well. Policies proposed, developed, or implemented by individuals who won elections with more general proposals may experience a backlash when the time comes to address the details thereof. Without access to this more detailed layer of interest and behavioral detail which more closely explains voter attitudes towards various issues, it can be hard to assess how a given campaign will be received or how it should be constructed to best resonate with the greatest portions of a population.

Consider the Patient Protection and Affordable Care Act, also known as Obamacare, passed in 2010: many who have opposed it have done so for different reasons, which range widely from "it goes too far" to "it doesn't go far enough." This level of nuance as to the reasons people state a given preference is typically lost in questions on the topic, although it should still be noted that directly addressing this issue wouldn't necessarily yield quality data due to the numerous problems associated with questionnaire format survey research. If true values of individual support levels for such policies are known, or even if we assume that to be the case for rhetorical purposes, then an ability to cross-reference this data with additionally nuanced information such as the favorability metrics for specific sections of the law would allow for much more robust analysis. Robert Weissberg, Ph.D., wrote about the subtleties lost in polling in "Leaders Should Not Follow Opinion Polls":

> By commercial necessity, modern polling produce[s] instant results by reducing complicated, multifaceted issues to a few crude alternatives. Queries about the military budget typically focus on "increasing/decreasing/or no change" spending choices. No room exists for more sophisticated respondents who wants to cut some expenditures while expanding others. Nor does this typical question permit well-versed advice that reflects actual conditions - for example, increasing spending provided a *[sic]* bellicose dictators remain in power, but otherwise seek reductions. Worse, this

> commonplace format never asks for specific dollar figures. Two people can agree on cutting Pentagon budgets, but one desires a modest $100,000,000 largely symbolic cut while the other prefers lopping off $200,000,000,000. This numerical difference is critical politically, but disappears when the public's "voice" is crudely transmitted via the poll.[39]

Cross-referencing research findings with additional external data, such as information regarding how individual survey respondents use any given service (child care for example), would be a substantial boon for determining respondents' true revealed preferences regarding policies which affect that service. Under traditional methodologies, however, this generally isn't a viable option—in this scenario specifically, there are numerous legal, moral, and ethical barriers to conducting such an analysis. However, in situations where those barriers are not present, the problems that emerge from aggregating data from multiple sources will still present themselves.

The waterfall-style methodology of most social science research means that unless all these variables are anticipated in advance and incorporated into the study beforehand, a higher level of rigor is not possible. Digital collectors, on the other hand, operate on an ongoing basis and are a much more agile approach. Therefore, factors which were not considered from the outset of the project can be factored in at a later date without forcing researchers to go through the sampling process again or re-collect the initial dataset.

Stay on Target

All data that is identified, collected and processed must be relevant to the issue or issues being addressed. Asking questions (or requesting permissions, in the case of digital behavioral data collectors) that do not seem germane to an engagement can raise red flags in people's minds. This results in people opting out or tuning out[40] in a manner similar to what occurs when users of smartphone apps are pushed by the app or its developers to engage with a product more often than they are naturally inclined to do. In consequence, this introduces additional biases within the collected data.

For researchers in need of a lot of data, aggregating multiple topics into a single collection tool and allowing those using it to select for themselves how they engage with each subject as it becomes relevant to their lives allows for broad cross-analysis. Additionally, it produces a holistic dataset that gathers pieces of information which could be difficult to collect in isolation. While processing all such collected data in the same manner provides substantial internal comparability, one even larger benefit is that those participating can effectively tell the research team what the target is, allowing the team to tailor the incentives accordingly.

In an article titled "Your Facebook Fans Are Hiding Your Posts At An Alarming Rate," Ekaterina Walter notes that it can be difficult to identify subject matter relevant to broad audiences.[41] Her advice to "[b]e humble enough to admit you don't always know what your fans want to read—so ask what they want to see" is just as applicable to researchers as it is to internet content producers.

This process of gathering a user's interests to deliver appropriate incentives cannot be forced, lest we see the introduction of biases which are the result of provoking respondents to opt-out. Providing a platform wherein those who use it are able to completely customize and privately tailor their own experience does much of the research team's hard work for them. It allows researchers to go after very broad populations using a multitude of approaches, and it provides value based on what users tell researchers the targets should be in their specific instance. Since delivered value is provided responsively rather than personally by the researchers, this effectively completely automates the process.

When using this approach, researchers must be able to provide some immediate value to users in exchange for any given piece of information, regardless of what that piece of information is. This is not only an expectation held by most who are willing to turn over their data, but it is also a best practice for producing the sort of data sought to conduct rigorous social science.

There are many cases in which additional targeted data collection can substantially augment the value that can be provided by the collector. Fitness trackers again serve as an example. Those casually interested in tracking their fitness metrics may not be inclined to provide a tracker with regular updates to changes in their body weight, yet doing so in combination with other fitness data can allow a sufficiently advanced tracker to provide early warning signs of a number of possible health concerns[42] and alert the user when they might wish to consult with a physician about abnormalities.

An example of a collection attempt which may raise concern for users is location data synced to PIIs. For example, there is additional value for both users and researchers in, say, a fitness collector having access to one's location as this can provide much better figures for distances traveled, allow for computation of the length of one's stride, and refine details such as calories burned on a run. However, many may be reluctant to turn over this data unless the value for the user is clearly demonstrated in advance. This is especially so in the case of public or semi-public databases, where one's personal data is associated with their fitness information so others can find them and compete in social fitness competitions[43] or the like, though it has also already been demonstrated that this specific type of data is not a viable source of social science research data due to the biases present therein.

PIIs are an example of data which generally provides no value to researchers' scientific efforts. Traditional methodologies often require some PII so that respondents can be contacted, but alternative approaches to research can eliminate this need as individuals can be reached through their digital hangouts. This does not mean personal data should never be collected, only that it should never be sought. If participants seek value that can only be delivered by collecting personal information, that option should be made available but never required for participation.

Combining PIIs with other sensitive information such as location history or financial details often throws up red flags due to the possibility of fraud, identity theft, or even threats to one's physical security[44] that can arise if and when such a dataset containing them is compromised.[45] This is one obvious instance in which collection of this information should be voluntary for participants with a value-add in return. This additional value should be clearly illustrated prior to gathering such data. However, it would be ideal to avoid collecting PII entirely and providing any such value that could justify such collection by other means to ensure any *observer effects* are kept to a minimum.

Demonstrating the value that can be provided in return for a specific additional data point—and only then providing a prompt whereby that data point can be collected after a user has expressed interest in receiving that added value—keeps data collection "on target" as far as all parties involved are generally concerned. This process flow increases the likelihood that users will agree to provide this data and substantially decreases the negative reactions experienced by those who do not want that to provide more information than is absolutely necessary for them to get what they want out of their engagement with the collector.

Anonymous collection can also help overcome some user hesitation, especially when substantial value can still be delivered in return.[46] This is another reason why narrowing collection to only those pieces of information necessary to conduct research is important. When little to no data is gathered or included in a database which links individual digital profiles to real-world identities, the risks from and possibility of a breach or leak are greatly reduced.[47] Such an event may damage research efforts or undermine the research team by making publically available a comprehensive dataset, but the fallout will be contained by only collecting the "on target" data needed for their efforts and may even improve user trust by demonstrating the researchers' adherence to anonymity.

Broad behavior and engagement tracking aren't necessarily "off target." A metric like frequency of intoxicant use may be relevant to an investigation regarding social behaviors in certain settings, but is unlikely to result in any additional value which can be delivered to users. Researchers who need this data point and are able to provide valuable insights in return— such as data on how weight will be affected by the caloric intake resulting from consuming different types of alcoholic beverages—can offer to provide those insights to users if users provide information about their beverage consumption frequency. In order to prevent the introduction of error into the dataset, though, any such prompts should only be shown in response to a given user engaging with a collector in a manner which suggests they would be receptive, or at least not put off, by such a request.

If a research effort is unable to make someone's life better, even marginally so, in exchange for data, the notion of a behavioral quantitative data model as a superior source of social science research inputs falls apart. In that case, social scientists might as well continue using questionnaire data as their primary sources, as it is much harder to ensure the accuracy of collected data which fails to provide demonstrable value to the person providing it in return.

Requesting information without a good *prima facie* reason merely reintroduces *sampling bias* and *self-selection bias* and their accompanying problems. Since these are major sources of concern regarding the integrity of social science data, allowing such issues to resurface in a medium that is otherwise relatively predisposed to excluding them effectively constitutes a form of scientific malfeasance. In the social sciences in particular, adhering to these data collection best practices of keeping data collection on target, providing value in return for data, not forcing the process, and building datasets with data that is objectively measurable, internally comparable, pertinent to the subject matter, and has static meaning, is necessary for the sake of data integrity.

Chapter 9 - Ongoing Continuous Efforts are Superior

Unlike the hard physical sciences, conditions in the social sphere are more or less in a constant state of flux. Two colliding atoms will always behave in ways which follow from the laws governing their interactions, and two chemicals will produce the same sort of reaction when mixed in the same solution.[1]

The tenants of the natural sciences are based around this concept that two objects will react identically to identical stimuli at any point in time. Within the social sciences, however, this is not so clear-cut; oftentimes, the same person will react differently to the same stimuli at different points in time due to changes in their personal preferences and the effects of external events.

One of the many issues faced by traditional social science research methodologies that have centered around surveys is that, as Kate Kelley, Belinda Clark, Vivienne Brown, and John Sitzia describe in their article "Good practice in the conduct and reporting of survey research" published in *International Journal for Quality in Health Care*, they "are designed to provide a 'snapshot of how things are at a specific time'."[2] Furthermore, there is "no attempt to control conditions or manipulate variables."[3]

The data collected through survey research are usually discrete rather than continuous,[4] which limits their use and depreciates their value. The lack of continuous measurement—a method in which information is captured over an ongoing time period and with a more granular level of detail—means that the value of such research is largely limited to broad generalizations and simple go/no go suggestions regarding specific courses of action.

While there are organizations that attempt to build ongoing panels in order to re-engage the same individuals in a larger sample pool over time,[5] there are a number of problems associated with this approach. As one would likely expect, most of the issues with panels are centered around the same concerns that plague survey-based social science research in general. Unfortunately, the process of creating a panel oftentimes compounds many of these problems.

This is a discrete form of data collection masquerading as continuous. A series of distinct snapshots are not only much harder to capture; they provide much less detail. Consider the difference between a set of photos taken in rapid succession then combined in an animated picture format, and a regular video file. A burst of images making up the animated picture certainly has a use, but it conveys much less information than a continuous stream of video and audio data.

In addition to the general bias and data error issues associated with traditional survey methodologies, there are multiple other concerns which arise from using survey panels. Survey response rates have been dropping substantially throughout the 21st century and are already particularly low,[6] oftentimes hovering in the single digits. A 100% response rate for follow-up surveys is almost impossible to achieve. This means that each subsequent survey sent to a panel will see lower and lower overall response metrics, introducing additional *self-selection bias* each time a survey is distributed.

Using panels also tends to exacerbate another form of *self-selection bias* in the response data, as there is a specific type of person who actively agrees to participate in an ongoing series of surveys prior to knowing anything about them.[7] When all of these effects are compounded, the resulting reduction in data quality more than counters the benefits and cost savings which are generally employed as justifications for using survey panels.

Continuous measurement of large populations—which themselves consist of a great many smaller groups or subsets—allows for identification of trends, changes in perspectives, and comparative analysis to all be conducted much more robustly than can be done with a series of snapshots. Piecing together multiple point-in-time examinations of a phenomenon leaves substantial gaps in the data. Researchers often attempt to fill in these gaps with their own interpretations,[8] but their explanations are generally based on that particular researcher's own perspectives and may not be reproduced by another researcher conducting the same study.[9]

Another related folly is attempting to gather data to represent a snapshot of a single moment in time by collecting data over multiple points in time, which is about as effective as attempting to determine whether there is gold in an area by surveying adjacent areas; the odds that either will work are low, yet researchers are counting on it when deploying surveys for longer periods of time, and when they ask about past or anticipated future events. This is akin to attempting to communicate with a toddler who can only answer questions with a "yes" or a "no"—trying to determine the reason it is crying by asking a series of increasingly detailed questions takes time, and the act of doing so can change the reason; maybe the child was initially hungry, but is now more upset that it has been unable to communicate this need and is no longer thinking about food.[10]

The snapshots approach assumes all the influential variables are known and accounted for in a given investigation. The presumption is that the "camera" (survey) is pointed at the right frame (sample) and uses all the right settings (asks the right questions and does so correctly) such that what is captured will be sufficiently detailed so that all necessary information can be extracted from the resulting image. This is rarely the case, which continuous, ever-expanding collection and analysis addresses by capturing greater quantities of quality data, enabling social researchers to approximate the level of rigorous experimental controls employed by the natural sciences.

The more agile, continuous-collection approach to research eliminates many issues associated with re-sampling by taking what could be thought of as a panoramic video, which ensures that appropriately representative groups and all requisite data are included within the dataset. This practice also substantially reduces the problems associated with timing and responsiveness, as a lack thereof does not constitute error or bias but rather represents valuable data itself.

Since these agile collection methods do not employ question-and-answer format research, the data gathered is eminently more comparable over time and less subject to the biases introduced by the survey approach. This agile approach has a significant advantage over a waterfall approach in that a very large portion of participants can be retained, effectively allowing for recycling and reusing of samples and data. There will always be some attrition over time,[11] but since the nature of this approach allows for an application of the law of large numbers,[12] the negative effects of this phenomenon can be mitigated.

Constantly growing the sample and consistently refreshing the data therefrom is something that can only be achieved via the agile approach of continuous digital behavioral data collection. This methodology, when employed in a manner which adequately samples the entire population, maintains strength in the face of opt-outs and the biases that would otherwise be introduced into the dataset.

Motu Facillimo ex Notitia Continua (Agility through Continuous Data)

When collected data is quantified in a comparable time-series structure, the resulting dataset has innumerate benefits over traditional approaches. This does not mean that data can be quantified after the fact and retain the same benefits as data that was quantified upon collection, but rather that the latter type of data is notably superior in comparison to other formats for the purposes of scientific analysis.

Unlike traditional survey research practices centered around waterfall methodologies—which have been shown to be both riddled with inefficiencies and prone to errors—approaches borne out of an agile mindset in combination with large, purpose-built datasets allow for much quicker project execution without sacrificing quality. Additionally, repeating any given research project further reduces the timeline to a mere sliver of that which one would encounter when using a traditional approach.

It can take weeks to simply "field" a survey alone. The National Business Research Institute suggests that those conducting such research "leave [an] online survey in deployment for at least a couple of weeks to give time to send announcement emails, invitation emails, reminder emails, and finally, thank you emails."[13] Infosurv Research, a self-described "leading survey company,"[14] concurs by stating that "[a] survey typically requires 2-10 business days"[15] in the field.

Other steps in the survey research process generally take similar amounts of time, meaning that most survey research projects take well over a month to complete. While the process can be sped up, doing so generally results in either substantial financial cost or a degradation of data quality. For leaders whose primary interest is to be seen "doing something" this may be sufficient, but is should be unacceptable for those committed to getting things right and making improvements.

An additional factor which must be taken into consideration when conducting a survey research project is the fact that one survey is rarely enough. Especially when attempting to determine whether certain events have altered how people think or behave, multiple surveys are generally required in order to provide a "before and after" perspective.[16] This, in theory, allows researchers and analysts to assess the effectiveness of a program or policy. However, as with many other aspects of traditional survey research methodologies, this practice is fraught with concerns that potentially invalidate their findings.

Because of the time required to execute surveys, controlling for external intervening factors is very difficult. Surveys lack variable controls by their very nature,[17] and while this is also true of pure behavioral monitoring, a continuous set of data allows for more refined analysis that can be used in conjunction with very large datasets to introduce more rigor to social science research.

Figure 9.1 – Survey Data-Oriented Research Project Timeline

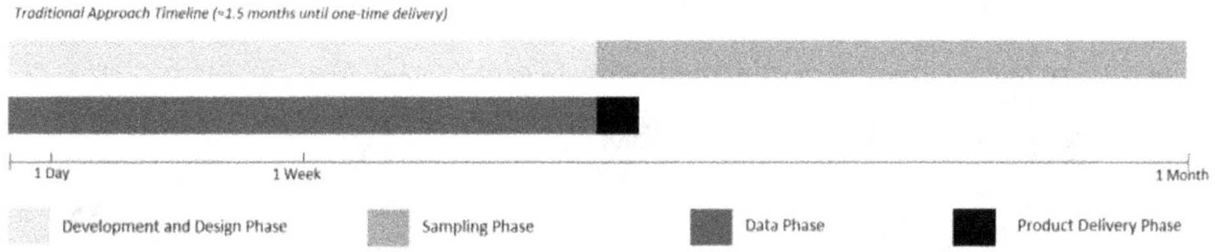

Reaching the same population sample (or an identically representative sample of the population) for a follow-up survey can present a substantial hurdle as well. Data gathered over time which presents findings from two distinct groups is not internally comparable and can effectively invalidate any results produced from that dataset. However, controlling for this scenario can be very difficult without the morally dubious tactic of using the force of law to compel a response.

In order to better understand why using data from distinct yet similar groups violates internal comparability, imagine that someone attempts to ask both of their next-door neighbors how they feel about the noise levels coming from the home of the asker. The asker only reaches one neighbor, who says that the asker's house is rather loud and that it could be quieter. The asker tries to keep the noise down for two weeks and then reaches out to the neighbors again. This time they only reach the other neighbor, who has no problem with the noise level.

These two snapshots of data collected in response to the same question tell the person asking very little about how effective their attempts to be quieter were. Both neighbors were part of the same population, but these data points cannot provide any definitive conclusions about change over time. This same principle applies to survey research efforts more broadly, where an inability to reach the same set of respondents multiple times can have a substantial negative impact on the quality of data collected and the findings produced.[18]

A much more rapid response, one that even approaches real-time, is possible when researchers don't need to actively recruit a sample. Eliminating questions further reduces the time a research project requires by removing the step of crafting the questions themselves, a process that also happens to be very time and labor intensive. Replacing this step with identification of relevant subject matter for which behavioral data is needed can reduce a two-week process to one that takes just a few days, possibly less.

Figure 9.2 – 80 Minute Exposure vs 20 Second Exposure Photo Comparison

© RoyceBair.com

Additionally, events which occur over the course of fielding a survey may influence the responses collected. Oftentimes this does not pose a substantial problem because people are unlikely to change habits or perspectives on the timescales over which most surveys are conducted, but in some scenarios this time delay can have a strong effect on research results. Political opinion polls often operate on much tighter timelines than other social science research efforts, for example, yet in races which see stunning revelations or announcements,[19] any polls being conducted at the time are likely to have highly skewed results.[20] In such cases, data collected at the start of the deployment period is less internally comparable to data collected towards the end. Snapshots in time, as surveys purport to be, need to be precise in order to have value. A photo taken with a long exposure time can be very visually appealing, and can even provide some valuable insights, but it often comes at the cost of lost detail.[21]

A series of pictures does not provide a very clear perspective, leaving much up to interpretation. Videos are a better format for more accurate analysis due to the continuous nature of the data they provide. Likewise, surveys which serve as snapshots in time aren't designed around this data collection model and thus leave out large amounts of potentially vital information. Continuously-aggregated data is more like a video file than a flat image. In cases where moment-in-time data are required, this information can be clipped like individual frames from a video.

One example of this principle in action is how athletes watch videos of performances to learn and improve from them in a process known as "film study".[22] They don't look at groupings of photographs but instead watch full plays. Looking at two snapshots of a single play from a football game—one shot prior to hiking the ball at the 50-yard line and the other taken after a touchdown is scored on that play—tells viewers little about how the offensive team was able to score or about how the defense can better protect against that play next time. Continuous monitoring via a video stream, which starts prior to the play and ends following the touchdown, provides far more detail and actionable intelligence that can be used to augment future performance.

Research methodologies centered around continuous data collection help to greatly reduce the "missing" data issues associated with surveys. Since each data point from each moment in time is distinctly captured and identifiable as such, it can be analyzed and used to produce any number of momentary snapshots that may be sought regardless of the format in which they are needed. This means that the same dataset can be used to produce the data equivalent of both images in Figure 9.2, and far more, whenever the need for either arises.

Continuous data collection also enables continuous delivery of value to clients in addition to the value-driven incentives which are provided to users. Switching to data which is collected quantitatively allows clients to receive updates to any reporting and analysis for which dashboard and algorithms have already been constructed in near-real-time. It may take slightly longer to obtain initial data on a subject matter which was not already been tracked by the researcher's collection mechanisms, but once a pertinent dataset with continual growth is established, the flexibility afforded is vast.

In many cases, since the data collected is fully quantified and need not be "adjusted" in the manner that traditional methodologies often employ, dashboards containing specific reports and perspectives on the data can be constructed in ways traditional methodologies can never facilitate. These can allow clients to navigate through needed information on their own. This ability enables such clients to rapidly generate their own findings without the need for the handoffs that arise in the traditional waterfall-style approaches.

Figure 9.3 – Behavioral Data-Oriented Research Project Timelines

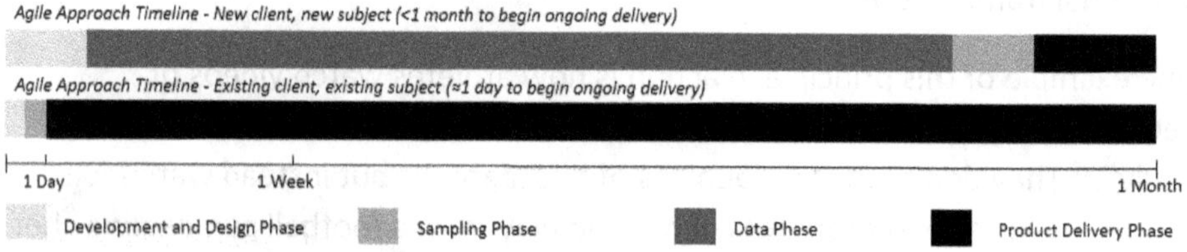

Once initial setup is complete, the need for additional labor on behalf of the research team is minimal. This substantially reduces the costs associated with delivering refined intelligence/knowledge to clients, which in turn enables the team to invest more heavily in improving the breadth and depth of the data which is collected. It also augments the value delivered to users of the data collection tools. The research team's resources can more heavily focus on expanding and refining the data collection process rather than "adjusting" data or analyzing that which has been collected. Clients who require additional support or analysis can always contract with the research firm to conduct such work, but when this process is no longer an integral step, all parties can be far more responsive. The research process is effectively automated, with human intervention required only at a high level.

Reuse is Cost-Effective and the Key to High Quality Time-Series Data

Another benefit of continual digital data collection over traditional survey research is retroactive analysis. While data cannot be "created" by the research team to backfill missing periods and still be considered legitimate, additional examination of previously-collected quantified data in light of new revelations is feasible in ways that are much more difficult to do with survey data. This difference becomes much more pronounced the further in time from the initial point of collection that such a retrospective is requested.

This agility is in large part enabled by the fact that digital behavioral monitoring reuses research data and participants. Therefore, respondents need not be identified or solicited each time data is required, a valuable asset. Some established research firms have attempted to build panels which can be similarly mined for potential respondents to occasional surveys, but this approach is far more effective when employed in conjunction with continuous, natively-quantified behavioral data.

A useful natural sciences analogy would be that of a weather station continuously monitoring an area and generating data on meteorological activity. Weather stations collect data on an ongoing basis, continuously "sampling" the larger region to provide a complete meteorological picture of the vicinity in question. Their data are combined with information from other stations in order to identify patterns and predict behaviors on multiple scales. Identically quantified and structured data from multiple stations within each region are always being refreshed, bestowing an internally comparable time-series quality upon the sample data. One-time use weather stations which needed to be re-deployed regularly would not be very helpful.

While some needs can be anticipated, one never knows exactly what will need to be researched in the future. Sample reusability, especially with continuously refreshed data, allows a research team to respond much more rapidly once needs are identified since the data have already been gathered. Reusability is also a very important factor when it comes to opening up social science researchers' access to time-series data. If participants within a sample cannot be continually reached over extended periods, then access to time-series data for those participants is lost. Therefore, any additional information collected becomes another addition to a collection of snapshots with substantially less value, much closer to that of survey panels.

A very large dataset of comparable time-series data from the same participants also enables a form of quasi-experimental inquiry[23] to be employed. Researchers generally cannot randomly assign those who use the data collectors into control and experimental groups to test responses to a specific stimulus.

However, when stimuli occur in the real-world, those affected can be placed into one group, and an equally representative but unaffected group can serve as a control. Behavioral data from these two groups can then be compared to examine the effects of the stimulus. While quasi-experimental designs offer many benefits when random assignment into test or control groups is not possible, the results may be subject to some interpretation problems which Barry Gibbons and Joan Herman wrote about in their journal article *True and Quasi-Experimental Designs*, published in Practical Assessment, Research & Evaluation:

> The nonequivalent, posttest only design consists of administering an outcome measure to two groups or to a program/treatment group and a comparison. For example, one group of students might receive reading instruction using a whole language program while the other receives a phonetics-based program. After twelve weeks, a reading comprehension test can be administered to see which program was more effective.
>
> ...
>
> The nonequivalent group, pretest-posttest design partially eliminates a major limitation of the nonequivalent group, posttest only design. At the start of the study, the researcher empirically assesses the differences in the two groups. Therefore, if the researcher finds that one group performs better than the other on the posttest, s/he can rule out initial differences (if the groups were in fact similar on the pretest) and normal development (e.g. resulting from typical home literacy practices or other instruction) as explanations for the differences.[24]

When researchers have sufficiently large amounts of data available, and when that data is not tainted by quality issues to any significant degree, then working backwards to approximate scientific standards becomes possible. Individuals affected by stimuli can be monitored in the same manner as those unaffected, both groups can be proactively sampled so as to be equally representative, and the outcomes can then be compared. While it does not rise to the level of a true controlled experiment,[25] this process does allow researchers to approximate that level of rigor in a field where applying such scientific standards is otherwise impractical.

Furthermore, a survey panel approach to recycling samples only distributes subsequent surveys to portions of the overall panel, and researchers must hope that participants will respond in representative proportions. Collectors gathering data continuously can make all the information for which they wish to collect behavioral responses available to all those who use a given tool, knowing that even a lack of interaction by users provides valuable research data.

Ongoing engagement with participants is superior to building a panel of survey respondents with whom researchers must regularly attempt to reconnect. This is especially the case when an attempt to reconnect comes somewhat out of the blue and pertains to a completely different subject matter to that which was originally discussed.

It is substantially cheaper and easier to retain an existing business client than it is to onboard a new one.[26] This principle can be applied to obtaining data from an individual research participant as well. Continuing to work with those who have already provided data increases the likelihood that these individuals will provide new data when such information is needed by the researchers, especially when commensurate additional value can be provided in exchange.

This recyclability is great for researchers and for their clients. Data which examine how views and priorities vary for the same individuals over time can provide substantial insights into how markets and public opinion respond to external events and are affected by the progression of time. It enables additional insights based on other data collected, including data which may not previously have been thought to have any correlation to the subject under consideration.

This is one reason why it is important to have a broad appeal and to build very large, representative samples. Large datasets which contain comparable, natively quantified data that covers a wide cross-section of human behaviors can reveal less intuitive patterns and help researchers identify correlations, including those which surveys might have trouble exposing. Any such findings can then be examined more rigorously by additional scientific study designed to replicate the observed correlations independently.

With a large enough dataset, researchers can expect enough continuity within the userbase to provide a baseline of data that can be used when examining other smaller groups. This baseline information can provide context and comparative value in determining how various groups differ. The larger and more inclusive the dataset becomes, the more this principle applies; having continuity of data throughout increasingly smaller groupings within the general population serves to augment findings on every level because it provides valuable points of reference (both current and historical) which allow for a robust comparative analysis.

When individuals do stop providing data entirely, new participants with identical profiles can be added in to a cluster to serve as a replacement of sorts, either temporarily or permanently. This is not an ideal tactic, but it is a far better patch than the weighting or adjustments employed in traditional survey research. A continually-growing sample set reduces the threat of data degradation from losing individual participants and largely eliminates the need for additional action on the part of the research team to recruit replacements.

Continuous collection methods cannot entirely eliminate gaps in collected data, as there will always be individual participants who leave the collector and return at a later date, usually when they are prompted to re-engage in some manner. However, these gaps can provide some additional valuable data that largely cannot be obtained by traditional means. For example, they may tell researchers when certain populations are no longer sufficiently interested in or affected by the primary subject matter.

It's not only likely that there will be churn–it is inevitable.[27] There will undoubtedly be participants who opt out of using the collector at some point, regardless of the level of value that collector provides. This is the case for nearly all mobile software, especially when that software can be downloaded free of charge. However, unlike survey panelists—who cannot be legally re-contacted after opting out without violating privacy laws—users can be re-engaged even when they opt out of continuous data collectors.

Aggressive efforts to re-engage opt-outs can be employed, though such efforts are unlikely to prove highly effective. Someone who has already used a service and determined it did not meet their needs is unlikely to change their mind in response to repeated pleas to reconsider.[28] Moreover, users who do re-engage after aggressive recruitment efforts may taint the data with malicious use of deliberate misinformation. Intentional falsification does occur, and persistence interpreted as nagging can provoke this response. In recruiting participants in such a manner, researchers perturb the system they are attempting to measure. Since behaviors are being monitored, a lack of engagement is subsequently still valuable data. Pushing individuals to re-engage when they are not naturally inclined to do so introduces error into the data as a result.

Digital advertising technologies can come off as creepy, especially if people feel that advertisements are stalking them around the internet. Large buttons and calls to action in service of a product that someone already rejected can turn them off even more. Any engagement is likely to be accidental, or even malicious[29] if a person becomes so fed up with being targeted by one's ads that they click simply to cause the advertiser to spend money fruitlessly. Worse, using these techniques to re-engage past users can bring about the appearance that their anonymity has been violated, regardless of whether that is true.

Approaches which are less aggressive, and which carry less emphasis on reacquisition, hold greater promise. Those approaches are often primarily focused on preventing the collector's existence from lapsing out of a former user's memory. For this tactic to be successful, the prior relationship between the research team and the user must be positive, and researchers must bring something new to the table[30] which the former users find more enticing than the previously-offered value.

To prevent attempts to re-engage from fostering a hostile mindset, advertising technologies are best employed with less of an emphasis on driving engagement with the medium itself or on being seen by specific individuals. Advertisements on the internet are generally served on a cost-per-click (CPC) basis, a cost per thousand views (CPM) basis, a cost-per-action or acquisition (CPA) basis,[31] or a cost-per-install (CPI) basis in the case of mobile applications.[32]

Under a CPC system, advertisers pay much less per advertisement served on ads that get very low click rates. Deliberately designing ads which will be run on a CPC basis to be more subdued and have low click rates can very cheaply keep something in the back of someone's mind when strategically placed in an echo chamber that person frequents.

Broad Appeal

For any social science research dataset to be viable and have predictive power, it must be either be representative of the entire population being examined, or it must be large enough for representative portions to exist within it.[33] For a dataset to strongly represent each sub-group within the general population, it must be very large. This requires that the collector be sufficiently attractive to each sub-group, and that it induces the membership of each of those groups to organically acquire the collector. This doesn't mean the research team shouldn't or can't engage in efforts to raise awareness of the collector's value to users, but it is necessary to execute this step with care.

The two ways by which a message reaches its intended audiences are by broadcasting and narrowcasting.[34] Most people are very familiar with broadcast communications, as they have formed the basis of most data transmissions since the inception of telecommunications. A single message is crafted and designed to appeal to the greatest number of people possible, with slight alterations based on the medium.

For a long time, this was the only practical means of generating brand awareness via telecommunication technologies. It was relatively difficult to judge the effectiveness of broadcast communications considering the difficulty in determining who exactly was exposed to a given advertisement and what actions they took afterwards.

The proliferation of television channels, numbering in the hundreds and thousands, first enabled narrowcasting, though those TV advertising efforts largely remained based around a broadcast model. A single message was crafted for television audiences, though the multitude of channels each with their unique programming allowed for selective distribution of this broadcast message to the viewers most likely to be receptive to the message.[35] Advertisers largely continue using broadcasting to this day, despite the fact that many have sought to use narrowcasting[36] due to how much more effective it can be.

The dawn of the internet had an even greater effect on narrowcast advertising. Furthermore, internet advertising nearly *requires* narrowcast messaging to be effective. Using the same advertisement repeatedly regardless of how a prospect came to the attention of the advertiser is not only a recipe for advertising fatigue, but it also fails to make use of the greatest advantages internet advertising has to offer: personalizing content for relevance.[37]

Personalization drastically increases conversion from a passive prospect to an active engaged participant.

A lot of advertisers still fail to take advantage of this capacity and continue to use very similar advertisements across all digital avenues. Running a series of campaigns to narrowly target a single message to a wide variety of groups believed to be receptive thereto fails to make full use of the ways the internet enables narrowcasting. Delivering irrelevant content which fails to properly identify the value which can be offered to the individual viewing the ad has an effect, but a substantially diminished one.[38] In the internet advertising era there is effectively no excuse for wasting resources in this manner when developing personalized content has been shown to be much more effective.

While both narrowcast and broadcast messaging can be employed with digital advertising technologies, instances where broadcasting is a superior option are uncommon. Subtle broadcasts can be effective for staying connected with and reacquiring former users who are already familiar with the value offered and merely need to be occasionally reminded that the product exists. However, finding new participants to flesh out representation and grow the robustness of the sample requires a different approach, one which narrowcasting on a massive scale is best suited to accomplish due to its much higher success rates at producing conversions from a pool of prospects.

Since the "sample" of the entire population within the dataset must be large enough for representative samples of sub-groups to exist in large enough quantities that bolster the anonymity of each user, narrowcasting to each group with messaging that resonates with them specifically[39] is an ideal approach to building the needed participant base. Of course, it is still important to avoid aggressively pushing for adoption of the collector.

Appealing to such a broad spectrum of individuals in ways that sufficiently piques each of their interests is far more effective though narrowcasting, as broadcasting cannot be sufficiently descriptive so as to have a strong impact on one group without producing negative effects on other groups.[40] What is relevant to one individual or group thereof may be entirely irrelevant to others, making use of the same message for all audiences inappropriate.[41]

Additionally, the more effective a specific message is at inducing action within one group of individuals, the more it may provoke backlash amongst other groups. For example, a broadcast message advertising all of Planned

Parenthood's offered services[42] will produce drastically different results between different individuals which could polarize and potentially alienate viewers. If the same advertisement were narrowcast to show more conservative audiences a version with an emphasis on their patient education services while more liberal viewers saw one focused on emergency contraception, the same general pitch could better appeal to both groups.

Researchers can turn the general concept that causes *self-selection bias* on its head. The tendency of people to congregate in echo chambers,[43] amplified in the digital era, can benefit those who need to reach a multitude of diverse groups. Narrowcast messages can be tailored to directly appeal to that group without extensive concern for how members of other groups would react.

Once a point of interest within a specific echo chamber has been identified, researchers can introduce relevant content into this chamber until a critical mass has been reached and the chamber itself popularizes the researcher's collectors. This does not mean aggressively saturating that chamber with messaging intended purely to drive collector adoption. Instead, it means that researchers should provide value that those within that chamber appreciate, and they should tie this value to the services offered by the collection mechanisms. Such ties need not exist within every iota of value delivered via messaging; in fact, only occasionally introducing such connections is far more effective over the long term.

The process of narrowcasting *en masse* requires that researchers engage in a wide variety of different digital social environments. This can be described as a Venn diagram-style approach to sampling, continually adding additional circles which overlap with each other until each group is adequately represented. Ideally, the number of circles will be sufficiently large that each individual falls into more than one, which allows for ever-growing incentives for any given individual to participate, as the intersectional value delivered becomes more and more personalized to each potential user.

Reaching out to specific groups in order to build a comprehensive representation of the entire study population is made possible by reaching out to every, or effectively every, sub-group. Members of the National Rifle Association and members of the Gun Owners of America represent different subsets of gun owners with different inclinations that congregate in their own particular echo chambers, neither of which may be representative of the entire population of gun owners. Likewise, the broader group of gun owners are decidedly not representative of the entire population.

This narrowcasting approach requires caution; it could easily backfire if a message escapes the echo chamber which was its intended target, or if it misses the target and ends up in a location where it is counterproductive. Messages should endeavor to avoid becoming inflammatory; even though such messaging may be effective at recruiting some participants, it can turn just as many away.

Inflammatory messaging could also drastically degrade the quality of the participant pool's representativeness in numerous ways.[44] Individuals who participate in an echo chamber only tangentially due to relatively minor associations with that group may share such a message within their other circles, counteracting the positive effects of messages narrowcast to those initial circles. The damage this causes could be reduced by ensuring that messaging and value which could be considered inflammatory is not directly linked to the collector or the research team, but ensuing relative neutrality is a much safer approach.

Since less energy and fewer resources need to be dedicated towards conducting data adjustments when using this approach, much more emphasis can be placed on expanding the appeal of participation. The more relevant information that users are given, the more likely it is that they will be inclined to use the collector to receive the incentives it provides.

When the subject matter of the research is sufficiently broad, the likelihood that it will be applicable to a given individual increases substantially. This in turn makes the dataset more robust over time by broadening initial appeal and reducing opt-outs by those who have participated at any point in the past. Additionally, greater coverage provides better value to those using data collectors and in turn improves the quality of the data collected. This occurs because there is more information available for comparative analysis, trend identification, and quasi-experimental research.

There are generally a substantial number of classifications that apply to any one individual, a concept often referred to in modern parlance as intersectionality. Though that term generally carries political connotations related to studies of oppression or discrimination and is often used explicitly in reference to race or sex,[45] the general principle behind it is extensive and commonly recognized: each individual person is considered unique and was so long before the advent of genetics proved it to be true. No two people share all the same classifications, so any given messaging will resonate differently with each person.

Expanding the coverage of value and aspects of life addressed within a collector increases the chance that any one individual will start using the collector once it covers the intersection which most applies to them. As more value can be directly provided on a personal level to each unique individual, the attractiveness of the collector grows and becomes enticing to larger audiences.

By not specifically recruiting for a survey where the respondents naturally expect to be giving up their data while receiving little if anything in return, a substantial impetus for self-selection is largely avoided because participants receive direct value. In this scenario, *sampling bias* poses a much greater issue than does self-selection, but large samples with sufficiently broad coverage can reduce or even eliminate the risks this tactic presents.

Appealing to sufficiently large portions of the general population so that complete representation is assured is a key factor in enabling active, proportional sampling. This offers a way in which one of the major issues plaguing the entirety of social sciences, lack of replicability within studies,[46] can finally start to be addressed. It is critical to create an environment in which researchers and scientists can reproduce not only the findings of others, but also the findings of their own work.[47] A lack of confirmation means that the outcomes could be attributed to random chance, experimental error, misinterpretation, biases within the data, or any number of other issues that effectively invalidate them.

These practices allow for studies and examinations to be conducted much more rapidly, cheaply, and in ways which are much more scientifically sound. Not only is this approach far more agile, but it also largely eliminates the need for data adjustments. Adjustments are primarily made to account for unrepresentative data, but if the dataset is large enough, such representativeness can nearly be assured. A sizable dataset which resembles a random sample can itself be sampled in any numbers of ways, probabilistic or non-probabilistic.[48]

Some re-clustering of individual user data profiles may be sometimes necessary in order to address issues related to churn. However, when large enough samples reach broad enough cross-sections of the population and data is collected continuously, this can be done rather effectively. The broader the array of coverage and data subsequently collected, the more accurate re-clustering will be and the less frequently it need be done, as broader coverage creates greater value and provides greater incentives for participants to continue using the collector.

Chapter 10 - Social Science Must Modernize to Grow Up

One of the most significant stated benefits of using a probability sample of the population in question is that, if the sample selection is truly random,[1] the findings should be generalizable–they should reflect the preferences of the larger population. This principle means that researchers should be able to take their results at face value, and that the true values should fall within the calculated margins of error.

If researchers have to adjust the results from a probability sample, the benefits of using this approach are utterly destroyed. Researchers who adjust results from probability samples implicitly acknowledge that their sample was not representative, and oftentimes that not all members of the population had an equal chance of being included within that sample.[2] When this is the case, a true probability sample is not possible, regardless of what it is called.

Very little good can come from deliberately introducing error into a dataset, yet researchers do this all the time. While on the surface this is done to ostensibly correct for bias and error, in practice this magnifies the problems which are already present in the findings. Researchers have little way of controlling for these issues. This goes against the core of scientific principles regarding controlled experimentation,[3] which makes it hard to call much social research a science at all. While conducting true experimental research in the social realm still poses many hurdles, social researchers can start to bridge the gap ethically by using methods which enable quasi-experimental methods.

Surveys are already notoriously lacking in controls, and adjustments made by researchers invalidate what scientific rigor remained, reducing the research quality to little more than shots in the dark at relatively large targets. Despite this, they still manage to miss the mark far more than would be expected, even by the laxest of standards. This should no longer be considered acceptable. With the degree and amount of pure quantitative information at our disposal, it is now possible to start raising the bar, thereby holding social science to a standard worthier of the 'science' label.

The cost per data point is much lower than it was in the past,[4] comparatively and absolutely, and data can oftentimes be freely obtained directly from the source in ways which minimize bias. This allows researchers and scientists to selectively acquire every piece of information they need to test a given social hypothesis. Social sciences can use the unprecedented economic and technical capabilities provided by the internet to directly mine quantified human behavioral data from highly representative cross-sections of the population, rather than attempting to aggregate such information from other sources.

This development of cost effective means to anonymously and unobtrusively study diverse groups which are broadly representative of the entire population, and each of its segments, without the specter of legal consequences has exciting potential. Well-tailored implementations can produce highly accurate descriptive and predictive models for forecasting or explaining people's reactions to stimuli, a hallmark of scientific stringency.

Past efforts to accomplish this objective have been fraught with issues. Those problems can be sidestepped entirely by abandoning outdated practices which are no longer effective at producing results. The validity and predictive strength of the social sciences will be substantially augmented by adopting methodologies more in line with the rigor of the physical sciences and discarding those antiquated approaches which have guided social science research for over a century.[5]

The social sciences have maintained a separate set of standards from the natural sciences for long enough. While the differences may have been borne out of necessity, this is no longer the case. Practices which are approaching obsolescence should not be continued simply because they are the way things have always been done. Humanity has entered an era where we can start to apply the principles refined over hundreds of years which have produced great successes in studying and explaining natural phenomenon to better understand arguably far more complex social phenomenon.[6]

Humans have been studying ourselves for every bit as long as we have been studying the world in which we live, but refinements in the way we examine the former have come far more slowly than those which are used to address the latter. Scientists have been building bigger and better tools to study how the universe works for centuries,[7] epitomized by the Enlightenment and the Scientific Revolution, but advances in the study of ourselves have been comparatively lacking.

Humanity has been able to quantify the natural world in ways that allow for models to be built which accurately predict future events based on known inputs. By contrast, our explanations of and models predicting our own behavior are much more qualitative, not only often failing to align with observed events but often struggling to definitively explain the past. The lack of an ability to conduct controlled experimentation in social sciences combined with a generally poor understanding of how our minds operate has resulted in a dark age which more recent developments can end.

The natural sciences were not always so refined; the causes of observed phenomenon were ascribed to supernatural causes for millennia. The divergence between the approaches used by the natural and social sciences grew out of the fact that it has taken much longer for humanity to develop the tools needed to research its own behavior. Now, technological advances can provide insight into the synthesis of behavior and psychology, allowing researchers to examine the drivers of human activity in ways less prone to error.

While research into public opinions and market behaviors has ventured into this realm, a lack of any sort of experimental protocols in these practices has largely precluded these fields from being regarded as truly scientific. The impact of these limitations have been felt by many a failed campaign—corporate, political, or otherwise—all of which would benefit greatly from the application of quantitative scientific methodologies beyond statistical inference.

While scholars have warned against the use of natural science approaches in service of the social sciences, the primary justification for this argument is that, as Ludwig von Mises wrote in his book "Money, Method, and the Market Process" published in 1990, "[t]he experience to which the natural sciences owe all their success is the experience of the experiment" and the lack of subjective interpretation of facts.[8] These are very valid positions, but they are ones which did not account for the rise of modern technological solutions. Sufficiently vast quantities of high-quality research data, unaffected by subjective interpretation, can approximate controlled experimentation, as those affected by a given stimuli can be identified, isolated, and compared against an unaffected control group.

Reality is constantly conducting "experiments" in that each individual has different experiences throughout life. Identifying those who share any given experience and comparing them to others in large enough numbers can yield results with rigor on par with the controlled experiments seen in the natural sciences. While this is not true controlled experimentation, a sufficiently large dataset which is properly constructed and structured can allow social scientists to get *close*, much closer than has ever been possible before.

Now that the means for such research have arrived, there is no good reason to continue relying primarily on old methods. Doing so is the equivalent of natural scientists employing the theories of alchemy, astrology, or phrenology to explain observed phenomenon in an era where chemistry, physics, and neurology have proven far more reliable.

Just as qualitative supernatural and pseudo-scientific descriptions gave way to quantitative direct observance and mathematical modeling to explain the natural world, so too must qualitative solicitations and bias-prone datasets be replaced by true behavioral models within the social realm. Long-standing theories which were built off individual case studies and examinations of comparatively small portions of the population—especially where the researchers themselves inadvertently affected the data collected—largely amount to guesswork which often fails to hold up to scrutiny.

Generalizing models which are produced from the observed behaviors of psychiatric patients and college students[9] to the entirety of humanity makes about as much sense as generalizing the material properties of all the elements from the data generated by in-depth observations of lithium and iron. This has long been a standard method of producing research data, but the dawn of the digital age makes such a limited approach no longer necessary. When individual details of each person's life can be catalogued, there is no reason to introduce bias by observing only specific subsets of the population.

A wholesale revolution may not be necessary to fill the increasing gap between reality and survey research, but novel approaches are indeed needed in order to bridge these divides. Traditional methodological approaches are inherently flawed, as they increasingly struggle to reliably sample representative portions of the population and extract data without inducing numerous biases. Combined with the growing issues surrounding data privacy and confidentiality, linguistic interpretation, incentives for accuracy, and stated versus revealed preferences, older practices are ill-equipped for the brave new world of the 21st century. Old habits die hard, though, and researchers tend to stick to what they know as much as any other person does.

In recognition of the value which the digital collection of data provides, social scientists are looking to harness the vast troves of information generated electronically by technology firms, but they do not do so effectively. This data is severely tainted in a number of ways—including but not limited to those same growing concerns which negatively affect the quality of survey research data—and are thus are generally not viable for the type of research which scientists seek to conduct. Outsourcing scientific data collection to organizations which do not collect scientific data does little to enable research that will stand up to in-depth scrutiny.

Researchers continue to rely on outdated and obsolete practices, even when using digitally-collected data. Too often, they use methodologies built upon those old protocols, which they attempt to incrementally modify to account for different collection standards. Consequently, the results contain the same issues that plague traditional surveys conducted in this era. Accuracy is more often arrived at by happenstance rather than by the application of rigorous and sound scientific principles, threatening the legitimacy of those principles as they continue to be associated with practices that are unscientific at their core.

The scientific principles are indeed sound, but the "GiGo" principle also applies. As the saying goes, "Garbage in, garbage out." When all the inputs are garbage, so too will the outputs be worthless regardless of any adjustments, corrections, and algorithms applied in attempts to smooth over the issues. Only when the data itself is of high quality and truly representative of reality can research results also have these attributes. Therefore, numerous substantial changes in the collection process are necessary in the vast majority of cases.

The overhaul needed to address these problems cannot be based upon approaches from the 20th century. They cannot rely on statements made by individuals, use platforms where social aspects are an important factor, or be tied to the individual identities of those from whom the data is being collected. These issues alone invalidate nearly all the data currently being generated in a digital format. Only means which track actual preferences in an anonymous format can compensate for the errors and biases which tend to manifest in people's digital footprints.

Purpose-built collection mechanisms which address all of the issues facing traditional approaches are needed in order to take social sciences to the next level. Creating such a new source for data collection is no easy feat—it requires a substantial investment of time by highly-skilled individuals who are both aware of those mechanism's needs and capable of addressing them adequately.

Such tools are needed to promote the social sciences from a pseudo-scientific collection of qualitative standards to a truly scientific, natively quantified discipline. They also greatly promote efficiency, profitability, and investment in further refining the quality of our understanding of ourselves. Well-built tools provide enhanced value in every direction; research clients, research participants, researchers themselves, and society at large all benefit from the adoption of tools which substantially reduce the friction associated with each stage the research process.

It is only a matter of time before this shift in the social sciences arrives. The traditional methodologies will continue to provide value while the needed improvements are developed and fielded. However, given their wholesale inadequacy, the sooner this crutch can be discarded, the sooner we can start building a more comprehensive understanding of why people behave the way they do.

Index

I

J

K

L

M

N

O

P

Q

R

S

T

U

V

W

Z

About the Author

Steve Wood holds a BA and MA in Political Science from the University of Cincinnati. He moved to Washington, DC after graduating during the Great Recession to work for grassroots advocacy groups managing data, conducting research (often by survey), and creating publications from his findings. After several years in the region, a tech startup located in Utah hired him away before being acquired later that same year. His experiences during that time prompted him to launch his own startup, ATLAS Mobile Technologies (atlasmobile.tech), to keep people informed of changes and differences in laws which affect them, as well as connect them with legal counsel when they need it most to minimize violations of their rights. He worked on this company while consulting as a data/research expert, and was employed by the admissions office of what soon became the state's largest university by headcount creating technological solutions to augment their recruiting efforts, until moving to Colorado to be closer to family then subsequently further back east for the same reason. He loves mountains and hates humidity.

To contact or learn more about Steve, visit his website at http://steve-wood.us

Endnotes

Chapter 1

[1] Zukin, C. (2015, June 20). What's the Matter With Polling? *The New York Times*. Retrieved from https://nyti.ms/1GyPSmU

[2] DeTurck, D. (n.d.). Case Study I: The 1936 Literary Digest Poll. *University of Pennsylvania*. Retrieved from https://www.math.upenn.edu/~deturck/m170/wk4/lecture/case1.html

[3] Cantril, H. (1937). How Accurate Were the Polls? *The Public Opinion Quarterly*, Vol. 1, No. 1, 97-109. Retrieved from http://www.jstor.org/stable/2744805

[4] The United Press. (1936, November 2). Straw Vote Fight Arouses Interest. *The Pittsburgh Press*. Retrieved from https://news.google.com/newspapers?id=fkYbAAAAIBAJ&sjid=IU8EAAAAIBAJ&pg=2555,806060&dq=literary-digest&hl=en

[5] Peters, G. (2016). Election Year Presidential Preferences. *The American Presidency Project*. Retrieved from http://www.presidency.ucsb.edu/data/preferences.php

[6] Dickey, D. (2012). United States presidential election, 1976. *Wikipedia - Historical polling for United States presidential elections*. Retrieved from https://en.wikipedia.org/wiki/Historical_polling_for_United_States_presidential_elections#United_States_presidential_election.2C_1976

[7] RealClearPolitics Staff. (2016, November 8). General Election: Trump vs. Clinton vs. Johnson vs. Stein. *RealClearPolitics Polls*. Retrieved from https://www.realclearpolitics.com/epolls/2016/president/us/general_election_trump_vs_clinton_vs_johnson_vs_stein-5952.html

[8] Rasmussen Reports Staff. (2016, November 7). White House Watch: Clinton Edges Ahead. *Rasmussen Reports*. Retrieved from http://www.rasmussenreports.com/public_content/politics/elections/election_2016/white_house_watch_nov7

[9] RealClearPolitics Staff. (2016, November 8). Florida: Trump vs. Clinton vs. Johnson vs. Stein. *RealClearPolitics Polls*. Retrieved from https://www.realclearpolitics.com/epolls/2016/president/fl/florida_trump_vs_clinton_vs_johnson_vs_stein-5963.html

[10] RealClearPolitics Staff. (2016, November 8). Pennsylvania: Trump vs. Clinton vs. Johnson vs. Stein. *RealClearPolitics Polls*. Retrieved from https://www.realclearpolitics.com/epolls/2016/president/pa/pennsylvania_trump_vs_clinton_vs_johnson_vs_stein-5964.html

[11] RealClearPolitics Staff. (2016, November 8). Michigan: Trump vs. Clinton vs. Johnson vs. Stein. *RealClearPolitics Polls*. Retrieved from https://www.realclearpolitics.com/epolls/2016/president/mi/michigan_trump_vs_clinton_vs_johnson_vs_stein-6008.html

[12] Ipsos Public Affairs. (2016, November 7) Core Political Daily Tracker 11.07.2016. *Reuters*. Retrieved from https://www.realclearpolitics.com/docs/2016/2016_Reuters_Tracking_-_Core_Political_Daily_11.07_.16_.pdf

[13] Monmouth University Polling Institute. (2016, November 7). Clinton

Leads by 6 Points. *Monmouth University*. Retrieved from https://www.monmouth.edu/polling-institute/reports/MonmouthPoll_US_110716/
[14] The Economist/YouGov Poll. (2016, November 7). November 4 - 7, 2016. *The Economist*. Retrieved from https://d25d2506sfb94s.cloudfront.net/cumulus_uploads/document/l37rosbwjp/econTabReport_lv.pdf
[15] Wisconsin: Trump vs. Clinton vs. Johnson vs. Stein. *RealClearPolitics Polls*. Retrieved from https://www.realclearpolitics.com/epolls/2016/president/wi/wisconsin_trump_vs_clinton_vs_johnson_vs_stein-5976.html
[16] Lester, W. (1998, November 1). 'Dewey Defeats Truman' Disaster Haunts Pollsters. *Los Angeles Times*. Retrieved from http://articles.latimes.com/1998/nov/01/news/mn-38174
[17] Bradner, E. (2017, June 10). Poll: Ossoff leads Handel 51-44 in most expensive House race ever. *CNN Politics*. Retrieved from http://www.cnn.com/2017/06/09/politics/georgia-house-poll-jon-ossoff-karen-handel/index.html
[18] RealClearPolitics Staff. (2017, June 20). Georgia 6th District Run-Off Election- Handel vs. Ossoff. *RealClearPolitics Polls*. Retrieved from https://www.realclearpolitics.com/epolls/2017/house/ga/georgia_6th_district_runoff_election_handel_vs_ossoff-6202.html#polls
[19] FOX 5 Atlanta Staff. (2017, June 16). New FOX 5 Poll: Ossoff, Handel Race Too Close to Call. *FOX 5 Atlanta*. Retrieved from http://www.fox5atlanta.com/news/261896863-story
[20] Trafalgar Group. (2017, June 19). GA CD6 Special Election Survey Conducted 6/17-6/18. *Trafalgar Group*. Retrieved from https://drive.google.com/file/d/0B4lhKxf9pMitSUE2X2ItLWhoYVU/view
[21] RealClearPolitics Staff. (2017, May 25). 2017 Montana At-Large District Special Election - Gianforte vs. Quist vs. Wicks. *RealClearPolitics Polls*. Retrieved from https://www.realclearpolitics.com/epolls/2017/house/mt/2017_montana_atlarge_district_special_election_gianforte_vs_quist_vs_wicks-6209.html
[22] RealClearPolitics Staff. (2017, November 8). Virginia Governor - Gillespie vs. Northam. *RealClearPolitics Polls*. Retrieved from https://www.realclearpolitics.com/epolls/2017/governor/va/virginia_governor_gillespie_vs_northam-6197.html#polls
[23] Virginia Quantitative Research. (2017, November 3). DAILY TRACKING TOPLINES: OCT 30 - Nov 2, 2017. *the polling company*. Retrieved from https://www.realclearpolitics.com/docs/VA_TPC_Topline_Oct_30-Nov_2.pdf
[24] Rasmussen Reports Staff. (2017, November 3). Election 2017: Virginia Governor. *Rasmussen Reports*. Retrieved from http://www.rasmussenreports.com/public_content/politics/elections/election_2017/virginia/election_2017_virginia_governor
[25] Wilson, H. (2017, November 3). RC Poll: Northam and Gillespie deadlocked; Lieutenant Governor and Attorney General races also tied. *Roanoke College*. Retrieved from

https://www.roanoke.edu/about/news/rc_poll_politics_nov_2017
[26] Trafalgar Group Staff. (2017, November 4). Virginia Governor Survey Conducted 10/31/17-11/02/17. *Trafalgar Group*. Retrieved from https://www.realclearpolitics.com/docs/Trafalgar_VA_Gov_11-4-17.pdf
[27] Tuchfarber, A. Personal conversation dated July 14, 2017
[28] Royce, W. (1970, August). Managing the Development of Large Software Systems. *IEEE WESCON 26*. Retrieved from https://www.cs.umd.edu/class/spring2003/cmsc838p/Process/waterfall.pdf
[29] Lella, A., & Lipsman, A. (2014, August 21). The U.S. Mobile App Report. *comScore*. Retrieved from https://www.comscore.com/Insights/Presentations-and-Whitepapers/2014/The-US-Mobile-App-Report
[30] Groups Plus Staff. (2008). FAQs about Focus Groups. *Groups Plus*. Retrieved from http://www.groupsplus.com/pages/faq.htm
[31] SIS International Research Staff. (2017). Focus Group about Business and Politics, $150 Incentive. *SIS International Research*. Retrieved from https://www.sisinternational.com/focus-group-business-politics-150-incentive/
[32] SIS International Research Staff. (2017). Compensated Interviews Richmond, VA Between $150-300 Dollars. *SIS International Research*. Retrieved from https://www.sisinternational.com/compensated-interviews-richmond-va-150-300-dollars/
[33] SIS International Research Staff. (2017). Focus Groups for Truckers in Atlanta, Dallas, Los Angeles and Chicago $250. *SIS International Research*. Retrieved from https://www.sisinternational.com/focus-groups-truckers-atlanta-dallas-los-angeles-chicago/
[34] SIS International Research Staff. (2017). Consumer Focus Group $150 Dollar Compensation. *SIS International Research*. Retrieved from https://www.sisinternational.com/consumer-focus-group-150-dollar-compensation/
[35] SIS International Research Staff. (2017). Phone Interview, Get Paid $100 Dollars for 30-40 Minutes. *SIS International Research*. Retrieved from https://www.sisinternational.com/compensated-telephone-interview-get-paid-100-incentive/
[36] SIS International Research Staff. (2017). App Test NYC $50 Dollar Compensation. *SIS International Research*. Retrieved from https://www.sisinternational.com/app-test-nyc-50-dollar-compensation/
[37] SIS International Research Staff. (2017). Russian and Chinese Speakers in NYC $50 incentive. *SIS International Research*. Retrieved from https://www.sisinternational.com/russian-chinese-speakers-nyc-50-incentive/
[38] SIS International Research Staff. (2017). San Francisco Short Interview, Get Paid $50 Dollars for 20 Minutes. *SIS International Research*. Retrieved from https://www.sisinternational.com/san-francisco-short-interview-get-paid-50-dollars-20-minutes/
[39] SIS International Research Staff. (2017). Fitness Study for Women $500

Dollar Incentive. *SIS International Research*. Retrieved from https://www.sisinternational.com/fitness-study-women-500-dollar-incentive/

[40] SIS International Research Staff. (2017). Childcare Workers, Babysitters, Nanny's, Grandparents...For Online Survey $50 Dollar Incentive. *SIS International Research*. Retrieved from https://www.sisinternational.com/childcare-workers-babysitters-nannys-grandparents-online-survey-50-dollar-incentive/

[41] Hagglund, D. (2009, April 6). Six guidelines for compensating research participants. *Dimensional Research*. Retrieved from http://dimensionalresearch.com/blog/2009/04/06/market-research-how-should-you-compensate-participants/

[42] *Ibid*

[43] Sopo, C. (2013, September 22). How much does it cost to commission a national opinion poll? *Quora*. Retrieved from https://www.quora.com/How-much-does-it-cost-to-commission-a-national-opinion-poll

[44] Nielsen, J. (1998, January 1). Estimated Cost of Running a Focus Group. *Nielsen Norman Group*. Retrieved from https://www.nngroup.com/articles/focus-group-cost/

[45] Science Buddies. (2017). Sample Size: How Many Survey Participants Do I Need?. *Science Buddies*. Retrieved from https://www.sciencebuddies.org/science-fair-projects/project_ideas/Soc_participants.shtml

[46] Stine, M. (2010, September 7). Waste #4: Handoffs. *DZone*. Retrieved from https://dzone.com/articles/waste-4-handoffs

[47] *ibid*

[48] Friesen, M., White, S., & Byers, J. (2008, April). Chapter 34 Handoffs: Implications for Nurses. *Patient Safety and Quality: An Evidence-Based Handbook for Nurses*. Retrieved from https://www.ncbi.nlm.nih.gov/books/NBK2649/

[49] U.S. Army Corps of Engineers. (2007, May 12). APPENDIX D Legal Definition of "Traditional Navigable Waters". *U.S. Army Corps of Engineers Jurisdictional Determination Form Instructional Guidebook*. Retrieved from http://www.usace.army.mil/Portals/2/docs/civilworks/regulatory/cwa_guide/app_d_traditional_navigable_waters.pdf

[50] Arizona Legislature. (2015). Title 13 - Criminal Code § 13-2919 Automated telephone solicitation; violation; classification. *2015 Arizona Revised Statutes*. Retrieved from http://law.justia.com/codes/arizona/2015/title-13/section-13-2919

[51] Pew Research Center Staff. (2017). Collecting survey data. *Pew Research Center*. Retrieved from http://www.pewresearch.org/methodology/u-s-survey-research/collecting-survey-data/

Chapter 2

[1] Federal Trade Commission. (2016, August). Q&A for Telemarketers & Sellers About DNC Provisions in TSR. *U.S. Federal Trade Commission*. Retrieved from https://www.ftc.gov/tips-advice/business-center/guidance/qa-telemarketers-sellers-about-dnc-provisions-tsr

[2] Blumberg, S. J., & Luke, J. V. (2007, May 14). Wireless Substitution: Early Release of Estimates Based on Data from the National Health Interview Survey, July – December 2006. *Centers for Disease Control and Prevention*. Retrieved from https://www.cdc.gov/nchs/data/nhis/earlyrelease/wireless200705.pdf

[3] Blumberg, S. J., & Luke, J. V. (2018, June 7). Wireless Substitution: Early Release of Estimates Based on Data from the National Health Interview Survey, July – December 2017, pg 2. *Centers for Disease Control and Prevention*. Retrieved from https://www.cdc.gov/nchs/data/nhis/earlyrelease/wireless201806.pdf

[4] *Ibid*

[5] Smith, A. & Anderson, M. (2018, March 1). Methodology. *Pew Research Center*. Retrieved from http://www.pewinternet.org/2018/03/01/social-media-use-2018-methodology/

[6] Blumberg, S. J., & Luke, J. V. (2017, May 4). Wireless Substitution: Early Release of Estimates Based on Data from the National Health Interview Survey, July – December 2016. *Centers for Disease Control and Prevention*. Retrieved from https://www.cdc.gov/nchs/data/nhis/earlyrelease/wireless201705.pdf

[7] Clement, S. (2016, September 6). How the Washington Post-SurveyMonkey 50-state poll was conducted. *The Washington Post*. Retrieved from https://www.washingtonpost.com/news/post-politics/wp/2016/09/06/how-the-washington-post-surveymonkey-50-state-poll-was-conducted/

[8] The Marist Poll. (2017, March). How the Survey was Conducted, pg 33. *McClatchy-Marist Poll*. Retrieved from https://www.documentcloud.org/documents/3532285-McClatchy-Marist-Poll-National-Nature-of-the.html

[9] Barthel, M. (2017, May 10). Americans' Attitudes About the News Media Deeply Divided Along Partisan Lines. *Pew Research Center*. Retrieved from http://www.journalism.org/2017/05/10/democrats-republicans-now-split-on-support-for-watchdog-role/

[10] Jackson, N., & Sparks, G. (2017, March 31). A Poll Finds Most Americans Don't Trust Public Opinion Polls. *The Huffington Post*. Retrieved from http://www.huffingtonpost.com/entry/most-americans-dont-trust-public-opinion-polls_us_58de94ece4b0ba359594a708

[11] *Ibid*

[12] The Marist Poll. (2017, March). How the Survey was Conducted, pg 32. *McClatchy-Marist Poll*. Retrieved from https://www.documentcloud.org/documents/3532285-McClatchy-Marist-Poll-National-Nature-of-the.html

[13] The Media Insight Project. (2018, June 11). Levels of trust and how Americans feel about the fairness and accuracy of the press. *The American Press Institute*. Retrieved from https://www.americanpressinstitute.org/publications/reports/survey-research/fairness-accuracy-of-press/

[14] The Marist Poll. (2017, March). How the Survey was Conducted. *McClatchy-Marist Poll*. Retrieved from https://www.documentcloud.org/documents/3532285-McClatchy-Marist-Poll-National-Nature-of-the.html

[15] Nickerson, R. (1998). Confirmation Bias: A Ubiquitous Phenomenon in

Many Guises. *Review of General Psychology*, Vol 2, No. 2, 175-220. Retrieved from http://psy2.ucsd.edu/~mckenzie/nickersonConfirmationBias.pdf

[16] Shearer, E. & Matsa. K. E. (2018, September 10). News Use Across Social Media Platforms 2018. *Pew Research Center*. Retrieved from http://www.journalism.org/2018/09/10/news-use-across-social-media-platforms-2018/

[17] Ipsos Poll Data. (2017, March 28). Ipsos Public Affairs: BuzzFeed Facebook News 3-28-2017. *Ipsos Public Affairs*. Retrieved from https://www.documentcloud.org/documents/3559451-Ipsos-Buzzfeed-News-Facebook-News-Survey-Topline.html

[18] American Press Institute Staff. (2017, May 24). People have more trust in 'my' media than 'the' media. *American Press Institute*. Retrieved from https://www.americanpressinstitute.org/publications/reports/survey-research/my-media-more-trusted-than-the-media/

[19] Keeter, S., Hatley, N., Kennedy, C., & Lau, A. (2017, May 15). What Low Response Rates Mean for Telephone Surveys. *Pew Research Center*. Retrieved from http://www.pewresearch.org/2017/05/15/what-low-response-rates-mean-for-telephone-surveys/

[20] GSS Staff. (n.d.). Response Rate and Field Period. *General Social Survey*. Retrieved from http://gss.norc.org/Documents/other/GSS Response Period and Field Period.pdf

[21] Czajka, J., & Beyler, A. (2016, June 15). Declining Response Rates in Federal Surveys: Trends and Implications. *Mathematica Policy Research*. Retrieved from https://aspe.hhs.gov/system/files/pdf/255531/Decliningresponserates.pdf

[22] Center for Behavioral Health Statistics and Quality. (2016, September). 2015 National Survey on Drug Use and Health: Methodological summary and definitions, Table B.3. *Substance Abuse and Mental Health Services Administration*. Retrieved from https://www.samhsa.gov/data/sites/default/files/NSDUH-MethodSummDefsHTML-2015/NSDUH-MethodSummDefsHTML-2015/NSDUH-MethodSummDefs-2015.pdf

[23] Czajka, J., & Beyler, A. (2016, June 15). Declining Response Rates in Federal Surveys: Trends and Implications, pg a.11. *Mathematica Policy Research*. Retrieved from https://aspe.hhs.gov/system/files/pdf/255531/Decliningresponserates.pdf

[24] Hill, H. A., Elam-Evans, L. D., Yankey, D., Singleton, J. A., & Dietz, V. (2016, October 7). Vaccination Coverage Among Children Aged 19–35 Months — United States, 2015. *Center for Disease Control and Prevention*. Retrieved from https://www.cdc.gov/mmwr/volumes/65/wr/mm6539a4.htm

[25] Czajka, J., & Beyler, A. (2016, June 15). Declining Response Rates in Federal Surveys: Trends and Implications, pg a.16. *Mathematica Policy Research*. Retrieved from https://aspe.hhs.gov/system/files/pdf/255531/Decliningresponserates.pdf

[26] American Community Survey. (n.d.). Response Rates. *U.S. Census Bureau*. Retrieved from https://www.census.gov/acs/www/me

thodology/sample-size-and-data-quality/response-rates/
[27] *Ibid*
[28] IRS Statements and Announcements. (2013, October 8). Reminder: Oct. 15 Tax Deadline Remains During Appropriations Lapse. *Internal Revenue Service*. Retrieved from https://www.irs.gov/uac/newsroom/reminder-oct-15-tax-deadline-remains-during-appropriations-lapse
[29] The Rutherford Institute. (2017, February 23). Constitutional Q&A: American Community Survey. *Rutherford Institute*. Retrieved from https://www.rutherford.org/publications_resources/legal_features/constitutional_qa_american_community_survey
[30] Bolling, K., & Smith, P. (2017, June 29). Declining Response Rates and their Impact, pg 4-6. *Social Research Association*. Retrieved from http://the-sra.org.uk/wp-content/uploads/keith-bolling-and-patten-smith-declining-response-rates-and-their-impact.pdf
[31] *Ibid*, pg 11-12
[32] National Academy of Sciences (2013). Nonresponse in Social Science Surveys: A Research Agenda. *National Academy of Sciences*. Retrieved from https://www.nap.edu/read/18293/chapter/3
[33] *Ibid*
[34] European Union. (2011, May). EU Cookies Directive. *TermsFeed*. Retrieved from https://termsfeed.com/blog/eu-cookies-directive/
[35] Miller, A. (2016, August 24). Ad Fatigue Kills Your Campaigns. We've Found the Solution. *ReFUEL4*. Retrieved from http://blog.refuel4.com/blog/2016/08/25/ad-fatigue-kills-campaigns-weve-found-solution
[36] American Psychological Association. (2006, March 20). Multitasking: Switching costs. *American Psychological Association*. Retrieved from http://www.apa.org/research/action/multitask.aspx
[37] *Ibid*
[38] Sun, L. (2018, June 30). Survey shows most Americans uncomfortable with companies selling their data: A Foolish Take. *USA Today*. Retrieved from https://usat.ly/2tCKlfN
[39] Federal Trade Commission. (2009, September). CAN-SPAM Act: A Compliance Guide for Business. *Federal Trade Commission*. Retrieved from https://www.ftc.gov/tips-advice/business-center/guidance/can-spam-act-compliance-guide-business
[40] Canadian Radio-television and Telecommunications Commission. (2017, June 13). Canada's Anti-Spam Legislation. *Government of Canada*. Retrieved from http://fightspam.gc.ca/eic/site/030.nsf/eng/home
[41] *Ibid*
[42] SimplyCast Staff. (n.d.). Can you explain CASL?. *SimplyCast*. Retrieved from https://www.simplycast.com/interactive-marketing-support/faqs/can-you-explain-casl/
[43] Robinson, G. (2016, January 13). Market Research Under CASL. *Informz*. Retrieved from http://www.informz.com/blog/deliverability/market-research-under-casl/
[44] European Parliament and Council. (2002, July 12). Directive 2002/58/EC of

the European Parliament and of the Council of 12 July 2002 concerning the processing of personal data and the protection of privacy in the electronic communications sector (Directive on privacy and electronic communications). *European Union*. Retrieved from http://eur-lex.europa.eu/LexUriServ/LexUriServ.do?uri=CELEX:32002L0058:en:HTML

[45] European Union. (2011, May). EU Cookies Directive. *TermsFeed*. Retrieved from https://termsfeed.com/blog/eu-cookies-directive/

[46] Cornell Law School. (n.d.). EU Member State Laws Implementing the E-Privacy Directive. *Cornell Law School*. Retrieved from https://www.law.cornell.edu/wex/inbox/eu_member_state_laws_implementing_e-privacy_directive

[47] Anderson, J., & Rainie, L. (2017, October 19). The Future of Truth and Misinformation Online. *Pew Research Center*. Retrieved from http://www.pewinternet.org/2017/10/19/the-future-of-truth-and-misinformation-online/

[48] Clement, S. (2016, September 6). How the Washington Post-SurveyMonkey 50-state poll was conducted. *The Washington Post*. Retrieved from https://www.washingtonpost.com/news/post-politics/wp/2016/09/06/how-the-washington-post-surveymonkey-50-state-poll-was-conducted/

[49] Karlson, K. (2016, July 22). 12 Speedy Ways to Overcome Ad Fatigue (And Keep Down Your Cost-per-action). *AdEspresso*. Retrieved from https://adespresso.com/academy/blog/overcome-ad-fatigue-keep-cpa-down/

[50] Statistic Brain. (2016, July 2). Attention Span Statistics. *Statistic Brain*. Retrieved from http://www.statisticbrain.com/attention-span-statistics/

[51] Henning, J. (2013, December 24). Is the Ideal Survey Length 20 Minutes?. *Research Access*. Retrieved from http://researchaccess.com/2013/12/survey-length/

[52] Wilson, K., & Korn, J. H. (2007, 5 June). Attention During Lectures: Beyond Ten Minutes. *Teaching of Psychology*. 34 (2): 85–89. doi:10.1080/00986280701291291.

[53] Pew Research Center. (2012, May 15). Assessing the Representativeness of Public Opinion Surveys. *Pew Research Center*. Retrieved from http://www.people-press.org/2012/05/15/assessing-the-representativeness-of-public-opinion-surveys/

[54] GSS Staff. (n.d.). Frequently Asked Questions. *National Opinion Research Center (NORC)*. Retrieved from http://gss.norc.org/faq

[55] GSS Staff. (n.d.). Response Rate and Field Period. *National Opinion Research Center (NORC)*. Retrieved from http://gss.norc.org/Documents/other/GSS Response Period and Field Period.pdf

[56] Pew Research Center. (2012, May 15). Assessing the Representativeness of Public Opinion Surveys. *Pew Research Center*. Retrieved from http://www.people-press.org/2012/05/15/assessing-the-representativeness-of-public-opinion-surveys/

[57] Jensen, T. (2017, July 18). Health Care a Mine Field for Republicans;

Many Trump Voters in Denial on Russia. *Public Policy Polling*. Retrieved from http://www.publicpolicypolling.com/pdf/2017/PPP_Release_National_71817.pdf
[58] FluidSurveys Team. (2015, January 26). Survey Priming – How Your Question Order is Giving Your Survey Bias. *FluidSurveys*. Retrieved from http://fluidsurveys.com/university/survey-priming-question-order-giving-survey-bias/
[59] Pew Research Center Staff. (n.d.). Frequently asked questions. *Pew Research Center*. Retrieved from http://www.pewresearch.org/methodology/u-s-survey-research/frequently-asked-questions/
[60] Sigelman, L. (1981). Question-Order Effects on Presidential Popularity. *Public Opinion Quarterly*, Vol. 45 199-207. Retrieved from http://citeseerx.ist.psu.edu/viewdoc/download?doi=10.1.1.841.9142&rep=rep1&type=pdf
[61] Sexton, R. (2010, April 8). Election 2010: Tackling the Shy Tory problem. *The Guardian*. Retrieved from https://www.theguardian.com/commentisfree/2010/apr/08/general-election-2010-polls
[62] Biegelsen, A. (2008, January 9). Obama's Wilder Lesson. *Style Weekly*. Retrieved from https://web.archive.org/web/20081007113727/http:/www.styleweekly.com/article.asp?idarticle=16054
[63] Khachigian, K. (2008, November 2). Don't Blame the Bradley Effect. *The Washington Post*. Retrieved from http://www.washingtonpost.com/wp-dyn/content/article/2008/10/30/AR2008103002396.html
[64] Tarrance, Jr., V. L. (2008, October 13). The Bradley Effect - Selective Memory. *RealClearPolitics*. Retrieved from https://www.realclearpolitics.com/articles/2008/10/the_bradley_effect_selective_m.html
[65] The Associated Press. (2008, November 7). Poll Data Doesn't Reflect Bradley Effect. *CBS News*. Retrieved from http://www.cbsnews.com/news/poll-data-doesnt-reflect-bradley-effect/
[66] Mount, H. (2004, November 4). Republicans shyly make their presence felt. *The Telegraph UK*. Retrieved from http://www.telegraph.co.uk/comment/personal-view/3612634/Republicans-shyly-make-their-presence-felt.html
[67] Sturgis, P., Baker, N., Callegaro, M., Fisher, S., Green, J., Jennings, W., Kuha, J., Lauderdale, B., & Smith, P. (2016, March). Report of the Inquiry into the 2015 British general election opinion polls, pg 70. *Market Research Society and British Polling Council*. Retrieved from http://eprints.ncrm.ac.uk/3789/1/Report_final_revised.pdf.
[68] Sexton, R. (2010, April 8). Election 2010: Tackling the Shy Tory problem. *The Guardian*. Retrieved from https://www.theguardian.com/commentisfree/2010/apr/08/general-election-2010-polls
[69] Sturgis, P., Baker, N., Callegaro, M., Fisher, S., Green, J., Jennings, W., Kuha, J., Lauderdale, B., & Smith, P. (2016, March). Report of the Inquiry into the 2015 British general election opinion polls, pg 70. *Market Research Society and British Polling Council*. Retrieved from

http://eprints.ncrm.ac.uk/3789/1/Report_final_revised.pdf

Chapter 3

[1] AllPsych Staff. (n.d.). Dr. Christopher L. Heffner. *AllPsych Network*. Retrieved from https://allpsych.com/about/drheffner/
[2] Heffner, C. (2017). Research Methods Chapter 8.6 The Correlation. *AllPsych Network*. Retrieved from https://allpsych.com/researchmethods/correlation/
[3] Suarez, M. (n.d.). Causal Inference in Quantum Mechanics: A Reassessment. *University of Pittsburgh Philosophy of Science Archive*. Retrieved from http://philsci-archive.pitt.edu/3229/1/SuarezCausalInference.pdf
[4] Ratner, B. (n.d.). The Correlation Coefficient: Definition. *DM STAT-1*. Retrieved from http://www.dmstat1.com/res/TheCorrelationCoefficientDefined.html
[5] *Ibid*
[6] Lavrakas, P. (2008). Encyclopedia of Survey Research Methods, Priming. *Sage Research Methods*. Retrieved from http://methods.sagepub.com/reference/encyclopedia-of-survey-research-methods/n399.xml
[7] Weiner, M. (2015). A Natural Experiment: Inadvertent Priming of Party Identification in a Split-Sample Survey. *Survey Practice*, Vol. 8, No. 6. Retrieved from http://www.surveypractice.org/index.php/SurveyPractice/article/view/312/html_47#fn1
[8] History.com Staff. (2009). Watergate Scandal. *History.com*. Retrieved from http://www.history.com/topics/watergate
[9] History.com Staff. (2009). Nixon resigns. *History.com*. Retrieved from http://www.history.com/this-day-in-history/nixon-resigns
[10] Vannette, D. (2015, June 17). Biased Data Are Bad Data: How to Think About Question Order. *Qualtrics*. Retrieved from https://www.qualtrics.com/blog/biased-data-is-bad-data-how-to-think-about-question-order/
[11] Eveland, V., & Sekely, W. (2001) Effect Of Response Position And Number Of Responses On Response Selection. *University of West Georgia*. Retrieved from http://www.westga.edu/~bquest/2001/response.htm
[12] *Ibid*
[13] Ansolabehere, S., & Schaffner, B. (2013). Distractions, pg 2. *University of Massachusetts*. Retrieved from http://people.umass.edu/schaffne/distractions_FinalDraft.pdf
[14] *Ibid*, pg 7
[15] *Ibid*
[16] *Ibid*
[17] *Ibid*, pg 22
[18] *Ibid*
[19] *Ibid*
[20] Craven, J. (2016, November 7). Here's What Could Happen If Donald Trump Doesn't Accept The Election Results. *Huffington Post*. Retrieved from http://www.huffingtonpost.com/entry/donald-trump-accept-election-results_us_582094f8e4b0aac6248591c7
[21] Schow, A. (2016, November 28). The Left's Miraculous Change of Heart on

Accepting Election Results. *Observer*. Retrieved from http://observer.com/2016/11/the-lefts-miraculous-change-of-heart-on-accepting-election-results/
[22] Ansolabehere, S., & Schaffner, B. (2013). Distractions. *University of Massachusetts*. Retrieved from http://people.umass.edu/schaffne/distractions_FinalDraft.pdf
[23] Cornell Law School. (n.d.). Leading question. *Cornell Law School Legal Information Institute*. Retrieved from https://www.law.cornell.edu/wex/leading_question
[24] Cornell Law School. (n.d.). Rule 611. Mode and Order of Examining Witnesses and Presenting Evidence. *Cornell Law School Legal Information Institute*. Retrieved from https://www.law.cornell.edu/rules/fre/rule_611
[25] Di Bella, J. (2009, June 11). The Effects of Leading Questions. *JeffBoulton.ca*. Retrieved from http://www.jeffboulton.ca/mdm_project/03.pdf
[26] Jensen, T. (2017, July 18). Health Care a Mine Field for Republicans; Many Trump Voters in Denial on Russia. *Public Policy Polling*. Retrieved from http://www.publicpolicypolling.com/pdf/2017/PPP_Release_National_71817.pdf
[27] British English Online Staff. (2016). British English vs American English. *British English Online*. Retrieved from http://www.britishenglishonline.com/british-english-vs-american-english/british-english-vs-american-english/
[28] MacMillian Dictionary Staff. (n.d.). Pissed - Definitions and Synonyms. *MacMillian Dictionary*. Retrieved from http://www.macmillandictionary.com/us/dictionary/american/pissed
[29] American Psychological Association Staff. (2018). Violence. *American Psychological Association*. Retrieved from http://www.apa.org/topics/violence/
[30] Barrett, L. F. (2017, July 14). When is Speech Violence?. *New York Times*. Retrieved from https://www.nytimes.com/2017/07/14/opinion/sunday/when-is-speech-violence.html
[31] Cambridge Advanced Learner's Dictionary & Thesaurus Staff. (n.d.). Violence. *Cambridge University*. Retrieved from http://dictionary.cambridge.org/dictionary/english/violence
[32] Gramlich, J. (2017, February 21). 5 facts about crime in the U.S. *Pew Research Center*. Retrieved from http://www.pewresearch.org/fact-tank/2017/02/21/5-facts-about-crime-in-the-u-s/
[33] CQ Press. (2012). Guide to U.S. Foreign Policy: A Diplomatic History, Page 628. *Sage Publications*. Retrieved from https://books.google.com/books?id=Udd1AwAAQBAJ&pg=PA628&lpg=PA628&dq=%22I+pledge+to+you+that+we+shall+have+an+honorable+end+to+the+war+in+Vietnam.%22&source=bl&ots=6vZ4kkAywO&sig=vAZbD-iUphFavkp_g8stvlB65o8&hl=en&sa=X&ved=0ahUKEwjQjp60srTVAhUj6oMKHYi8DKkQ6AEIUDAI#v=onepage&q=%22I%20pledge%20to%20you%20that%20we%20shall%20have%20an%20honorable%20end%20to%20the%20war%20in%20Vietnam.%22&f=false

[34] Jensen, T. (2017, July 18). Health Care a Mine Field for Republicans; Many Trump Voters in Denial on Russia. *Public Policy Polling*. Retrieved from http://www.publicpolicypolling.com/pdf/2017/PPP_Release_National_71817.pdf
[35] Lin, J., Quan, D., Sinha, V., Bakshi, K., Huynh, D., Katz, B., & Karger, D. (2003, September). What Makes a Good Answer? The Role of Context in Question Answering. *MIT AI Laboratory*. Retrieved from https://groups.csail.mit.edu/infolab/publications/Lin-etal-INTERACT03.pdf
[36] Insights Association Staff. (2016, September 12). "Push polls" - Deceptive Advocacy/Persuasion Under the Guise of Legitimate Polling. *Insights Association*. Retrieved from http://www.insightsassociation.org/issues-policies/best-practice/push-polls-deceptive-advocacypersuasion-under-guise-legitimate-polling
[37] AAPOR Staff. (June 2007/October 2015). AAPOR Statements on "Push" Polls. *American Association for Public Opinion Research*. Retrieved from http://www.aapor.org/Standards-Ethics/Resources/AAPOR-Statements-on-Push-Polls.aspx
[38] Obeidallah, D. (2014, November 7). We've Been on the Wrong Track Since 1972. *Daily Beast*. Retrieved from http://www.thedailybeast.com/weve-been-on-the-wrong-track-since-1972
[39] Gallup Organization Staff. (2018, August 12). Satisfaction With the United States. *Gallup Organization*. Retrieved from http://www.gallup.com/poll/1669/general-mood-country.aspx
[40] McLeod, S. (2008). Likert Scale. *SimplyPsychology*. Retrieved from https://www.simplypsychology.org/likert-scale.html
[41] Changing Minds Staff. (n.d.). Likert Scale. *ChangingMinds.org*. Retrieved from http://changingminds.org/explanations/research/measurement/likert_scale.htm
[42] Tsand, K. K. (2012). The use of midpoint on Likert Scale: The implications for educational research. *Hong Kong Teachers' Centre Journal*, Vol. 11. Retrieved from http://edb.org.hk/HKTC/download/journal/j11/HKTCJv11_11-B02.pdf
[43] Bertram, D. (n.d.). Likert Scales. *University of Belgrade*. Retrieved from http://poincare.matf.bg.ac.rs/~kristina/topic-dane-likert.pdf
[44] Tsand, K. K. (2012). The use of midpoint on Likert Scale: The implications for educational research. *Hong Kong Teachers' Centre Journal*, Vol. 11. Retrieved from http://edb.org.hk/HKTC/download/journal/j11/HKTCJv11_11-B02.pdf
[45] Grimm, P. (2010, December 15). Social Desirability Bias. *Wiley International Encyclopedia of Marketing*. Retrieved from http://onlinelibrary.wiley.com/doi/10.1002/9781444316568.wiem02057/abstract;jsessionid=B943E329A303A0ACCB16CB292D18A8B7.f01t01
[46] Brown, J. D. (2000). What issues affect Likert-scale questionnaire formats? *JALT Testing & Evaluation SIG Newsletter*, Vol. 4, No. 1, 27-30. Retrieved from http://hosted.jalt.org/test/PDF/Brown7.pdf

[47] Wogan, T. (2015, May 26). Do atoms going through a double slit 'know' if they are being observed? *Physics World*. Retrieved from http://physicsworld.com/cws/article/news/2015/may/26/do-atoms-going-through-a-double-slit-know-if-they-are-being-observed

Chapter 4

[1] Crichton, M. (2002, April 26). Why Speculate? *International Leadership Forum*. Retrieved from http://web.archive.org/web/20081225081603/http:/www.crichton-official.com:80/speech-whyspeculate.html
[2] Ballotpedia Contributors. (n.d.) Georgia's 6th Congressional District. *Ballotpedia*. Retrieved from https://ballotpedia.org/Georgia%27s_6th_Congressional_District
[3] *Ibid*
[4] Bluestein, G. (2017, June 19). Spending in Georgia Sixth race pushes past $50 million. *Atlanta Journal-Constitution*. Retrieved from http://politics.blog.ajc.com/2017/06/19/the-race-for-georgias-6th-district-now-costs-more-than-50m/
[5] Ballotpedia Contributors. (n.d.) Georgia's 6th Congressional District special election, 2017. *Ballotpedia*. Retrieved from https://ballotpedia.org/Georgia%27s_6th_Congressional_District_special_election,_2017
[6] Ballotpedia Contributors. (n.d.) Georgia's 6th Congressional District special election, 2017/Polls. *Ballotpedia*. Retrieved from https://ballotpedia.org/Georgia%27s_6th_Congressional_District_special_election,_2017/Polls
[7] Beckel, M. (2017, June 16). The money behind the most expensive U.S. House race in history. *IssueOne*. Retrieved from https://www.issueone.org/money-behind-expensive-u-s-house-race-history/
[8] CBS News. (2017, July 29). Results Show Kid Rock Has A Chance In U.S. Senate Race. *CBS News Detroit*. Retrieved from http://detroit.cbslocal.com/2017/07/29/results-show-kid-rock-has-a-chance-in-u-s-senate-race/
[9] Breiner, A. (2017, August 1). Kid Rock polling as top Republican for Michigan Senate seat. *Tribune News Service*. Retrieved from https://www.thestar.com/news/world/2017/08/01/kid-rock-polling-as-top-republican-for-michigan-senate-seat.html
[10] RealClearPolitics Staff. (2017). Michigan Senate - Kid Rock vs. Stabenow. *RealClearPolitics Polls*. Retrieved from https://realclearpolitics.com/epolls/2018/senate/mi/michigan_senate_kid_rock_vs_stabenow-6214.html
[11] Abadi, M. (2017, August 2). Mark Zuckerberg has hired a Democratic pollster. *Business Insider*. Retrieved from http://www.businessinsider.com/is-mark-zuckerberg-running-for-president-in-2020-pollster-2017-8
[12] Krishna, S. (2017, August 3). Zuckerberg hires Clinton pollster, totally not running for president. *Engadget*. Retrieved from https://www.engadget.com/2017/08/0

3/zuckerberg-hires-democratic-pollster/

[13] Martosko, D. (2017, August 2). Could Democrats get Congress back in 2018? New poll shows them ahead by 7 points after Obamacare repeal failure and week of White House chaos. *Daily Mail*. Retrieved from http://www.dailymail.co.uk/news/article-4754088/Democrats-lead-congressional-poll-retake-House.html

[14] Monmouth University. (2017, November 6). Two Point Race For Governor. *Monmouth University Polling Institute*. Retrieved from https://www.monmouth.edu/polling-institute/reports/MonmouthPoll_VA_110617/

[15] Blanton, D. (2017, November 6). Fox News Poll: Race for Virginia governor remains tight. *Fox News*. Retrieved from http://www.foxnews.com/politics/2017/11/06/fox-news-poll-race-for-virginia-governor-remains-tight.html

[16] Virginia Quantitative Research. (2017, November 6). DAILY TRACKING TOPLINES: Nov 2-5, 2017. *the polling company, inc*. Retrieved from https://www.realclearpolitics.com/docs/VA_TPC_Topline_Nov_2-5.pdf

[17] Hall, P. (2017, November 5). Emerson College Poll: VA Governor's Race Tightens as Northam Leads Gillespie by Three Points. Voters Oppose "Sanctuary Cities," Majority are Pro-Choice. *Emerson College*. Retrieved from https://gallery.mailchimp.com/5d83bc45f4839ff4fb96bb8b8/files/be0b846e-c534-43b3-8be7-ec4cb7d2fb08/ECPS__VA_Press_release.pdf

[18] Brown, P. A., & Rubenstein, P. S. (2017, November 6). Democrat Has 9-Point Likely Voter Lead In Virginia, Quinnipiac University Poll Finds; Big Gender And Racial Gaps. *Quinnipiac University*. Retrieved from https://poll.qu.edu/virginia/release-detail?ReleaseID=2497

[19] Rasmussen Reports Staff. (2017, November 3). Election 2017: Virginia Governor. *Rasmussen Reports*. Retrieved from http://www.rasmussenreports.com/public_content/politics/elections/election_2017/virginia/election_2017_virginia_governor

[20] Kidd, Q., & Bitecofer, R. (2017, November 6). Northam holds 6-point lead over Gillespie, 51%-45%, as independents and moderates break for Democrat. *The Judy Ford Wason Center for Public Policy*. Retrieved from http://wasoncenter.cnu.edu/wp-content/uploads/2017/11/Nov-6-Report-Final-1.pdf

[21] Trafalgar Group. (2017, November 3). Virginia Governor Survey Conducted 10/31/17-11/02/17. *The Trafalgar Group*. Retrieved from https://www.realclearpolitics.com/docs/Trafalgar_VA_Gov_11-4-17.pdf

[22] The New York Times Upshot/Siena College Poll. (2017, November 3). The New York Times Upshot/Siena College Poll Oct 29-Nov 2, 2017. *Siena College*. Retrieved from https://www.siena.edu/assets/files/news/VA1117_Crosstabs.pdf

[23] Gravis Marketing. (2017). Crosstabs. *Gravis*. Retrieved from https://www.realclearpolitics.com/docs/Gravis_VA_Gov_2017.pdf

[24] Virginia Quantitative Research. (2017, November 3). DAILY TRACKING TOPLINES: Oct 30 - Nov 2, 2017. *the polling company, inc*. Retrieved from https://www.realclearpolitics.com/docs/VA_TPC_Topline_Oct_30-Nov_2.pdf
[25] Wilson, H. (2017, November 3). RC Poll: Northam and Gillespie deadlocked; Lieutenant Governor and Attorney General races also tied. *Roanoke College*. Retrieved from https://www.roanoke.edu/about/news/rc_poll_politics_nov_2017
[26] Gatlin, G. (2017, November 2). Suffolk Poll of Virginia Governor's Race Shows Democrat Northam with an Edge over Republican Gillespie, 47 Percent to 43 Percent. *Suffolk University*. Retrieved from http://www.suffolk.edu/academics/10740.php
[27] Virginia Department of Elections (2017, November 17). 2017 November General. *Virginia Department of Elections*. Retrieved from http://results.elections.virginia.gov/vaelections/2017 November General/Site/Statewide.html
[28] Brown, P. A., & Rubenstein, P. S. (2017, November 6). Democrat Has 9-Point Likely Voter Lead In Virginia, Quinnipiac University Poll Finds; Big Gender And Racial Gaps. *Quinnipiac University*. Retrieved from https://poll.qu.edu/virginia/release-detail?ReleaseID=2497
[29] Kidd, Q., & Bitecofer, R. (2017, November 6). Northam holds 6-point lead over Gillespie, 51%-45%, as independents and moderates break for Democrat. *The Judy Ford Wason Center for Public Policy*. Retrieved from http://wasoncenter.cnu.edu/wp-content/uploads/2017/11/Nov-6-Report-Final-1.pdf
[30] Blanton, D. (2017, December 11). Fox News Poll: Enthused Democrats give Jones lead over Moore in Alabama. *Fox News*. Retrieved from http://www.foxnews.com/politics/2017/12/11/fox-news-poll-enthused-democrats-give-jones-lead-over-moore-in-alabama.print.html
[31] Hall, P. (2017, December 11). Emerson College Poll: Moore with Significant 9-point Lead in Final Poll. *Emerson College*. Retrieved from https://www.realclearpolitics.com/docs/Emerson_College_Alabama_Dec_11.pdf
[32] Murray, P. (2017, December 11). Alabama: Turnout Big Question in Senate Race. *Monmouth University Poll*. Retrieved from https://www.monmouth.edu/polling-institute/reports/MonmouthPoll_AL_121117/
[33] Trafalgar Group. (2017, December 8). Alabama US Senate Special Election Conducted 12/6-7/17. *The Trafalgar Group*. Retrieved from https://www.realclearpolitics.com/docs/Trafalgar_Group_Alabama_Senate_Dec_9th.pdf
[34] Kaplan, D. (2017, December 9). Alabama Polling. *Gravis Marketing*. Retrieved from https://www.realclearpolitics.com/docs/Gravis_Alabama_Dec_9th.pdf
[35] Journey, R. (2017, December 5). EXCLUSIVE: Roy Moore's lead over Doug Jones increases in new poll. *WBRC Fox 6 News*. Retrieved from http://www.wbrc.com/story/37000237/exclusive-roy-moores-lead-over-doug-jones-increases-in-new-poll

[36] Gravis Marketing. (2017, December 5). Alabama Senate. *Gravis Marketing*. Retrieved from https://www.realclearpolitics.com/docs/Gravis_Alabama_Senate_Dec_5th_2017.pdf
[37] Seattle Office of Labor Standards. (2015). Seattle's Minimum Wage. *City of Seattle*. Retrieved from http://www.seattle.gov/Documents/Departments/LaborStandards/OLS-MW-multiyearChart.pdf
[38] Jardim, E., Long, M., Plotnick, R., van Inwegen, E., Vigdor, J., & Wething, H. (2017, June/October[rev]). Minimum Wage Increases, Wages, and Low-Wage Employment: Evidence from Seattle. *National Bureau of Economic Research (NBER)*. Retrieved from http://www.nber.org/papers/w23532
[39] Thompson, L., & Martinez, A. (2014, June 2). Seattle City Council approves historic $15 minimum wage. *Seattle Times*. Retrieved from http://www.seattletimes.com/seattle-news/seattle-city-council-approves-historic-15-minimum-wage/
[40] *Ibid*
[41] Person, D. (2017, June 26). The City Knew the Bad Minimum Wage Report Was Coming Out, So It Called Up Berkeley. *Seattle Weekly*. Retrieved from http://www.seattleweekly.com/news/seattle-is-getting-an-object-lesson-in-weaponized-data/
[42] McMorris, B. (2017, July 31). Union PR Firm, Seattle Mayor Coordinated on Pro-$15 Minimum Wage Berkeley Study. *Washington Free Beacon*. Retrieved from http://freebeacon.com/issues/union-pr-firm-seattle-mayor-coordinated-pro-15-minimum-wage-berkeley-study/
[43] Sawant, K. (2016, September 20). Open Letter to Professor Jacob Vigdor, Evans School of Public Policy and Governance. *Seattle City Council*. Retrieved from https://www.documentcloud.org/documents/3111708-Councilmember-Sawant-Letter-to-Dr-Vigdor-Amended.html
[44] Silver, N. (2010, June 29). BREAKING: Daily Kos to Sue Research 2000 for Fraud. *FiveThirtyEight*. Retrieved from https://fivethirtyeight.com/features/breaking-daily-kos-to-sue-research-2000/
[45] Leek, J., & Peng, R. (2015) Opinion: Reproducible research can still be wrong: Adopting a prevention approach. *Proceedings of the National Academy of Sciences of the United States of America*, Vol 112, No. 6, 1645-1646. Retrieved from http://www.pnas.org/content/112/6/1645.full
[46] *Ibid*
[47] Trochim, W. M. K. (2006, October 20). Probability Sampling. *Web Center for Social Research Methods*. Retrieved from https://www.socialresearchmethods.net/kb/sampprob.php
[48] McGill University. (n.d.). Margin of Error. *McGill School of Computer Science*. Retrieved from https://www.cs.mcgill.ca/~rwest/wikispeedia/wpcd/wp/m/Margin_of_error.htm
[49] Mercer, A. (2016, September 8). 5 key things to know about the margin of error in election polls. *Pew Research Center*. Retrieved from http://www.pewresearch.org/fact-tank/2016/09/08/understanding-the-margin-of-error-in-election-polls/

[50] Smith, R. L. (2010). Determining the sample size. *University of North Carolina at Chapel Hill*. Retrieved from https://www.unc.edu/~rls/s151-2010/class23.pdf

[51] American Association for Public Opinion Research. (2017). Margin of Sampling Error/Credibility Interval. *American Association for Public Opinion Research*. Retrieved from http://www.aapor.org/Education-Resources/Election-Polling-Resources/Margin-of-Sampling-Error-Credibility-Interval.aspx

[52] Niles, R. (n.d.). Survey Sample Sizes and Margin of Error. *RobertNiles*. Retrieved from http://www.robertniles.com/stats/margin.shtml

[53] RealClearPolitics Staff. (2016, November 8). General Election: Trump vs. Clinton. *RealClearPolitics Polls*. Retrieved from https://www.realclearpolitics.com/epolls/2016/president/us/general_election_trump_vs_clinton-5491.html#polls

[54] Clinton, J., Hartig, H., Psyllos, S., & Lapinski, J. (2016, November 7). Poll: On Eve of Election Day, Clinton Maintains Her
Edge Over Trump. *NBC News*. Retrieved from https://www.nbcnews.com/storyline/data-points/poll-eve-election-day-clinton-maintains-her-edge-over-trump-n678816

[55] Hartig, H., Lapinski, J., & Psyllos, S. (2016, October 31). Poll: Clinton Maintains National Lead Over Trump Despite FBI Letter. *NBC News*. Retrieved from http://www.nbcnews.com/storyline/data-points/poll-clinton-maintains-national-lead-over-trump-despite-fbi-letter-n675771

[56] Hartig, H., Lapinski, J., & Psyllos, S. (2016, October 25). Poll: Republican Party Fractured as Hillary Clinton Maintains Solid Lead. *NBC News*. Retrieved from http://www.nbcnews.com/storyline/data-points/poll-republican-party-fractured-hillary-clinton-maintains-solid-lead-n672001

[57] Hartig, H., Lapinski, J., & Psyllos, S. (2016, October 18). Poll: Clinton Maintains Solid National Lead. *NBC News*. Retrieved from http://www.nbcnews.com/storyline/data-points/poll-clinton-maintains-solid-national-lead-n667751

[58] Hartig, H., Lapinski, J., & Psyllos, S. (2016, October 10). Poll: More Voters Say Trump Doesn't Respect Women After Lewd Tape Surfaces. *NBC News*. Retrieved from https://www.nbcnews.com/storyline/data-points/poll-more-voters-say-trump-doesn-t-respect-women-after-n663296

[59] Hartig, H., Lapinski, J., & Psyllos, S. (2016, October 4). Poll: Hillary Clinton Holds National Lead Over Donald Trump. *NBC News*. Retrieved from http://www.nbcnews.com/storyline/data-points/poll-hillary-clinton-holds-national-lead-over-donald-trump-n658721

[60] Hartig, H., Lapinski, J., & Psyllos, S. (2016, September 26). Poll: Clinton Leads Trump Among Likely Voters Ahead of First Debate. *NBC News*. Retrieved from https://www.nbcnews.com/storyline/data-points/poll-clinton-leads-trump-among-likely-voters-ahead-first-debate-n654531

[61] Hartig, H., Lapinski, J., & Psyllos, S. (2016, September 20). Hillary Clinton Regains Momentum Against Donald Trump: Poll. *NBC News*. Retrieved from http://www.nbcnews.com/storyline/data-points/hillary-clinton-regains-momentum-against-donald-trump-poll-n650926

[62] Hartig, H., Lapinski, J., & Psyllos, S. (2016, September 13). Poll: Clinton's Lead Narrows Among Independents, Voters Nationally. *NBC News*. Retrieved from http://www.nbcnews.com/politics/2016-election/poll-clinton-s-lead-narrows-among-independents-voters-nationally-n646911

[63] Hartig, H., Lapinski, J., & Psyllos, S. (2016, September 6). Clinton Holds Steady Against Trump as Campaign Enters Final Weeks: Poll. *NBC News*. Retrieved from http://www.nbcnews.com/politics/2016-election/clinton-holds-steady-against-trump-campaign-enters-final-weeks-poll-n642931

[64] Hartig, H., Lapinski, J., & Psyllos, S. (2016, August 30). Poll: Donald Trump Chips Away at Hillary Clinton's National Lead. *NBC News*. Retrieved from http://www.nbcnews.com/politics/2016-election/poll-donald-trump-chips-away-hillary-clinton-s-national-lead-n639591

[65] Hartig, H., Lapinski, J., & Psyllos, S. (2016, August 23). Trump Faces Hurdle With Minority Voters as Clinton Maintains Lead, Poll Shows. *NBC News*. Retrieved from http://www.nbcnews.com/politics/2016-election/trump-faces-hurdle-minority-voters-clinton-maintains-lead-poll-shows-n636061

[66] Hartig, H., Lapinski, J., & Psyllos, S. (2016, August 18). Poll: Clinton Maintains Big Lead as Voters Doubt Trump's Temperament. *NBC News*. Retrieved from http://www.nbcnews.com/politics/2016-election/poll-clinton-maintains-big-lead-voters-doubt-trump-s-temperament-n631351

[67] Hartig, H., Lapinski, J., & Psyllos, S. (2016, August 9). Poll: Clinton Opens Up Double-Digit Lead Over Trump. *NBC News*. Retrieved from http://www.nbcnews.com/politics/2016-election/poll-clinton-opens-double-digit-lead-over-trump-n625676

[68] Hartig, H., Lapinski, J., & Psyllos, S. (2016, August 2). Poll: Clinton Support Spikes Following Democratic Convention. *NBC News*. Retrieved from http://www.nbcnews.com/politics/2016-election/poll-clinton-support-spikes-following-democratic-convention-n621071

[69] Hartig, H., Lapinski, J., & Psyllos, S. (2016, July 26). Poll: No Post-Convention Bounce for Donald Trump. *NBC News*. Retrieved from http://www.nbcnews.com/politics/2016-election/poll-no-post-convention-bounce-donald-trump-n616426

[70] Huffington Post. (2016, July 18). 2016 General Election - Clinton 46%, Trump 45%. *Huffington Post*. Retrieved from http://elections.huffingtonpost.com/pollster/polls/nbc-surveymonkey-24929

[71] USC Dornsife Center for Economic and Social Research. (n.d.) Understanding America Study. *University of Southern California*. Retrieved from http://cesrusc.org/election/

[72] Smith, R. (2012, October 20). Big Oil Isn't as Profitable as Everyone Thinks. *AOL*. Retrieved from https://www.aol.com/2012/10/20/big-oil-isnt-as-profitable-as-everyone-thinks/

[73] American Petroleum Institute. (n.d.) Oil and Gas Industry Profit Margins Compared to All U.S. Industry Over the Last Five Years. *University of Texas*. Retrieved from http://www.beg.utexas.edu/energyecon/energy-inc/members/Course_Modules/Module_III_RM/API profit margins.pdf

[74] Biery, M. E. (2015, September 20). Oil, Gas Producers' Margins Sputter To 2%. *Forbes*. Retrieved from https://www.forbes.com/sites/sageworks/2015/09/20/oil-gas-producers-margins-sputter-to-2/#1813471717f3

[75] Ballotpedia Contributors. (n.d.) Georgia's 6th Congressional District. *Ballotpedia*. Retrieved from https://ballotpedia.org/Georgia%27s_6th_Congressional_District_special_election,_2017/Polls

[76] Breiner, A. (2017, August 1). Poll Shows Kid Rock as Republican Front-Runner, 8 Points Behind Stabenow. *Roll Call*. Retrieved from http://www.rollcall.com/news/politics/poll-shows-kid-rock-republican-front-runner-8-points-behind-stabenow

[77] Trafalgar Group. (2017, July 28). MI U.S. Senate Election Survey Conducted 7/25-27/17. *The Trafalgar Group*. Retrieved from https://drive.google.com/file/d/0B4lhKxf9pMitRFpUd3lHV21ZdGs/view

[78] RealClearPolitics Staff. (2017). Michigan Senate - Kid Rock vs. Stabenow. *RealClearPolitics Polls*. Retrieved from https://realclearpolitics.com/epolls/2018/senate/mi/michigan_senate_kid_rock_vs_stabenow-6214.html

[79] Hall, P. (2017, November 13). Emerson College Poll: Moore Leads Jones 55%-45% in Alabama Senate Race. Majority of Voters Not Shaken By Bombshell Moore Allegations. *Emerson College*. Retrieved from https://gallery.mailchimp.com/5d83bc45f4839ff4fb96bb8b8/files/993dd909-e98c-43f3-88e4-74f0deb686c7/ECP_PR_Alabama_11.13.pdf

[80] JMC Analytics and Polling. (2017, November 12). Alabama Senate Poll Results. *JMC Analytics*. Retrieved from http://winwithjmc.com/wp-content/uploads/2017/11/Alabama-Senate-Executive-Summary-General-Election-Poll-2.pdf

[81] Trafalgar Group. (2017, July 28). MI U.S. Senate Election Survey Conducted 7/25-27/17. *The Trafalgar Group*. Retrieved from https://drive.google.com/file/d/0B4lhKxf9pMitRFpUd3lHV21ZdGs/view

[82] Reed, L. (2012, October 3). If Incentives Matter, We Might Be in Trouble. *Foundation for Economic Education*. Retrieved from https://fee.org/articles/if-incentives-matter-we-might-be-in-trouble/

Chapter 5

[1] Sargent, G. (2017, May 1). Why did Trump win? New research by Democrats offers a worrisome answer. *The Washington Post*. Retrieved from https://www.washingtonpost.com/blogs/plum-line/wp/2017/05/01/why-did-

trump-win-new-research-by-democrats-offers-a-worrisome-answer/

[2] Merica, D. (2016, August 15). Clinton super PAC to temporarily stop airing ads some battleground states. *CNNPolitics*. Retrieved from http://www.cnn.com/2016/08/15/politics/hillary-clinton-super-pac-advertising/index.html

[3] Merriam-Webster Staff. (2017, December 6). Red Herring. *Merriam-Webster*. Retrieved from https://www.merriam-webster.com/dictionary/red herring

[4] Skelley, G. (2017, June 1). Just How Many Obama 2012 Trump 2016 Voters Were There? *University of Virginia Center for Politics*. Retrieved from http://www.centerforpolitics.org/crystalball/articles/just-how-many-obama-2012-trump-2016-voters-were-there/

[5] Olsen, H., Sides, J., Bowman, K. & Goldman, J. (2017, June 12). Voter Study Group 2016 Election VOTER Study Executive Summary. *The Democracy Fund*. Retrieved from https://www.voterstudygroup.org/reports/2016-elections/executive-summary

[6] *Ibid*

[7] Williams, R. (2014, August 26). Is There a Limit to the Friendships We Can Maintain? *Psychology Today*. Retrieved from https://www.psychologytoday.com/blog/wired-success/201408/is-there-limit-the-friendships-we-can-maintain

[8] Barth, D. (2015, September 4). 2015 Envelope Mandatory Messaging Test Preliminary Report. *U.S. Census Bureau*. Retrieved from https://www.census.gov/library/working-papers/2015/acs/2015_Barth_01.html

[9] U.S. Census Bureau Staff. (2017, March 16). American Community Survey (ACS) Mandatory vs. Voluntary Methods. *U.S. Census Bureau*. Retrieved from https://www.census.gov/programs-surveys/acs/methodology/mandatory-voluntary-methods.html

[10] Costa, K. (2012, May 15). The American Community Survey Is Under Attack. *Center for American Progress*. Retrieved from https://www.americanprogress.org/issues/general/news/2012/05/15/11567/the-american-community-survey-is-under-attack/

[11] Social Science Space Staff. (2015, March 3). American Community Survey Back in the Frying Pan. *Social Science Space*. Retrieved from https://www.socialsciencespace.com/2015/03/american-community-survey-back-in-the-frying-pan/

[12] Rampell, C. (2012, May 19). The Beginning of the End of the Census? *The New York Times*. Retrieved from http://www.nytimes.com/2012/05/20/sunday-review/the-debate-over-the-american-community-survey.html

[13] Tech Terms Staff. (2015, March 4). GIGO. *Tech Terms*. Retrieved from https://techterms.com/definition/gigo

[14] Bethlehem, J. (n.d.). Weighting Adjustment. *Applied Survey Methods*. Retrieved from http://www.applied-survey-methods.com/weight.html

[15] M., V. (2011, August 30). Weighting Data - A Few Cautions. *Research & Marketing Strategies, Inc*. Retrieved from https://rmsresults.com/2011/08/30/what-is-weighting-data-in-market-research-a-few-cautions/

[16] Bethlehem, J. (n.d.). Weighting Adjustment. *Applied Survey Methods*. Retrieved from http://www.applied-survey-methods.com/weight.html
[17] Young, R. & Johnson, D. (2012). To Weight or Not to Weight, That is the Question: Survey Weights and Multivariate Analysis. *American Association for Public Opinion Research*. Retrieved from http://www.aapor.org/AAPOR_Main/media/AnnualMeetingProceedings/2012/03_-Young-Johnson_A2_Weighting-paper_aapor-2012-ry.pdf
[18] Potter, F. J. (1990, May). Methods for Extreme Weights in Sample Surveys, pg 16. *University of North Carolina at Chapel Hill*. Retrieved from http://www.stat.ncsu.edu/information/library/mimeo.archive/ISMS_1990_1875T.pdf
[19] Fotini, T., Evangelia, V., & Michail, V. (2013, November). Weighting of responses in the Consumer Survey: Alternative approaches – Effects on variance and tracking performance of the Consumer Confidence Indicator. *Foundation for Economic and Industrial Research*. Retrieved from http://ec.europa.eu/economy_finance/db_indicators/surveys/documents/workshops/2013/el-iobe_m._vassileiadis_-_thematic_group_on_weighting_approaches_(cs)_-_paper_(iobe-el).pdf
[20] U.S. Census Bureau Staff. (2014, January). American Community Survey Design and Methodology. *U.S. Census Bureau*. Retrieved from https://www2.census.gov/programs-surveys/acs/methodology/design_and_methodology/acs_design_methodology_ch11_2014.pdf
[21] Researchscape Staff. (2016, September 20). Weighting Survey Results. *Researchscape*. Retrieved from http://www.researchscape.com/blog/weighting-survey-results
[22] Humes, K. R., Jones, N. A., & Ramirez, R. R. (2011, March). Overview of Race and Hispanic Origin: 2010. *U.S. Census Bureau*. Retrieved from https://www.census.gov/prod/cen2010/briefs/c2010br-02.pdf
[23] Izrael, D. (n.d.). Raking Survey Data (a.k.a. Sample Balancing). *Abt Associates*. Retrieved from http://www.abtassociates.com/Expertise/Surveys-and-Data-Collection/Raking-Survey-Data-(a-k-a--Sample-Balancing).aspx
[24] IBM Staff. (n.d.). The Floppy Disk. *IBM*. Retrieved from http://www-03.ibm.com/ibm/history/ibm100/us/en/icons/floppy/breakthroughs/
[25] Marr, B. (2015, September 30). Big Data: 20 Mind-Boggling Facts Everyone Must Read. *Forbes*. Retrieved from https://www.forbes.com/sites/bernardmarr/2015/09/30/big-data-20-mind-boggling-facts-everyone-must-read/#2dd23f9a17b1
[26] Dragland, Å. (2013, May 22). Big Data, for better or worse: 90% of world's data generated over last two years. *ScienceDaily*. Retrieved from https://www.sciencedaily.com/releases/2013/05/130522085217.htm
[27] Loechner, J. (2016, December 22). 90% Of Today's Data Created In Two Years. *Center for Media Research*. Retrieved from https://www.mediapost.com/publications/article/291358/90-of-todays-data-created-in-two-years.html
[28] Walker, B. (2015, April 5). Every Day Big Data Statistics - 2.5 Quintillion Bytes of Data Created Daily. *Voucherland*.

Retrieved from http://www.vcloudnews.com/every-day-big-data-statistics-2-5-quintillion-bytes-of-data-created-daily/

[29] Turner, V. (2014, April). The Digital Universe of Opportunities: Rich Data and the Increasing Value of the Internet of Things. *IDC*. Retrieved from https://www.emc.com/leadership/digital-universe/2014iview/executive-summary.htm

[30] Walker, B. (2015, April 5). Every Day Big Data Statistics - 2.5 Quintillion Bytes of Data Created Daily. *Voucherland*. Retrieved from http://www.vcloudnews.com/every-day-big-data-statistics-2-5-quintillion-bytes-of-data-created-daily/

[31] Cisco Visual Networking Index: Global Mobile Data Traffic Forecast Update, 2016–2021 White Paper. *Cisco*. Retrieved from https://www.cisco.com/c/en/us/solutions/collateral/service-provider/visual-networking-index-vni/mobile-white-paper-c11-520862.html

[32] Vincent, J. (2016, August 24). Does Facebook think you're liberal or conservative? Here's how to find out. *The Verge*. Retrieved from https://www.theverge.com/circuitbreaker/2016/8/24/12621784/facebook-political-preferences-ads

[33] Bellis, M. (2017, March 26). The Invention of Radio. *ThoughtCo*. Retrieved from https://www.thoughtco.com/invention-of-radio-1992382

[34] Apicella, C. L., Marlowe, F. W., Fowler, J. H., & Christakis, N. A. (2012, January 26). Social networks and cooperation in hunter-gatherers. *Nature*, 481, 497-501. Retrieved from http://www.nature.com/nature/journal/v481/n7382/full/nature10736.html?foxtrotcallback=true

[35] *Ibid*

[36] Falcone, R. (n.d.). In machines we trust? *Institute of Cognitive Sciences and Technologies*. Retrieved from http://www.istc.cnr.it/question/machines-we-trust

[37] Ashby, N. (2006, July 18). Relativistic Effects in the Global Positioning System. *American Association of Physics Teachers*. Retrieved from https://www.aapt.org/doorway/TGRU/articles/Ashbyarticle.pdf

[38] Kondik, K. (2017, April 26). Center for Politics Poll Takes Temperature of Trump Voter at 100-Day Mark. *UVA Today*. Retrieved from https://news.virginia.edu/content/center-politics-poll-takes-temperature-trump-voters-100-day-mark

[39] Cisco Staff. (2017, February 7/March 28). Cisco Visual Networking Index: Global Mobile Data Traffic Forecast Update, 2016–2021 White Paper. *Cisco*. Retrieved from https://www.cisco.com/c/en/us/solutions/collateral/service-provider/visual-networking-index-vni/mobile-white-paper-c11-520862.html

Chapter 6

[1] Facebook Staff. (2017). How does Facebook suggest tags? *Facebook*. Retrieved from https://www.facebook.com/help/122175507864081

[2] Singh, A., Patil, D., Reddy, G. M., & Omkar, S. N. (2017, August 30). Disguised Face Identification (DFI) with Facial KeyPoints using

Spatial Fusion Convolutional Network. *arXiv*. Retrieved from https://arxiv.org/pdf/1708.09317.pdf
[3] American Heritage Dictionary of the English Language, Fifth Edition. (2016). Hashtag. *The Free Dictionary*. Retrieved from http://www.thefreedictionary.com/hashtag
[4] Fox News Staff. (2011, September 15). Obama Campaign's 'Attack Watch' Becomes Victim of Conservative Mockery. *Fox News*. Retrieved from http://www.foxnews.com/politics/2011/09/15/attack-watch-becomes-victim-conservative-mockery.html
[5] O'Rourke, S. (2018, May 29). Are you addicted to social media? *RTE Radio 1*. Retrieved from https://radio.rte.ie/radio1highlights/social-media-addiction-sean-orourke/
[6] Falcone, R. (n.d.). In machines we trust? *Institute of Cognitive Sciences and Technologies*. Retrieved from http://www.istc.cnr.it/question/machines-we-trust
[7] Sidner, C., Lee, C., & Lesh, N. (2017, September 8). The Role of Dialogue in Human Robot Interaction. *Researchgate*. Retrieved from https://www.researchgate.net/publication/228752181_The_Role_of_Dialogue_in_Human_Robot_Interaction
[8] Scott, T. M. (n.d.). The Observer in Modern Physics. *National Aeronautics and Space Administration - Glenn Research Center*. Retrieved from https://www.grc.nasa.gov/WWW/K-12/Numbers/Math/Mathematical_Thinking/observer.htm
[9] The Economist Staff. (2006, May 20). Herbert Simon. *The Economist*. Retrieved from http://www.economist.com/node/13350892
[10] Business Dictionary Staff. (n.d.). Satisficing. *Business Dictionary*. Retrieved from http://www.businessdictionary.com/definition/satisficing.html
[11] CityDictionary Staff. (n.d.). CityDictionary - The Dictionary with Local Flavor. *CityDictionary*. Retrieved from http://www.citydictionary.com/
[12] Vaux, B. (2007, July 30). What is the distinction between dinner and supper? *Harvard Dialect Survey*. Retrieved from http://dialect.redlog.net/staticmaps/q_96.html
[13] Vaux, B. (2007, July 30). What is your *general* term for a big road that you drive relatively fast on? *Harvard Dialect Survey*. Retrieved from http://dialect.redlog.net/staticmaps/q_79.html
[14] Vaux, B. (2007, July 30). What is 'the City'? *Harvard Dialect Survey*. Retrieved from http://dialect.redlog.net/staticmaps/q_95.html
[15] Vaux, B. (2007, July 30). What is your *general* term for the rubber-soled shoes worn in gym class, for athletic activities, etc.? *Harvard Dialect Survey*. Retrieved from http://dialect.redlog.net/staticmaps/q_73.html
[16] Vaux, B. (2007, July 30). What do you call an easy course? *Harvard Dialect Survey*. Retrieved from http://dialect.redlog.net/staticmaps/q_83.html
[17] Carbon, S. B. (2012, January 6). An Updated Definition of Rape. *U.S. Department of Justice, Office on*

Violence Against Women. Retrieved from https://www.justice.gov/archives/opa/blog/updated-definition-rape
[18] Truman, J. L., & Morgan, R. E. (2016, October). Criminal Victimization, 2015. *U.S. Department of Justice, Bureau of Justice Statistics*. Retrieved from https://www.bjs.gov/content/pub/pdf/cv15.pdf
[19] Pew Research Center Staff. (n.d.). Questionnaire design. *Pew Research Center*. Retrieved from http://www.pewresearch.org/methodology/u-s-survey-research/questionnaire-design/
[20] Singer, E. (2004). Risk, Benefit, and Informed Consent in Survey Research. *Survey Research*, Vol. 35, No 2-3, 1-23. Retrieved from http://www.srl.uic.edu/Publist/Newsletter/2004/04v35n2-3.pdf
[21] Sterling, G. (2015, June 2). Survey: 99 Percent Of Consumers Will Share Personal Info For Rewards, But Want Brands To Ask Permission. *MarketingLand*. Retrieved from https://marketingland.com/survey-99-percent-of-consumers-will-share-personal-info-for-rewards-also-want-brands-to-ask-permission-130786
[22] Berry, S. H., Pevar, J. S., & Zander-Cotugno, M. (2010). The Use of Incentives in Surveys Supported by Federal Grants. *Council of Professional Associations on Federal Statistics*. Retrieved from http://www.copafs.org/seminars/use_of_incentives_in_surveys.aspx
[23] McLeod, S. (2015). Skinner - Operating Conditioning. *Simply Psychology*. Retrieved from https://simplypsychology.org/operant-conditioning.html
[24] NSSE Staff. (2014, October 21). Survey Incentive FAQ. *National Survey of Student Engagement*. Retrieved from http://nsse.indiana.edu/pdf/NSSE Survey Incentive FAQ.pdf
[25] Berry, S. H., Pevar, J. S., & Zander-Cotugno, M. (2010). The Use of Incentives in Surveys Supported by Federal Grants. *Council of Professional Associations on Federal Statistics*. Retrieved from http://www.copafs.org/seminars/use_of_incentives_in_surveys.aspx
[26] Lavrakas, P. J. (2010). Use of Incentives – Who, What, Where, When, Why, and How? *Council of Professional Associations on Federal Statistics*. Retrieved from http://www.copafs.org/seminars/use_of_incentives_five_questions.aspx
[27] NSSE Staff. (2014, October 21). Survey Incentive FAQ. *National Survey of Student Engagement*. Retrieved from http://nsse.indiana.edu/pdf/NSSE Survey Incentive FAQ.pdf
[28] Shore, L. M., Tetrick, L. E., Lynch, P., & Barksdale, K. (2006). Social and Economic Exchange: Construct Development and Validation. *Journal of Applied Social Psychology*, Vol. 36, No. 4, 837-867. Retrieved from https://www.researchgate.net/profile/Lynn_Shore/publication/227537354_Social_and_Economic_Exchange_Construct_Development_and_Validation/links/5a20d37d4585158865c519e2/Social-and-Economic-Exchange-Construct-Development-and-Validation.pdf
[29] Keusch, F., Batinic, B., & Mayerhofer, W. (2014, April). Motives for joining nonprobability online panels and their association with survey participation behavior, in: *Online Panel Research: A*

Data Quality Perspective (eds M. Callegaro, R. Baker, J. Bethlehem, A. S. Göritz, J. A. Krosnick and P. J. Lavrakas). Retrieved from http://onlinelibrary.wiley.com/doi/10.1002/9781118763520.ch8/summary

[30] Baradoy, L. (2015, May 8). 5 Survey Incentive Metrics for Getting Actionable Insights and Improving Response Rates. *Qualtrics*. Retrieved from https://www.qualtrics.com/blog/5-survey-incentive-metrics-for-getting-actionable-insights-and-improving-response-rates-2/

[31] Almuhimedi, H., Schaub, F., Sadeh, N., Adjerid, I., Acquisti, A., Gluck, J., Cranor, L., & Agarwal, Y. (2015, April 18). Your Location has been Shared 5,398 Times! A Field Study on Mobile App Privacy Nudging. *NormSadeh.com*. Retrieved from http://www.normsadeh.com/file_download/179

[32] Anderson, M. (2016, January 29). More Americans using smartphones for getting directions, streaming TV. *Pew Research Center*. Retrieved from http://www.pewresearch.org/fact-tank/2016/01/29/us-smartphone-use/

[33] Kaplan, D. (2016, April 22). Overwhelming Number Of Smartphone Users Keep Location Services Open. *GeoMarketing*. Retrieved from http://www.geomarketing.com/overwhelming-number-of-smartphone-users-keep-location-services-open

[34] SHRM Online Staff. (2011, September 6). Survey: Noncash Rewards Boost Performance and Morale. *Society for Human Resource Management (SHRM)*. Retrieved from https://www.shrm.org/ResourcesAndTools/hr-topics/benefits/Pages/NoncashRewards.aspx

[35] Berry, S. H., Pevar, J. S., & Zander-Cotugno, M. (2010). The Use of Incentives in Surveys Supported by Federal Grants. *Council of Professional Associations on Federal Statistics*. Retrieved from http://www.copafs.org/seminars/use_of_incentives_in_surveys.aspx

[36] Singer, E. (2002, October 3). The Use and Effects of Incentives in Surveys. *Stanford University*. Retrieved from https://iriss.stanford.edu/sites/default/files/singer_slides.pdf

[37] Magness, P. W., & Murhpy, R. P. (2015). Challenging the Empirical Contribution of Thomas Piketty's Capital in the Twenty-First Century. *Journal of Private Enterprise*, Spring 2015; GMU School of Public Policy Research Paper No. 15-2. Retrieved from https://papers.ssrn.com/sol3/Papers.cfm?abstract_id=2543012

[38] Sieber, J. E. (2006, June 13/2016, February 1). Privacy and Confidentiality: As Related to Human Research in Social and Behavioral Science. *National Bioethics Advisory Commission*. Retrieved from http://www.onlineethics.org/cms/17207.aspx#threats

[39] Halsall, A. K. (2017, September 19). Millennials may be history's most competent parents. Here's why. *Medium*. Retrieved from https://medium.com/winnie/millennials-may-be-historys-most-competent-parents-here-s-why-94a6cb2cf4bd

[40] Stevens, K. (2017, August 17). Internet Stats & Facts for 2017. *Hosting Facts*. Retrieved from

https://hostingfacts.com/internet-facts-stats-2016/
[41] Statista Staff. (2017). Number of smartphone users in the United States from 2010 to 2022 (in millions). *Statista*. Retrieved from https://www.statista.com/statistics/201182/forecast-of-smartphone-users-in-the-us/
[42] Chaffey, D. (2017, March 1). Mobile Marketing Statistics compilation. *Smart Insights*. Retrieved from http://www.smartinsights.com/mobile-marketing/mobile-marketing-analytics/mobile-marketing-statistics/
[43] Stevens, K. (2017, August 17). Internet Stats & Facts for 2017. *Hosting Facts*. Retrieved from https://hostingfacts.com/internet-facts-stats-2016/
[44] *Ibid*
[45] SurveyMonkey Staff. (n.d.). How to Create a Survey. *SurveyMonkey*. Retrieved from https://help.surveymonkey.com/articles/en_US/kb/How-to-create-a-survey
[46] SurveyMonkey Staff. (n.d.). SurveyMonkey Audience pricing. *SurveyMonkey*. Retrieved from https://www.surveymonkey.com/mp/audience/audience-pricing
[47] SurveyMonkey Staff. (n.d.). Get real-time feedback from people around the world. *SurveyMonkey*. Retrieved from https://www.surveymonkey.com/mp/audience/

Chapter 7

[1] Localytics Staff. (n.d.). About Localytics. *Localytics*. Retrieved from https://www.localytics.com/company/about/
[2] More With Mobile Staff. (2013, June 19). Prices and Value of Consumer Data. *More With Mobile*. Retrieved from http://www.more-with-mobile.com/2013/06/prices-and-value-of-consumer-data.html
[3] *Ibid*
[4] Cole, J. S., Sarraf, S. A., & Wang, X. (2015, May). Does use of survey incentives degrade data quality? *Indiana University Center for Postsecondary Research National Survey of Student Engagement*. Retrieved from http://nsse.indiana.edu/pdf/presentations/2015/AIR_Forum_2015_Cole_Sarraf_Wang_paper.pdf
[5]*Ibid*
[6] Keusch, F., Batinic, B., & Mayerhofer, W. (2014, April). Motives for joining nonprobability online panels and their association with survey participation behavior, in: *Online Panel Research: A Data Quality Perspective* (eds M. Callegaro, R. Baker, J. Bethlehem, A. S. Göritz, J. A. Krosnick and P. J. Lavrakas). Retrieved from http://onlinelibrary.wiley.com/doi/10.1002/9781118763520.ch8/summary
[7] Vidyarthi, A. (2006, June 29). How people behave differently when they are being watched. *RxPG News*. Retrieved from http://rxpgnews.com/behaviouralscience/How_people_behave_differently_when_they_are_being__4575_4575.shtml
[8] Molm, L. D., Takahashi, N., & Peterson, G. (2000). Risk and Trust in Social Exchange: An Experimental Test of a Classical Proposition. *AJS*, Vol. 105, No. 5, 1396-1427. Retrieved from https://www.researchgate.net/publicat

ion/234021759_Risk_and_Trust_in_Social_Exchange_An_Experimental_Test_of_a_Classical_Proposition
[9] Singer, E. (2002, October 3). The Use and Effects of Incentives in Surveys. *Stanford University*. Retrieved from https://iriss.stanford.edu/sites/default/files/singer_slides.pdf
[10] Statistic Brain. (2016, July 2). Attention Span Statistics. *Statistic Brain*. Retrieved from http://www.statisticbrain.com/attention-span-statistics/
[11] Hagglund, D. (2009, April 6). Six guidelines for compensating research participants. *Dimensional Research*. Retrieved from http://dimensionalresearch.com/blog/2009/04/06/market-research-how-should-you-compensate-participants/
[12] Berry, S. H., Pevar, J. S., & Zander-Cotugno, M. (2010). The Use of Incentives in Surveys Supported by Federal Grants. *Council of Professional Associations on Federal Statistics*. Retrieved from http://www.copafs.org/seminars/use_of_incentives_in_surveys.aspx
[13] Berry, S. H., Pevar, J. S., & Zander-Cotugno, M. (2008). Use of Incentives in Surveys Supported by Federal Grants - Working Paper. *RAND Corporation*. Retrieved from https://www.rand.org/content/dam/rand/pubs/working_papers/2008/RAND_WR590.pdf
[14] *Ibid*
[15] *Ibid*
[16] Smith, J. W. (n.d.). The Myth of 5,000 Ads. *Hill Holliday*. Retrieved from https://web.archive.org/web/20170813062217/http://cbi.hhcc.com/writing/the-myth-of-5000-ads/
[17] Vidyarthi, A. (2006, June 29). How people behave differently when they are being watched. *RxPG News*. Retrieved from http://rxpgnews.com/behaviouralscience/How_people_behave_differently_when_they_are_being__4575_4575.shtml
[18] Duffy, J. (2016, December 28). The 25 Best Fitness Apps of 2017. *PC Magazine*. Retrieved from https://www.pcmag.com/article2/0,2817,2485287,00.asp
[19] Eadicicco, L. (2014, October 9). A New Wave Of Gadgets Can Collect Your Personal Information Like Never Before. *Business Insider*. Retrieved from http://www.businessinsider.com/privacy-fitness-trackers-smartwatches-2014-10
[20] *Ibid*
[21] Dubey, S. (2016, May 18). 11 Types of Compelling Mobile Push Notifications That Delight Users. *MoEngage*. Retrieved from https://www.moengage.com/blog/11-types-of-compelling-mobile-push-notifications-that-delight-users/
[22] *Ibid*
[23] Molm, L. D., Takahashi, N., & Peterson, G. (2000). Risk and Trust in Social Exchange: An Experimental Test of a Classical Proposition. *AJS*, Vol. 105, No. 5, 1396-1427. Retrieved from https://www.researchgate.net/publication/234021759_Risk_and_Trust_in_Social_Exchange_An_Experimental_Test_of_a_Classical_Proposition
[24] O'Connell, C. (2015, December 10). 2015: The Year that Push Notifications Grew Up. *Localytics*. Retrieved from http://info.localytics.com/blog/2015-

the-year-that-push-notifications-grew-up
[25] *Ibid*
[26] O'Connell, C. (2016, January 20). The Inside View: How Consumers Really Feel About Push Notifications. *Localytics*. Retrieved from http://info.localytics.com/blog/the-inside-view-how-consumers-really-feel-about-push-notifications
[27] Zantal-Wiener, A. (2016, September 5/2017, July 28). 7 Types of Push Notifications Users Actually Enjoy. *HubSpot*. Retrieved from https://blog.hubspot.com/marketing/push-notification-types#sm.0001mtt508ki7dsiq6l1c4qodqcj3
[28] Dubey, S. (2016, May 18). 11 Types of Compelling Mobile Push Notifications That Delight Users. *MoEngage*. Retrieved from https://www.moengage.com/blog/11-types-of-compelling-mobile-push-notifications-that-delight-users/
[29] Williams, T. (n.d.). Getting Paid for Value Instead of Time. *Ignition Consulting Group*. Retrieved from http://www.ignitiongroup.com/getting-paid-for-value-instead-of-time/
[30] Dubey, S. (2016, May 18). 11 Types of Compelling Mobile Push Notifications That Delight Users. *MoEngage*. Retrieved from https://www.moengage.com/blog/11-types-of-compelling-mobile-push-notifications-that-delight-users/
[31] O'Connell, C. (2016, January 20). The Inside View: How Consumers Really Feel About Push Notifications. Localytics. Retrieved from http://info.localytics.com/blog/the-inside-view-how-consumers-really-feel-about-push-notifications
[32] Hatmaker, T. (2017, August 22). Users dump AccuWeather iPhone app after learning it sends location data to a third party. *TechCrunch*. Retrieved from https://techcrunch.com/2017/08/22/accuweather-revealmobile-ios/
[33] Molm, L. D., Takahashi, N., & Peterson, G. (2000). Risk and Trust in Social Exchange: An Experimental Test of a Classical Proposition. *AJS*, Vol. 105, No. 5, 1396-1427. Retrieved from https://www.researchgate.net/publication/234021759_Risk_and_Trust_in_Social_Exchange_An_Experimental_Test_of_a_Classical_Proposition
[34] Piketty, T. (2014, April). *Capital in the Twenty-First Century*. Retrieved from http://www.hup.harvard.edu/catalog.php?isbn=9780674430006
[35] Molm, L. D., Takahashi, N., & Peterson, G. (2000). Risk and Trust in Social Exchange: An Experimental Test of a Classical Proposition. *AJS*, Vol. 105, No. 5, 1396-1427. Retrieved from https://docs.google.com/viewerng/viewer?url=http://www.academicroom.com/sites/default/files/article/19/Linda+D.+Molm,+Risk+and+Trust+in+Social+Exchange.pdf
[36] Danupon. (2015). Trust is the building block of social exchange and role relationship. *Course Hero*. Retrieved from https://doc-0s-c4-apps-viewer.googleusercontent.com/viewer/secure/pdf/ar8g7cbp050okfokf5u37mm965nicpff/1srbcjr03flr9dc4cctjotaiglgs36sn/1506649200000/lantern/10204011717257916466/ACFrOgBXvwf0lQ1eFpN4By6pNtbgBRkRcMlhgGomVPtKemp_o0bhi2t9uk4I7_fuf2anxbCeY67Egp4tpppVNzYrQGFc5YbFSJ6xdEArgwJB1zSuybwSwnzRYmNeFlc=?print=true&nonce=ccp79ctbh3jfi&user=10204011717257

916466&hash=bprihmd5qg1roogi8k5kl4dl0a6s5e28
[37] Morrison, K. (2015, May 27). Survey: Many Users Never Read Social Networking Terms of Service Agreements. *AdWeek*. Retrieved from http://www.adweek.com/digital/survey-many-users-never-read-social-networking-terms-of-service-agreements/
[38] Nolan, K. (2015, January 22). Trust Concerns Deter Consumers from Providing Personal Information for Targeted Advertising. *Strategy Analytics*. Retrieved from https://www.strategyanalytics.com/access-services/ux-innovation/user-experience-strategies/reports/report-detail/trust-concerns-deter-consumers-from-providing-personal-information-for-targeted-advertising#.Wc5ZXbpFymQ
[39] Kuittinen, T. (2013, July 2). Paid App Sessions Actually Growing Faster Than Free App Sessions. *Forbes*. Retrieved from https://www.forbes.com/sites/terokuittinen/2013/07/02/paid-app-sessions-actually-growing-faster-than-free-app-sessions/#480240fc32af
[40] Nader, G. (n.d.). How Not to Sell Your App: Paid vs Free Apps. *AppsBuilder*. Retrieved from http://blog.apps-builder.com/paid-vs-free-apps/
[41] TheFreeDictionary.com. (n.d.). Spurious correlation. *TheFreeDictionary.com*. Retrieved from http://www.thefreedictionary.com/spurious+correlation
[42] Higgins, J. (2013, December 4). Ice cream doesn't cause drowning and other warnings about interpreting data. *Seattle Times*. Retrieved from http://blogs.seattletimes.com/educationlab/2013/12/04/ice-cream-doesnt-cause-drowning-and-other-warnings-about-interpreting-data/
[43] VersionOne Staff. (n.d.). The Benefits of Agile Software Development. *VersionOne*. Retrieved from https://www.versionone.com/agile-101/agile-software-development-benefits/

Chapter 8

[1] Wardman, M. (1988). A Comparison of Revealed Preference and Stated Preference Models of Travel Behaviour. *Journal of Transport Economics and Policy*, Vol. 22, No. 1, 71-91. Retrieved from http://www.jstor.org/stable/20052836
[2] Google Staff. (n.d.). Google Privacy & Terms, More Relevant Search Results. *Alphabet, Inc*. Retrieved from https://policies.google.com/privacy/example/more-relevant-search-results
[3] Darmanin, A. Personal conversation dated October 25, 2017
[4] O'Connell, C. (2015, December 10). 2015: The Year that Push Notifications Grew Up. *Localytics*. Retrieved from http://info.localytics.com/blog/2015-the-year-that-push-notifications-grew-up
[5] Walter, E. (2012, October 4). Your Facebook Fans Are Hiding Your Posts At An Alarming Rate. *Fast Company*. Retrieved from https://www.fastcompany.com/3001871/your-facebook-fans-are-hiding-your-posts-alarming-rate
[6] Jin, S. (2012, December 8). Big Data or Big Junk? *DoubleCloud*. Retrieved from http://www.doublecloud.org/2012/12/big-data-or-big-junk/

[7] Paranjape, N. (2014, April 6). Good Data vs. Bad Data: How to identify? *Efficiency 365*. Retrieved from https://efficiency365.com/2014/04/06/good-data-vs-bad-data-how-to-identify/

[8] Kale, S. (2016, July 28). Men on Tinder Explain Why They Swipe Right on Literally Everyone. *Vice*. Retrieved from https://broadly.vice.com/en_us/article/ae55xk/men-who-swipe-right-to-everyone-on-tinder-explain-themselves

[9] Carey-Simos, G. (2015, August 19). How Much Data Is Generated Every Minute On Social Media? *Wersm*. Retrieved from http://wersm.com/how-much-data-is-generated-every-minute-on-social-media/

[10] NOAA. (2018, February 6). Is there gold in the ocean? *National Oceanic and Atmospheric Administration*. Retrieved from https://web.archive.org/web/20171222025752/https://oceanservice.noaa.gov/facts/gold.html

[11] XE Staff. (2018, September 16). XE Currency Charts: XAU to USD. XE. Retrieved from https://www.xe.com/currencycharts/?from=XAU&to=USD&view=10Y

[12] International Monetary Fund. (2017, April). World Economic Data. *IMF*. Retrieved from https://www.imf.org/external/pubs/ft/weo/2017/01/weodata/WEOApr2017all.xls

[13] NOAA. (2018, February 6). Is there gold in the ocean? *National Oceanic and Atmospheric Administration*. Retrieved from https://web.archive.org/web/20171222025752/https://oceanservice.noaa.gov/facts/gold.html

[14] Perlman, H. (2016, December 2). Saline water: Desalination. *U.S. Geological Survey*. Retrieved from https://water.usgs.gov/edu/drinkseawater.html

[15] Turner, V. (2014, April). The Digital Universe of Opportunities: Rich Data and the Increasing Value of the Internet of Things. *IDC*. Retrieved from https://www.emc.com/leadership/digital-universe/2014iview/executive-summary.htm

[16] Harlowe, H. A. (2000, June 15). Identifying and Controlling for Sources of Bias & Error in Focus Group Assessment Research. *Analytica Consulting*. Retrieved from http://analyticaconsulting.co/wp-content/uploads/2012/02/Identifying-and-Controlling-for-Sources-of-Bias-in-focus-group-research.pdf

[17] Helmenstine, A. M. (2017, April 11). Acid-Base Chemical Reaction. *ThoughtCo*. Retrieved from https://www.thoughtco.com/mixing-acid-and-base-reaction-603654

[18] Roberts, D. (n.d.). Shapes of Distributions. *MathBitsNotebook.com*. Retrieved from http://www.mathbitsnotebook.com/Algebra1/StatisticsData/STShapes.html

[19] Rossi, G. B. (2014, May 20). Measurability, In: *Measurement and Probability*. Springer, Dordrecht. Retrieved from https://link.springer.com/chapter/10.1007/978-94-017-8825-0_1

[20] Rathke, J. (2007). Achieving Comparability of Secondary Data. *Research Design in Political Science*. Retrieved from https://link.springer.com/chapter/10.1057/9780230598881_6

[21] Quora. (2016). What is pertinent data? How is it used?. *Quora*. Retrieved from https://www.quora.com/What-is-pertinent-data-How-is-it-used
[22] Jensen, T. (2017, July 18). Health Care a Mine Field for Republicans; Many Trump Voters in Denial on Russia. *Public Policy Polling*. Retrieved from http://www.publicpolicypolling.com/pdf/2017/PPP_Release_National_71817.pdf
[23] Gagnon, S. (2017, December 12). How much of an atom is empty space? *Thomas Jefferson National Accelerator Facility*. Retrieved from https://education.jlab.org/qa/how-much-of-an-atom-is-empty-space.html
[24] U.S. Congress. (2013, January 14). Public Law 112-265 - Investigative Assistance for Violent Crimes Act of 2012. *Library of Congress*. Retrieved from https://www.congress.gov/112/plaws/publ265/PLAW-112publ265.pdf
[25] Rathke, J. (2007). Achieving Comparability of Secondary Data. *Research Design in Political Science*. Retrieved from https://link.springer.com/chapter/10.1057/9780230598881_6
[26] Follman, M., Aronsen, G., & Pan, D. (2012, July 20/2017, November 15). US Mass Shootings, 1982-2017: Data From Mother Jones' Investigation. *Mother Jones*. Retrieved from http://www.motherjones.com/politics/2012/12/mass-shootings-mother-jones-full-data/
[27] Follman, M., Aronsen, G., & Pan, D. (2012, July 20/2017, November 15). A Guide to Mass Shootings in America. *Mother Jones*. Retrieved from http://www.motherjones.com/politics/2012/07/mass-shootings-map/
[28] *Ibid*
[29] *Ibid*
[30] Young, R. & Johnson, D. (2012). To Weight or Not to Weight, That is the Question: Survey Weights and Multivariate Analysis. *American Association for Public Opinion Research*. Retrieved from http://www.aapor.org/AAPOR_Main/media/AnnualMeetingProceedings/2012/03_-Young-Johnson_A2_Weighting-paper_aapor-2012-ry.pdf
[31] Verma, S. (2009, January). Do consumers Respond Differently to Advertising Stimuli. *South Asian Journal of Management*, Vol. 16, 73-86. Retrieved from https://www.researchgate.net/publication/305603110_Do_consumers_Respond_Differently_to_Advertising_Stimuli
[32] Bornhövd, K., Quante, M., Glauche, V., Bromm, B., Weiller, C., & Büchel, C. (2002, June). Painful stimuli evoke different stimulus–response functions in the amygdala, prefrontal, insula and somatosensory cortex: a single-trial fMRI study. *Brain*, Vol. 125, No. 6, 1326–1336,. Retrieved from https://academic.oup.com/brain/article/125/6/1326/290417/Painful-stimuli-evoke-different-stimulus-response
[33] Collins English Dictionary - Complete & Unabridged 2012 Digital Edition. (n.d.). Habituation. *Dictionary.com*. Retrieved from http://www.dictionary.com/browse/habituation
[34] Intergovernmental Panel on Climate Change. (2007). Climate Change 2007: Synthesis Report In: IPCC Fourth Assessment Report. *Intergovernmental*

Panel on Climate Change. Retrieved from http://www.ipcc.ch/publications_and_data/ar4/syr/en/spms3.html

[35] NOAA's National Ocean Service Water Level Observation Network. (n.d.). Station FTPC1 - 9414290 - San Francisco, CA. *US Harbors*. Retrieved from http://ca.usharbors.com/monthly-tides/California-San Francisco Bay/San Francisco/2018-01

[36] Fowler, J. H., & Dawes, C. T. (2008, July). Two Genes Predict Voter Turnout. *The Journal of Politics*, Vol. 70, No. 3, 579-594. Retrieved from http://jhfowler.ucsd.edu/two_genes_predict_voter_turnout.pdf

[37] *Ibid*

[38] Joffe-Block, J. (2016, February 28). Sick Of Political Parties, Unaffiliated Voters Are Changing Politics. *NPRPolitics*. Retrieved from http://www.npr.org/2016/02/28/467961962/sick-of-political-parties-unaffiliated-voters-are-changing-politics

[39] Weissberg, R. (2002). Leaders Should Not Follow Opinion Polls. *Saddleback College*. Retrieved from http://www.saddleback.edu/faculty/agordon/documents/LeadersShouldNotFollowOpinionPolls.pdf

[40] Walter, E. (2012, October 4). Your Facebook Fans Are Hiding Your Posts At An Alarming Rate. *Fast Company*. Retrieved from https://www.fastcompany.com/3001871/your-facebook-fans-are-hiding-your-posts-alarming-rate

[41] *Ibid*

[42] Kistner, A., Lhommee, E., & Krack, P. (2014, June). *Frontiers in Neurology*, Vol. 5 84. Retrieved from https://www.frontiersin.org/articles/10.3389/fneur.2014.00084/full

[43] Pandey, R. (2016, July 5). Major S Health Update Introduces Together, Quick Measure, & More. *AndroidBeat*. Retrieved from http://www.androidbeat.com/2016/07/major-s-health-update-introduces-together-quick-measure/

[44] U.S. Army Maneuver Center of Excellence. (n.d.). Personally Identifiable Information (PII). *U.S. Army - Fort Benning*. Retrieved from http://www.benning.army.mil/garrison/dhr/content/PDF/PII BRIEFING.pdf

[45] As Equifax Amassed Ever More Data, Safety Was a Sales Pitch. *The New York Times*. Retrieved from https://www.nytimes.com/2017/09/23/business/equifax-data-breach.html

[46] Rainie, L. (2016, January 14). Privacy and Information Sharing. *Pew Research Center*. Retrieved from http://www.pewinternet.org/2016/01/14/privacy-and-information-sharing/

[47] Solove, D. (2014, June 25). Privacy and Data Security Violations: What's the Harm? *LinkedIn*. Retrieved from https://www.linkedin.com/pulse/20140625045136-2259773-privacy-and-data-security-violations-what-s-the-harm/

Chapter 9

[1] Douguet, N., Assemat, E. & Kokoouline, V. (2016, November). Complete symmetry characterization in collisions involving four identical atoms. *European Physics Journal D*, Vol. 70, 228. Retrieved from https://link.springer.com/article/10.1140/epjd/e2016-60587-9

[2] Kelley, K., Clark, C., Brown, V., & Sitzia, J. (2003, May). Good practice in the conduct and reporting of survey research. *International Journal for Quality in Health Care*, Vol. 15, No. 3, 261-266. Retrieved from https://www.academic.oup.com/intqhc/article/15/3/261/1856193/Good-practice-in-the-conduct-and-reporting-of
[3] *Ibid*
[4] Martz, E. (2017, April 7). Why Is Continuous Data "Better" than Categorical or Discrete Data? *Minitab*. Retrieved from http://blog.minitab.com/blog/understanding-statistics/why-is-continuous-data-better-than-categorical-or-discrete-data
[5] Gallup Staff. (n.d.). Inform your pressing decisions with insights from our panel. *Gallup Organization*. Retrieved from http://analytics.gallup.com/213695/gallup-panel.aspx
[6] Keeter, S., Hatley, H., Kennedy, C., & Lau, A. (2017, May 15). What Low Response Rates Mean for Telephone Surveys. *Pew Research Center*. Retrieved from http://www.pewresearch.org/2017/05/15/what-low-response-rates-mean-for-telephone-surveys/
[7] Keusch, F., Batinic, B., & Mayerhofer, W. (2014, April). Motives for joining nonprobability online panels and their association with survey participation behavior, in: *Online Panel Research: A Data Quality Perspective* (eds M. Callegaro, R. Baker, J. Bethlehem, A. S. Göritz, J. A. Krosnick and P. J. Lavrakas). Retrieved from http://onlinelibrary.wiley.com/doi/10.1002/9781118763520.ch8/summary
[8] Mathews, S. (2015). Analyzing Research Articles: A Guide for Readers and Writers. *University of North Carolina at Chapel Hill, School of Information and Library Science*. Retrieved from https://ils.unc.edu/courses/2015_spring/inls151_003/Analyzing_Research_Articles.pdf
[9] Weir, K. (2015, October). A reproducibility crisis? *American Psychological Association*. Retrieved from http://www.apa.org/monitor/2015/10/share-reproducibility.aspx
[10] Levinson, B. (n.d.). The Angry and Aggressive Child - Anger and Aggression. *The Hinks-Dellcrest Centre*. Retrieved from http://www.hincksdellcrest.org/ABC/Teacher-Resource/The-Angry-and-Aggressive-Child/Anger-and-Aggression.aspx
[11] Localytics Staff. (n.d.). Reboot: The Beginner's Guide to App Marketing. *Localytics*. Retrieved from http://ebooks.localytics.com/beginners-guide-to-app-marketing
[12] Sedor, K. (2015). The Law of Large Numbers and its Applications. *Lakehead University*. Retrieved from https://www.lakeheadu.ca/sites/default/files/uploads/77/images/Sedor Kelly.pdf
[13] National Business Research Institute. (n.d.). How Long Does it Take to Conduct an Employee Survey? *National Business Research Institute*. Retrieved from https://www.nbrii.com/faqs/employee-survey/long-take-conduct-employee-survey/

[14] Infosurv Research Staff. (n.d.). About Us. *Infosurv Research*. Retrieved from http://www.infosurv.com/survey-company/
[15] Infosurv Research Staff. (n.d.). Market Research FAQs. *Infosurv Research*. Retrieved from http://www.infosurv.com/faqs/market-research-faqs/
[16] National Business Research Institute. (n.d.). How Long Does it Take to Conduct an Employee Survey? *National Business Research Institute*. Retrieved from https://www.nbrii.com/faqs/employee-survey/long-take-conduct-employee-survey/
[17] Kelley, K., Clark, C., Brown, V., & Sitzia, J. (2003, May). Good practice in the conduct and reporting of survey research. *International Journal for Quality in Health Care*, Vol. 15, No. 3, 261-266. Retrieved from https://www.academic.oup.com/intqhc/article/15/3/261/1856193/Good-practice-in-the-conduct-and-reporting-of
[18] Lindsey, J. K. (2000). Dropouts in Longitudinal Studies: Definitions and Models. *Journal of Biopharmaceutical Statistics*, Vol. 10, No. 4, 503–525. Retrieved from http://c.ymcdn.com/sites/www.energypsych.org/resource/resmgr/imported/Dropout Data Management - Lindsey.pdf
[19] Davis, L. J. (2018, February 6). *The Unmaking of the President 2016: How FBI Director James Comey Cost Hillary Clinton the Presidency*
[20] Shepard, S. (2016, October 29). Will new FBI review dent Clinton's lead in the polls? Politico. Retrieved from https://www.politico.com/blogs/5-political-numbers-to-watch/2016/10/hillary-clinton-fbi-polls-230481
[21] Hoiberg, C. (2017, May). What is a Long Exposure? *Digital Photography School*. Retrieved from https://digital-photography-school.com/short-versus-long-exposure-landscape/
[22] Lillibridge, M. (2012, November 29). A Former Player's Perspective on Film Study and Preparing for an NFL Game. *Bleacher Report*. Retrieved from http://bleacherreport.com/articles/1427449-a-former-players-perspective-on-film-study-and-preparing-for-a-nfl-game
[23] Gibbons, B., & Herman, J. (1997). True and Quasi-Experimental Designs. *Practical Assessment, Research & Evaluation*, Vol. 5, No. 14. Retrieved from http://pareonline.net/getvn.asp?v=5&n=14
[24] *Ibid*
[25] *Ibid*
[26] Gallo, A. (2014, October 29). The Value of Keeping the Right Customers. *Harvard Business Review*. Retrieved from https://hbr.org/2014/10/the-value-of-keeping-the-right-customers
[27] Localytics Staff. (n.d.). Reboot: The Beginner's Guide to App Marketing. *Localytics*. Retrieved from http://ebooks.localytics.com/beginners-guide-to-app-marketing
[28] Abrams, Z., & Vee, E. (n.d.). Personalized Ad Delivery when Ads Fatigue: An Approximation Algorithm. *Stanford University*. Retrieved from http://theory.stanford.edu/~za/AdFatigue/AdFatigue.pdf
[29] Alexandrou, M. (n.d.). CPM vs. CPC vs. CPA. *Infolific*. Retrieved from

https://infolific.com/technology/internet/cpm-cpc-cpa/
[30] Kumar, V., Bhagwat, Y., & Zhang, X. (2015, August 7). What You Need to Know About Customer Win-Back. *Arizona State University Center for Services Leadership*. Retrieved from https://research.wpcarey.asu.edu/services-leadership/2015/08/07/what-you-need-to-know-about-customer-win-back/
[31] AdBoom Staff. (2015, April 2). CPM, CPC, CPL, CPA: Which Online Ad Models are Best?! *AdBoom*. Retrieved from http://adboomadvertising.com/blog/cpm-cpc-cpl-cpa-which-online-ad-models-are-best-2/
[32] Fitchett, C. (2015, July 24). A Mobile Ad Pricing Showdown: CPA vs CPM vs CPI. *Gimbal*. Retrieved from https://gimbal.com/mobile-ad-pricing-showdown/
[33] Austin Research Staff. (2014, July 30). The importance of representative samples and how to get them. *Austin Research*. Retrieved from http://austinresearch.co.uk/the-importance-of-representative-samples-and-how-to-get-them/
[34] Barasch, A., & Berger, J. (2013). Broadcasting and Narrowcasting: How Audience Size Impacts What People Share. *Marketing Science Institute*. Retrieved from http://www.msi.org/reports/broadcasting-and-narrowcasting-how-audience-size-impacts-what-people-share
[35] TV Tropes Staff. (n.d.). Repeating Ad. *TV Tropes*. Retrieved from http://tvtropes.org/pmwiki/pmwiki.php/Main/RepeatingAd
[36] Heitsch, R. (2011, May 9). Narrowcasting America. *Prezi*. Retrieved from https://prezi.com/cea_f0jguptp/cim200-research-presentation-narrowcasting-america/
[37] HyperTarget Marketing Staff. (2014, January 23). Narrowcast Marketing – A Way To Spend Less And Convert More. *HyperTarget Marketing*. Retrieved from https://hypertargetmarketing.com/blog/marketing/narrowcast-marketing-way-spend-less-convert/
[38] Dennis, A. R., Yuan, L., Hsieh, C. J., Feng, X., Hedge, A. P., & Webb, E. M. (2015). The Priming Effects of Relevant and Irrelevant Advertising in Online Auctions. *IEEE*. Retrieved from https://www.computer.org/csdl/proceedings/hicss/2015/7367/00/7367d394.pdf
[39] HyperTarget Marketing Staff. (2014, January 23). Narrowcast Marketing – A Way To Spend Less And Convert More. *HyperTarget Marketing*. Retrieved from https://hypertargetmarketing.com/blog/marketing/narrowcast-marketing-way-spend-less-convert/
[40] Weber, B. (2015, September). Inflammatory political rhetoric and hate speech in Bosnia and Herzegovina: political elites and the media. *Democratization Policy Council*. Retrieved from http://www.helsinki.org.rs/doc/AI-DPC BiH Security Risk Analysis Paper Series - 1_Hate Speech.pdf
[41] Dennis, A. R., Yuan, L., Hsieh, C. J., Feng, X., Hedge, A. P., & Webb, E. M. (2015). The Priming Effects of Relevant and Irrelevant Advertising in Online Auctions. *IEEE*. Retrieved from https://www.computer.org/csdl/proceedings/hicss/2015/7367/00/7367d394.pdf

[42] Planned Parenthood Staff. (2018). Our Services. *Planned Parenthood*. Retrieved from https://www.plannedparenthood.org/get-care/our-services

[43] Garimella, K., Morales, G. D. F., Gionis, A., & Mathioudakis, M. (2018, February 19). Political Discourse on Social Media: Echo Chambers, Gatekeepers, and the Price of Bipartisanship. *arXiv*. Retrieved from https://arxiv.org/pdf/1801.01665.pdf

[44] Weber, B. (2015, September). Inflammatory political rhetoric and hate speech in Bosnia and Herzegovina: political elites and the media. *Democratization Policy Council*. Retrieved from http://www.helsinki.org.rs/doc/AI-DPC BiH Security Risk Analysis Paper Series - 1_Hate Speech.pdf

[45] Oxford English Dictionary. (n.d.). Intersectionality. *Oxford University Press*. Retrieved from https://en.oxforddictionaries.com/definition/intersectionality

[46] Weir, K. (2015, October). A reproducibility crisis? *American Psychological Association*. Retrieved from http://www.apa.org/monitor/2015/10/share-reproducibility.aspx

[47] Baker, M. (2016, May 25/July 28). 1,500 scientists lift the lid on reproducibility. *Nature*. Retrieved from http://www.nature.com/news/1-500-scientists-lift-the-lid-on-reproducibility-1.19970

[48] Explorable.com Staff. (2009, May 17). Non-Probability Sampling. *Explorable.com*. Retrieved from https://explorable.com/non-probability-sampling

Chapter 10

[1] Hardon, A., Hodgkin, C., & Fresle, D. (2004). 5.4 Probability sampling methods for quantitative studies, in: *How to investigate the use of medicines by consumers*. World Health Organization. Retrieved from http://apps.who.int/medicinedocs/en/d/Js6169e/7.4.html

[2] Statistics Canada. (2013, July 23). Probability sampling. *Statistics Canada*. Retrieved from http://www.statcan.gc.ca/edu/power-pouvoir/ch13/prob/5214899-eng.htm

[3] Lathrop, K. (n.d.). A Controlled Experiment. *New Mexico Institute of Mining and Technology*. Retrieved from http://infohost.nmt.edu/~klathrop/controlled_experimnet.pdf

[4] More With Mobile Staff. (2013, June 19). Prices and Value of Consumer Data. *More With Mobile*. Retrieved from http://www.more-with-mobile.com/2013/06/prices-and-value-of-consumer-data.html

[5] von Mises, L., & Ebeling, R. M. (1990). *Money, Method, and the Market Process*. Mises Institute. Retrieved from https://mises.org/library/money-method-and-market-process/html/p/370

[6] *Ibid*

[7] History.com Staff. (2009). Enlightenment. *History.com*. Retrieved from http://www.history.com/topics/enlightenment

[8] von Mises, L., & Ebeling, R. M. (1990). *Money, Method, and the Market Process*. Mises Institute. Retrieved from https://mises.org/library/money-method-and-market-process/html/p/370

[9] Grohol, J. M. (2010, August 26). Psychology Secrets: Most Psychology Studies Are College Student Biased. *PsychCentral*. Retrieved from https://psychcentral.com/blog/archives/2010/08/26/psychology-secrets-most-psychology-studies-are-college-student-biased/

www.ingramcontent.com/pod-product-compliance
Lightning Source LLC
Chambersburg PA
CBHW050114280326
41933CB00010B/1093
* 9 7 8 1 7 3 2 8 8 9 7 0 5 *